Françoise de Bonneville

THE BOOK OF FINE LINEN

PREFACE BY MARC PORTHAULT

TRANSLATED FROM THE FRENCH BY DEKE DUSINBERRE

Flammarion

For Christian

Editorial Direction:
Ghislaine Bavoillot

Designed by
Marc Walter

Glossary translated by Bambi Ballard
Copyediting by Christine Schultz-Touge and Bernard Wooding
Picture research by Sabine Arqué-Greenberg
Typesetting by Octavo Editions, Paris
Photoengraving by Colourscan, France
Printed in Germany by Mohndruck, Gütersloh

Flammarion
26, rue Racine
75006 Paris

ISBN: 2-08013-557-0
No. d'édition: 1048
Dépôt légal: April 1994

CONTENTS

PREFACE

by Marc Porthault

Household linen once appeared in an infinite variety of fibers and weaves adorned with embroidery, lace and other exquisite refinements. Linen incarnated a complex tradition that reflected the differing sensibilities of various cultures, periods and places. Generations of craftsmen, spinners and weavers combined art with technology so that linen could transcend its utilitarian function. Little by little, refinement and comfort reached new heights.

Some household linen was so silken, so finely damasked, or so magnificently decorated that it inspired intense passion. It could also constitute a highly precious part of lavish interiors, rivalling works of art. More modest households, meanwhile, concentrated on assembling a trousseau designed to last a lifetime, for the sheets and tablecloths included in the bride's "hope chest" would become an important part of daily life. First, each piece of the trousseau would be patiently woven and painstakingly monogrammed, and later it would be lovingly maintained. Stacked in scented linen cupboards, it represented many families' only treasure. Yet however magnificent or modest household linen might be, it seemed to lack something. The conventional, austere whiteness of fine linen restricted its expressiveness to the glorification of fabric. While often pleasant or even delightful to touch, linen lacked a more playful, poetic dimension, it lacked a spirit capable of enchanting the eye and making life sweeter and more cheerful. In short, linen lacked color.

It was my mother, Madeleine Porthault, who decided to give linen color, enlivening the conventional whiteness of household linen with a palette of delicate, cheerful hues, mysteriously gleaned from the realm of flowers and the changing light of the seasons. A monochrome landscape suddenly came alive with color under the effect of a magic wand straight out of a fairy tale. Linen was no longer merely linen, it became a pleasure to mind, sight and touch. It begged to be stroked, embraced, cuddled because it was no longer simply beautiful, it was comforting. Linen could still be fancy for festive occasions, but its company was also impatiently sought at breakfast time, at bedtime, on getting out of the bath, on venturing into the sun. Impatiently sought, because its colorful palette magically conveyed the poetic sweetness of a given moment.

But Porthault's greatest accomplishment was probably in serving the tastes of others, in imagining their most intimate surroundings and dreams. And what "others"! All craftsmen are proud when the perfection of their work is recognized by the "great of this world." So it is hard not to consider the loyalty of the De Gaulles, the Kennedys and the Windsors—to name just a few from the past—as Porthault's finest reward. Today Porthault's calling is to decorate household linen with an infinite range of embroidered or printed patterns, adorned with airy, swirling details or embellished with delicate lace, whether in translucent blues, or pale greens, in cool, boreal shades, or in striking flashes of vivid, sunny color.

So let me invite you to sample this new approach to household linen, capping the long and fascinating history so skillfully recounted here by Françoise de Bonneville.

THE UNDYING PASSION FOR FINE LINEN

atiste, embroidery, lawn, and lace—women have never lost their passion for the frivolous secrets hidden away in lavender-scented linen cupboards. But the subject of fine linen is not so trifling as it might seem. People spend nearly half of their lifetimes caring for their bodies—eating, sleeping, washing—activities that are all linked to textiles and the use of sheets, towels, and tablecloths.

What exactly constitutes fine linen, that faithful servant of everyday tasks, trusty nighttime friend, and lifelong companion? Which fabrics are woven from hemp, flax, cotton, or silk? What are batiste, lawn, satin, and crêpe de Chine? Where do they come from? How were they passed down to us? And when were embroidery, lace, and damask all invented? These queries trigger an avalanche of further questions: When did household linen first appear? How long have bed sheets been used? Why is bathroom linen so recent? How did the rites and rituals associated with "table and bedtime etiquette" emerge? When did the concept of the trousseau appear, and what does it mean today? Why this age-old infatuation with linen? Who made it in the past and how was it cared for? What was the hidden meaning behind the patient weaving, embroidering, and monogramming of all those stacks of sheets and tablecloths prior to marriage? And, finally, does that pleasure of owning fine linen still exist, now that it is so often an impersonal, manufactured product?

Attempting to unravel this skein of questions makes it clear that, in sociologist André Georges Haudricourt's words, research into "any object, if studied correctly, brings all of society with it." This is perhaps even truer of household linen than of other objects, because behind the decoration exalting linen lies the intertwined thread composing it—the very thread of life that weaves a deep-seated link between textiles and humanity in a symbolism reaching back to the infancy of the human race.

Did you say frivolous, fine linen?

THE VANISHING
TRADITION OF THE
TROUSSEAU

Sheets and tablecloths, carefully folded and squarely stacked, have long been both cherished possessions and a delight to the eyes. Even if the towering *armoire*, warder of the traditional bridal trousseau, has practically disappeared from modern homes, it lives on in our imaginations as the sacred tabernacle of household linen. *Armoires*, better known in English as linen cupboards, are private affairs. Like jewelry boxes and writing desks, they hide life's little secrets—letters, yellowing photographs, or locks of hair tied with a ribbon—amid a pile of sheets or batiste handkerchiefs locked away under a heavy iron key. "Does there exist a single dreamer of words," wondered Gaston Bachelard in *The Poetics of Space*, "who does not respond to the word *armoire*?" *Armoire* is a grand word in French because it is simultaneously majestic and familiar, incarnating "a center of order that protects the house from uncurbed disorder. Here, order reigns, or rather, this is the reign of order. Order is not merely geometrical, it can also [record] family history. . . . Memories come crowding when we look back upon the shelf on which lace-trimmed batiste and muslin pieces lay on top of the heavier materials. . . ."

Yet linen cupboards are not as old as one might think. They first appeared at the end of the fourteenth century, as a piece of kitchen furniture. Back in the early Middle Ages, linen had generally been kept in chests that were easily taken along when the owner changed residence. These chests were made of wood covered with nailed leather and iron fittings, each with a locking key. Isabeau of Bavaria, wife of Charles VI (1380-1422), adored fine linen and had the supplier, Pierre du Fou, make countless chests to contain her celebrated collection of sheets and cloths. The queen continued to acquire linen to fill these chests, despite the political turmoil of the times, which culminated in the French defeat at the hands of the English king Henry V in the famous battle of Agincourt in 1415.

At the end of the fifteenth century, Charlotte of Savoy, the wife of King Louis XI of France, reserved a small chest for her most precious linen, woven in the rarest of fabrics and packed in dried rose petals.

Homes became more fixed as the Renaissance neared and trousseau chests within magnificent Tuscan palaces became actual pieces of furniture made of precious wood carved in bas-relief and painted in rich colors. At the same time, wardrobes grew taller in order to store clothing upright. The use of a special linen cupboard came later—a seventeenth-century painting by Pieter de Hooch depicts one in Holland, a land of linen if there ever was one. But it was only during the following century that it became a custom to make a wedding gift of a cupboard carved with symbols of abundance and fertility, containing the entire trousseau. By the 1800s, "the great linen century," it was *de rigueur* to display a cupboard full of monogrammed linen that a lifetime of use could not deplete. As Balzac wrote in *L'Interdiction*, "her linen had that rusty hue indicating a long sojourn in the cupboard, advertising the late Madame Popinot's obsession with linen; in Flemish fashion, she probably only bothered washing it twice a year." Yet this mound of white tablecloths, towels, and sheets marked in a corner with the blood-red thread of life, had begun accumulating long before—at the end of the Middle Ages. It is worth peeking into those chests and cupboards to discover what Bachelard described as "all those superabundant blessings that lie folded in piles" on the shelves of an *armoire* from another era.

THE HISTORY OF THE TROUSSEAU

What did the young princess Isabelle of France in 1397 have in common with a humble city girl in the year 1910? Nothing other than the eternal thread of

their trousseaux, containing similar pieces of cloth used for similar daily acts in nearly comparable proportions, but separated by a period of over five hundred years.

Isabelle of France received her trousseau at the age of seven, when she was promised in marriage to Richard II of England. It contained fourteen pairs of sheets, a dozen large cloths, two dozen smaller cloths, and several colored bedspreads in velvet and satin (including a white one embroidered with the four evangelists and an "Agnus Dei" encircled by the sun). The list ended with the touching addition of a few dolls. Five hundred years later, the typical trousseau advocated by a Parisian department store like Au Bon Marché included six pairs of sheets, two dozen pillowcases, three dozen table napkins, three tablecloths (two with matching napkins), a complete damask table setting for twelve, two dozen dishtowels; a dozen hand towels, two dozen bath towels, and six aprons.

In comparison, the inventory established in 1328 on the death of Clemence, daughter of King Charles I of Hungary, and widow of King Louis X of France, shows that she did not own much more than that. Her new linen amounted to five pairs of sheets, twelve handcloths, nine double-breadth bath towels, thirteen pieces of fine cloth (two for tablecloths and napkins), and finally three pieces of fustian totaling forty-six ells (a Paris ell was roughly forty-seven inches long). True enough, this was complemented by a list of "old linen" that included thirty-seven tablecloths and eighty-two handcloths. The only extravagance in the trousseau consisted of a pair of huge sheets, six breadths wide and six ells long, and a complete set of bedding in white *bougueran,* a term etymologically related to "buckram" but which at the time probably referred to fine linen or cotton.

Right up to the beginning of the twentieth century, tradition dictated that a trousseau include not only the bride's personal wardrobe, but also bedding and household linen and even what it was stored in—chests, cupboards, or other storage arrangements.

Back in the powerful duchy of Burgundy at the end of the Middle Ages, even a simple craftsman named Regnaud Chevallier (tailor, it should be said, to dukes), could own eighteen sheets (sixteen in linen), sixteen

tablecloths (twelve in linen), and twenty-three *tergeurs* or towels (ten in linen). Yet this was hardly comparable to the impressive numbers of sheets, tablecloths, and towels that would soon pile up in chests and cupboards beginning in the sixteenth century and continuing beyond the First World War.

Inventories of household linen often drawn up on the death of the owner are informative, yet give a poor picture of the original stock—linen wore out a great deal (damaged by the ash used as washing powder) and was constantly subject to theft (given its value). It was therefore regularly renewed down through the years, as demonstrated by records of orders placed with linen-drapers. Despite all these vagaries, what was left of a trousseau at the end of a life appears amazing today.

At the court of Versailles, household linen was rented, and only the personal trousseaux of the king and queen were purchased, being replaced once every three years. In his memoirs dated 1750, the duc de Luynes noted the expenditure of 30,000 francs by Queen Marie Leszczynska, wife of Louis XV, for the purchase of eighteen pairs of large sheets and twelve pairs of small sheets, eighteen undersheets, twelve mattress covers, six bleeding sheets, six dozen covers for warmers, three large Marseille foot covers (the finest of which was done in point d'Angleterre with brides), three small blanket covers in mesh and brides, eighteen pillowcases that matched the foot covers, followed by sixteen bedspreads (six of embroidered muslin with lace and six in white satin) and finally two taffeta-lined baskets and dozens of ells of ribbon made from colored satin and taffeta.

Today the word "trousseau," when used to refer to more than just the bride's personal wardrobe, tends to evoke the traditional ceremony of preparing linen years in advance, embroidering and monogramming it with the future spouses' initials. Linen was richly symbolic, conveying above all the wealth to be displayed before guests. This connotation took precedence and became a veritable institution in nineteenth-century Europe, where it represented an exaggerated expression of the ascendant bourgeoisie. "Dear Renée," wrote

Even dish towels have a certain nobility, especially old-fashioned ones. This still life (right) shows traditional dish towels and tablecloths of varying thickness, in pure linen or linen-and-cotton blends, in plain white, with red bands, or red cross-stitch embroidery. Folding sheets has always been one of the most animated of household chores. A room suddenly comes alive to the dance of expanses of cloth, the rustle and snap of fabrics, the fragrance of freshly washed linen. Cover of the 1924 catalogue from Les Grands Magasins du Printemps (below).

an exultant Louise in a Balzac tale about two young brides, "I now have a bride's trousseau! With everything stacked and scented." Michelle Perrot and Georges Ribeill have unearthed the private diary of Caroline Brame, a young Parisian aristocrat, who confessed in 1865 her sense of wonder before her friend's wedding gifts and trousseau, along with the almost mysterious fascination they provoked in her.

". . . And I went to see the trousseau, which is truly magnificent. Above all there are embroidered lace handkerchiefs that are delightful . . . sheets adorned with truly overly lavish lace, a coverlet with her magnificent coat of arms, and an infinite number of small, charming details."

Bourgeois European society even set up "trousseau funds" to enable the poorest of girls to have some household linen when they married; the girls would simply agree to contribute the sum of half a franc on a monthly basis, from age eight to twenty-one; they were then entitled, given charitable donations and subscriptions to the fund, to at least six sheets, six pillowcases, twelve dish towels, twelve hand towels, twelve bath towels, a complete table setting, and a few items of

personal clothing—a list which, these days, hardly seems impoverished.

A rural custom in southern France, specifically in the Orthe region between Béarn and the Basque country, held that the poorest fiancées would go from house to house requesting pieces of linen in order to stitch a little trousseau of their own prior to marriage. Whether humble or extravagant, the trousseau was always brought by the bride and generally remained her property in case of widowhood or remarriage.

Among affluent town-dwellers, the trousseau represented roughly five per cent of the total dowry. Items of linen in "rich" trousseaux were counted by "twelve dozens," and in more modest cases by "three dozens" even though, in principle, more frequent washing days, in towns at least, no longer made such hoards necessary. It should be noted that the habit of counting in multiples of three, six, twelve, and later eighteen, appeared during the eighteenth century. At the beginning of the twentieth century, the famous bridal shop La Cour Batave advocated the colossal figure of forty-eight pairs of sheets (not counting thirty pairs of sheets in coarser material for servants). But even though quantity was one of the signs of a "rich" trousseau, it was above all the quality of material and the

This wonderful ecru dish towel (right) of fairly sturdy linen has bands and initials in cross-stitch embroidery, and hems of laddered drawnwork. During the nineteenth century it became de rigueur for middle class families to have every item of the trousseau monogrammed, in imitation of aristocratic crests.

Nineteenth-century department stores radically altered the art of selling and the delights of buying. Customers could henceforth wander freely among the shelves to touch and compare. Going to one of these trade palaces became a favorite occupation of fashionable ladies, equal to a stroll in the park or taking tea with friends. The linen department at Harrods, London, in 1909 (right). The linen counter at Printemps department store, Paris, in 1890 (below).

January "white sales" are a department store invention originating in the late nineteenth century. The catalogues printed for the occasion were often magnificent, featuring the best graphic artists of the day, as in the Printemps white goods catalogue of 1913 (below).

decoration that justified the difference in price. In terms of table linen, for instance, the finest damask cloth came from Saxony or Armentières (northern France) after the decline of the Flemish textile center of Courtrai following the French Revolution. As for sheets, apart from the fineness of the linen cloth, the most costly were those with no middle seam. But it was above all lace insertions, which came back into fashion at the end of the First Napoleonic Empire (1804-1814), rivalling garlands of fancy needlework, intricate open-work, and complex monograms, that pushed cost up. It should not be forgotten that the trousseau also contained undergarments, always a pretence for a young woman's luxurious caprices.

In French cities, even though some mothers continued to buy cloth by the meter into the late nineteenth century, and had their daughter's linen stitched and embroidered by a linen maid or in certain convents, the Goncourt brothers commented in their *Journal* that "the most luxurious trousseaux of young women who bring six hundred thousand francs of dowry are made at Clairvaux [Abbey]. That's the inside story on all fine things in society." The appearance of department stores and factories would soon revolutionize purchasing habits, however. The new trade made traditional boutiques so suddenly and completely old-fashioned that the term became practically an insult, according to the *Journal des Modes*. The word boutique, of course, has now regained its former status.

By the end of the nineteenth century, department stores all had their "white goods" floor or "trousseau counter" where buyers would gather wide-eyed before displays that Balzac described as "commercial poetry." There one could find everything necessary to make up a complete trousseau. Zola recounted such a scene in *The Ladies' Paradise*:

"Denise entered the white goods gallery and headed for the handkerchiefs at the back. White paraded by in the form of white cottons, madapolams (fine calico), dimity (cotton damask), piqués, calicos, linens, nain-

sooks, muslins, and tarlatans. Then came linen in enormous mounds built of alternating pieces like stone blocks—sturdy linen, fine linen, in all widths, white or natural, pure linen, bleached in the field; then it began again, row after row of every sort of linen, an unending avalanche of white, of sheets, of pillowcases, of countless types of napkins, of tablecloths, of aprons and dish towels. . . ."

In addition to department stores, there were also textile "works" that specialized in trousseau items, such as La Cour Batave. It was founded in 1817 on rue de la Paix in Paris and became famous for its luxurious linen; it is now forgotten, and the only vestige is the house logo engraved on the façade of its former offices at number 60 rue Saint-Denis. Other examples include Les Galeries Modernes, the Dufayel firm, and less well known houses with sometimes silly names, such as Au Gagne-Petit (The Low-Earner), La Fille d'honneur (The Bridesmaid), Le Petit Chaperon Rouge (Little Red Riding Hood), Le Page Inconstant (The Unfaithful Page), and Le Pauvre Diable (the Poor Devil)! Several glamorous firms have

The sturdiness of fabrics—an important sales pitch—is amusingly illustrated on the cover of this catalogue for La Cour Batave (above), where white goods were displayed like works of art. All the sensual magic of linen is expressed in this "Roaring Twenties" poster (right) advertising white goods. Department stores of the day sold "complete trousseaux" as well as material by the yard for home-made trousseaux.

The exoticism of this catalogue cover (below) is not only for graphic effect. Egypt exported all of its cotton, a material that was on the verge of dethroning linen, which had reigned unchallenged over the realm of household fabrics for seven hundred years.

Making a choice (right)—the delights of looking, touching and assessing the infinite range of damask patterns spread out on the counter.

A turn-of-the-century catalogue (below) for white goods at Printemps department store.

Abundant labor was required to produce truly magnificent trousseaux. Many "hands" are seen here (above) completing a lavish trousseau for Lady May Cambridge, ordered from a London linen specialist, The White House. The firm was founded by a Frenchman in 1906, becoming an elegant symbol of the Entente Cordiale that reigned between Britain and France at that time.

The Printemps department store catalogue vaunted wonders like this rich batiste sheet (below) bordered with Colbert embroidery, a stitch-and-cut technique that rivalled Richelieu embroidery in the early twentieth century.

only recently shut their doors, and their names still ring in French ears; these include La Samaritaine de Luxe, La Grande Maison de Blanc, and A la Ville du Puy. Still others are bustling and prosperous even today, such as the Noël and Porthault firms.

At the time, all these stores would mark linen, embroidering it with the monogram of the future couple. For an added fee, the finished trousseau might even be washed a first time before delivery, in order to remove some of the stiffness of the fabric and make it more comfortable for its initial use.

Carefully ironed and folded, selected and prepared with excitement, this celebrated trousseau contained undergarments, sheets and splendid table linen bent under a crush of lace flounces, embroidery and open-work; during and after the Second Empire, it was supposed to be displayed at the same time as the collection of personal gifts with which the groom inundated his betrothed—pearls, gems, small furnishings, boxes, lace, furs, and all possible feminine frippery. The practice was pro-gressively abandoned as far as the trousseau went, because this display of intimate items made modest brides blush.

This custom was also followed in rural areas, where it acquired the status of a genuine rite. The linen would be arranged on the shelves of the bride's cupboard, ordered from a cabinetmaker for that purpose. The whiteness of the brand-new trousseau then gleamed on the shelves of the cupboard, opened on the wedding day to the delight of the guests. This huge piece of furniture shared pride of place in the nuptial bedroom with the fully made bed that since medieval times also constituted part of the bride's trousseau. In certain French provinces, the linen was placed in the cupboard by the bride's mother while her father assumed responsibility for throwing open the doors at the right moment, in a theatrical gesture accompanied by a ritual speech.

In the Orthe region, people observed a colorful custom called the *passade*. Before the wedding ceremony, the entire trousseau was carried from the

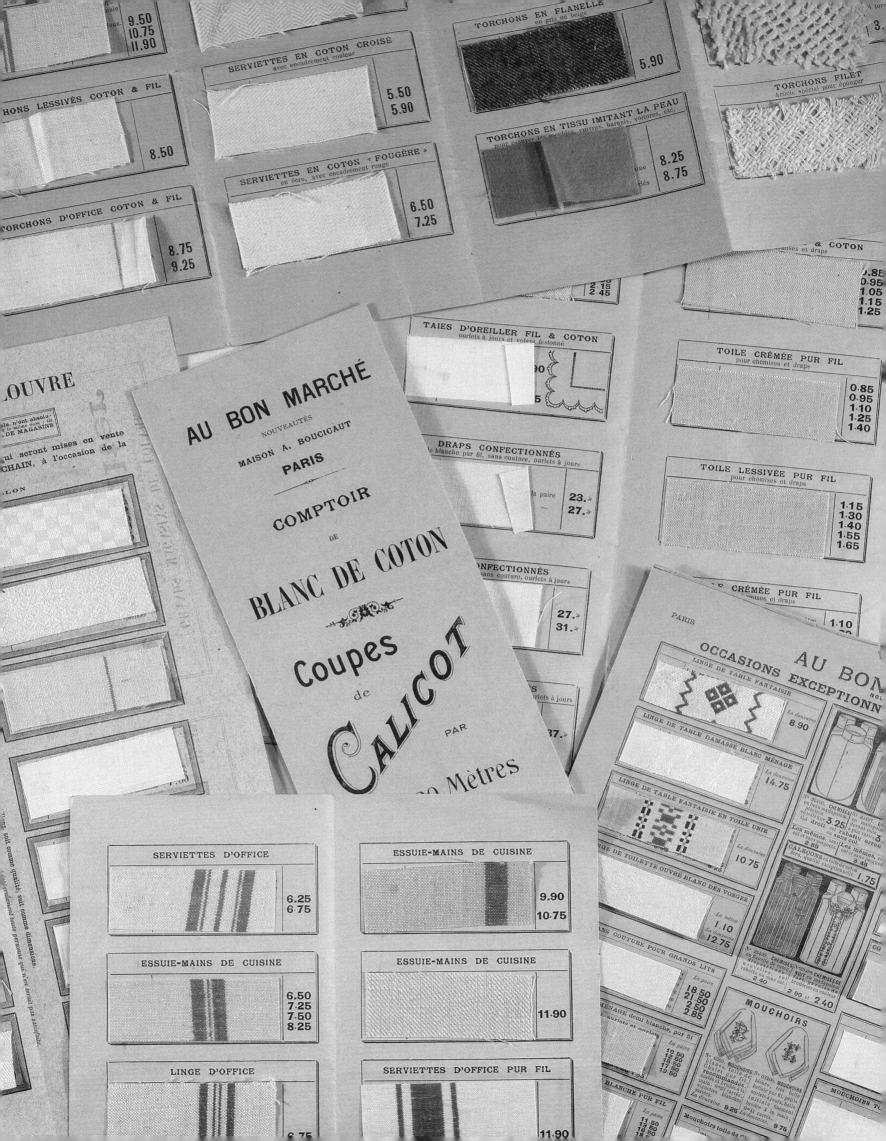

In the late nineteenth century, the linen departments of major stores began issuing mail-order catalogues, sometimes printed in hundreds of thousands of copies. A set of swatches (left)—each piece glued by hand—enabled buyers to see and touch the various types of cloth, from fine batiste to ticking, from pebble grain damasks to honeycomb weaves. Novelties were also featured, such as sturdy white calico newly imported from India and sold by the yard.

bride's home to that of the groom on a gaily decorated cart, while in Brittany it was transported in the cupboard itself. The "linen-bearing" cart was bedecked with flowers and boughs, and pulled by two festooned cows covered with a striped cape. The linen was piled on the cart by the bridesmaids who then accompanied it, one carrying a broom (symbol of housewifely duty) and the other carrying a distaff (symbol of fertility). Thus adorned, the procession crossed the village, heralding the wedding, offering drinks and singing songs enumerating the various objects that the young woman was bringing in her dowry. When the procession arrived, the mother of the bride put the sheets, tablecloths and towels in the cupboard, taking care to fold everything just right—that is, to give the illusion of greater numbers! Then the father opened the two doors, the village priest blessed the cupboard and bed, everyone made merry and the ceremony ended with a family meal at the future groom's house.

This trousseau had been prepared at least ten years earlier by the bride's mother, once the girl had made her First Communion or left school. Little by little, pieces of fabric were bought at the market, from trav-

eling salesmen, in stores during an occasional trip to a nearby town, or even from mail-order catalogues. In Zola's novel *The Ladies' Paradise*, known for the authenticity of its details, department store owner Mouret sends out 400,000 catalogues "translated into every language" to celebrate the opening of a new wing. These catalogues were abundantly illustrated with engravings and boasted "100,000 francs' worth of fabric" cut into swatches glued to the page so that customers could "feel" the various qualities of cloth.

It was at about this time that "modern ways" put a slow end to the old custom of fathers planting a few acres of flax and hemp for their daughters, who would spin their own yarn at home or at traditional village gatherings. The balls of yarn would then be woven on the family loom or given to the village weaver. Only the finest pieces of damask or linen finished with Venetian hemstitching were bought ready-made, and then handed over to professional embroiderers. The rest of the trousseau was, in theory, sewn and embroidered by the young woman, or at least monogrammed by her. Whether done privately at home or at a sewing bee, all her skill and pride went into this work.

The cover of an early twentieth-century catalogue (above) illustrates, in silhouette, an age-old symbol of femininity—a woman at the spinning wheel, assisted by her daughter.

Preparing the Trousseau *(left) photographed by Vincenzo Balocchi in 1916 shows a young woman bent over a white bedspread, a key item in every trousseau. At the beginning of the twentieth century, the bedspread would often be made of small squares of raised point needlework in geometric patterns executed with fine needles and mercerized cotton. The squares would then be stitched or crocheted together.*

These customs have practically disappeared from modern Western societies. Several wonderful traditions associated with the trousseau still exist, however. In Turkey, for instance, when a little girl is born, the undergarments that she will wear on her wedding day are placed in the bottom drawer of her dresser. With each birthday, various items are added to this trousseau. In Portugal, people in the port of Nazare and town of Leiria still prepare trousseaux years in advance of a wedding; at Castelo Branco, they always include the traditional bedspread embroidered with symbols of prosperity and fertility (now purchased ready-made, however, rather than embroidered by the fiancée herself).

Although the traditional refrains like "Sew, sew, sew my girl, for tomorrow you will wed" were still sung in the 1950s, these days words like stitch, embroider, and darn have become abstract and unfamiliar. The very concept of trousseau has become totally outmoded, except for a sector of the population brought up to be highly conventional or culturally sensitive to fine linen. Household linen is usually included in the wedding lists deposited at the large department stores that have taken over a mother's traditional role. Most people consider the acquisition of linen to be a necessity rather than a pleasure. It is usually bought in small quantities, is often of poorish quality and has to be frequently replaced since, in any event, it nows goes out of fashion just like everything else. Whether worn or not, used linen loses value and winds up being thrown away, whereas in the old days linen entered a whole cycle of diverse uses, from a brand-new state down to the condition of a shredded rag.

When cloth in good condition became victim of a snag or was beginning to appear worn, it would be carefully mended or darned. Darning entailed the veritable art of "re-weaving" with a needle. It occasionally produced masterpieces of camouflage, for highly skilled hands could even reconstruct the pattern of

The serenity of an afternoon devoted to caring for household linen, with sewing box close at hand and faithful dog curled up on his rug, is captured in this portrait by Alfred Smith (1851–1936) of his mother sewing (right).

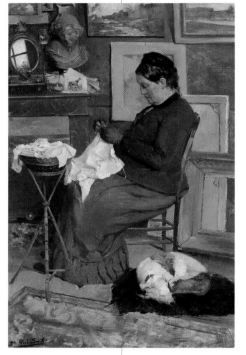

damask weave. When worn items contained sections in good condition, these would be cut out and reassembled in a patchwork, to be put to new uses. Finally, when linen was uniformly softened by years of use, it could still be used in the making of baby's diapers or linen for the ill. Once unusable, even as a dustcloth, it could always be torn into the strips used for bandages right up to the First World War. In the Poitou and Saintonge regions of France, a droll rug called a *lirette* has been woven ever since the eighteenth century; it consists of a warp of one or two sturdy yarns onto which are woven several layers of cloth scraps of varying colors. When good for no other use, shreds of fabric were recycled into paper pulp.

The consumer society has put an end to this life-cycle, although economic recession and the ecology movement have led to a rethinking of former methods of recycling. Meanwhile, there seems to be a change in consumer attitudes, favoring the purchase of better quality goods that last longer.

In the past several years, moreover, the January "white sales" invented by department stores in the late nineteenth century to reinforce new linen buying habits, seem to be meeting with increased success sparked by a renewed interest for domestic values in general. This has generated a recent trend toward linen-and-cotton or pure linen fabrics, as well as growing sales of white and unbleached material, for the first time since the arrival of colors and prints. The traditional trousseau, with its stocks of household linen designed to "last a lifetime," however, has vanished forever, not only from closets but also from consciousness. The doors of those heavy cupboards remain shut in family residences where their contents of white linen with interlacing monograms—once the pride of the mistress of the house—has imperceptibly fallen to the status of unused, old-fashioned object, even in France. Only people subject to nostalgia are still moved when they turn their heavy, magic key in the lock; yet, as

Whether in plain or pebbled weave, these old tablecloths and napkins (right) adorned with lace and openwork were used on the tea table. They perfectly incarnate the grand tradition of white linen prior to the arrival of color and prints.

Bachelard aptly noted, "if we give objects the friendship they [merit], we can not open a cupboard without a slight start. . . . "

OBSESSION WITH WHITE

". . . Beneath its russet wood, a [linen cupboard] is a very white almond. To open it is to experience an event of whiteness," continued philosopher-poet Bachelard. Prior to the vogue for multicolored "white goods," linen was always simply white, the natural color of flax that had been bleached by the sun. Everywhere flax was grown and its fibers woven, the taste for white has endured.

White, that colorless color, is also the combination of all seven colors of the spectrum. It therefore represents the potentiality of all colors, a sort of symbolic promise that has marked certain rites of passages for millennia. In ancient Rome, young boys would discard the red *pretexta* toga for a white *viril* one on reaching adolescence. The early Christians dressed in white for baptism. Priests don a white alb (from the Latin *alba*, "white") to say Mass; in the East, white is worn as a sign of mourning. In the mid-nineteenth century, the European bourgeoisie glorified the immaculate apparel of a child's First Holy Communion and a young woman's bridal gown. Nor should the antiseptic qualities associated with white be overlooked, such as white bandages supposed to favor healing.

This symbolism also stems from another tradition going back to classical times, which links purity not only to whiteness in general but to plant-based textiles in particular. Wool, even white, was banned from Egyptian temples; both Coptic priests and Druids were obliged to dress in white linen. It was probably the Roman Catholic church, however, that most heavily reinforced this ideal of pure, immaculate cloth, which was stressed to the point of becoming an obsession by the nineteenth century. In 1854, when Pius IX established the dogma of the Immaculate Conception, the Virgin Mary became the patron saint of linen maids. Moreover, the holy linen which comes in symbolic contact with body of Christ, that is to say the three communion cloths, had to be made exclusively from white hemp or flax, materials that symbolized purity of body and soul in the Holy Scriptures. As Victor Hugo asked rhetorically in *La Légende des Siècles*, "Wasn't Boaz attired in candid integrity and white linen?"

Communion cloths receive a blessing, and must remain spotlessly clean. Traditionally, they would be washed in three successive rinses and, in theory, only a priest was allowed to perform this task. The cloths could not be decorated, except for the "corporal" cloth which was embroidered with a small Greek cross in white or red thread.

The collective imagination was certainly struck by this purity of hemp and linen, this embroidery in white or red thread, this blessing of cloth and its ritual washing—and such rites were more or less transferred from the Catholic church to the bridal trousseau. The

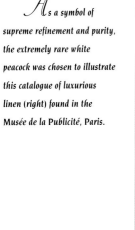

description of the display of white goods in Zola's nineteenth-century novel *The Ladies' Paradise* exploits this very metaphor:

". . . Then the white fell from the vaults—white blankets and white coverlets flapped in the air like church banners . . . And the wonder of this altar to the religion of white goods . . . was a tent made of white curtains. Muslins, gauzes, and lace in pale waves served as backdrop to the huge decoration which resembled both tabernacle and bed-alcove. It looked like a great white bed whose virginal expanse awaited the white princess, she who would come one day, all-powerful, in the white veil of a bride."

The "virginal whiteness" associated with the trousseau would progressively become the symbol of a young woman's virtue, as though the needlework (often learned from nuns) also taught a young woman the moral and family values required of every fiancée. The very contemplation of linen was part of the proper upbringing of girls, as advocated by Madame Léon Daudet in a book entitled *Comment Elever Nos Filles?*

"It is above all in front of the linen cupboard that a young girl will begin to sense the weightiness of household things. For is not the linen cupboard the most imposing representation of family security and stability? Behind its heavy doors are arranged piles of cool sheets, damask tablecloths, well-folded towels; nothing, in my opinion, is more restful to contemplate than a fine linen cupboard."

The virtue of needlework—hours spent leaning over white fabric, tugging a needle to make and decorate sheets and tablecloths—soon became assimilated with the idea of redemption. Nuns were fully aware of this when they employed wayward and repentant girls, not to mention convicts, in their institutions.

At the opposite extreme from the immaculate and

"virtuous" white so carefully ironed and folded in cupboards, however, there was also the rumpled, "intimate" white of love-making. Zola clearly alluded to this in his description of a store display that resembled both tabernacle and bed-alcove. He noted the whiteness not only of sheets, but also of undergarments. "There were slips, dressing gowns, peignoirs, long white garments, where one sensed the lazy mornings that stretched on after long evenings of tenderness."

Such garments were to be set against the pale skin that fulfilled the canons of beauty in those days, variously described as "ivory, satiny, pearly, milky, and snowy." The whiteness radiating from linen and flesh obsessed an entire society, to the extent of becoming one of the major motifs of symbolist literature.

MARKING THE TROUSSEAU

Another symbol of the traditional trousseau was the monogram of initials that intertwined like the arms of the young couple. Throughout the nineteenth century and, to a lesser extent, right into the 1950s, every item of household linen received this carefully embroidered seal. The habit disappeared with the decline of trousseaux, the appearance of fabrics more fragile

George Sand cultivated a genuine passion for household linen, and her lifestyle at Nohant required an enormous trousseau. She had damask napkins (right) embroidered very simply with her initials, in traditional cross-stitches of red thread. At the time, a red monogram was the sole authorized exception to the "all-white" rule—an exception permitted only at lunch.

Fancy white needlework was the uncontested queen of the trousseau in the nineteenth and early twentieth centuries, as magnificently illustrated by this batiste sheet dating from 1880 (right). The petals and leaves, embroidered in high relief, stand out from the sheet itself. In the 1950s, Grace Kelly had a sheet embroidered in the same way, with a blue hydrangea motif. This type of decoration, as light and insubstantial as the subject it depicts, is starched with sugar.

than linen, and notions of fashion that have dramatically shortened the life-span of linen items and rendered costly embroidery pointless.

Although marking linen is a very ancient tradition, it was not originally done for decorative purposes. When linen first began to be hoarded in the Middle Ages, sheets and "diaper cloth" (the term used at that time for both tablecloths and towels) were printed with indelible ink in one corner so that they could be identified. A fourteenth-century treatise on household management included a recipe for a liquid dye that would make a lasting mark on cloth—it was a decoction of grease, oil, and vinegar, boiled together and applied with the aid of a seal or stamp. In France, only the king's linen was actually embroidered. In 1380, during the reign of Charles V, a seamstress named Robinette la Couturière received an order for 194 diaper cloths "all to be marked with the fleur-de-lys and a sword."

Asselot, who was the linen maid to Isabeau of Bavaria and Charles VI, received payment for having "marked 158 cloths and towels with a demi fleur-de-lys, each piece marked on both ends," while Jehanne la Lorraine was paid for "fashioning eighty-four fleurs-de-lys in black thread." The color of the thread might vary—during the reign of Louis XII (1498-1515), the royal mark was three fleurs-de-lys embroidered in yellow. At Versailles in the seventeenth century, items belonging to Louis XIV were marked with a crown and two Vs for the main Versailles Château, or a T for the Trianon Château. Red thread remained the usual color, however, as evoked by George Sand in her memoirs about life at Nohant Château: "The large tablecloth of magnificent white bore on one of its corners the discreet mark of the maréchal de Saxe, the family ancestor, a small mark representing two crossed swords, embroidered in red thread."

Both embroidery and engraved seals were used to mark linen until the end of the eighteenth century. In 1779, a Paris engraver on rue Saint-Jacques offered customers a full range of stamps, along with the

"liquor" required to print initials in a way that would not alter the cloth in any way yet would resist successive washings.

It was above all in the nineteenth century, in imitation of royalty and nobility whose crests and arms had long personalized linen, that the embroidered monogram evolved into an ornament, especially on bed sheets. This habit of marking every item of household linen should be understood in the context of the rise of individualism and the almost ostentatious affirmation of self that characterized the nineteenth-century bourgeoisie. For want of crowns and coats of arms, the aspiring middle classes placed their initials on everything, from linen to silver, crystal, and china—to the delight of today's collectors and connoisseurs.

When the trousseau was being prepared during the betrothal period, which was usually the case in town, the future husband's initial was placed in front of the bride's. If the embroidery was done by the young girl long before marriage, it might be monogrammed with only the bride's initials, not just because those of the groom were unknown, but also as a sign of her personal property. This practice might also have stemmed from a sort of narcissism, since linen was one of the many symbols of the self, and it guaranteed that the name of the maternal forebear would not be completely forgotten by descendants—the monogram of her initials would stir their memory. Although the art of embroidery was generally transmitted from mother to daughter, during France's Third Republic (1870–1940) it was taught to girls in schools. The education culminated in a cross-stitched alphabetical sampler known as a *marquette*, of greater or lesser value depending on the skill of the embroiderer. French girls thus all acquired basic embroidery skills, even though the finest items in a trousseau were usually entrusted to the deft fingers of linen maids and professional embroiderers.

Top bed sheets were usually monogrammed in a raised satin-stitch roughly twelve inches from the openwork border that was visible on the turned-down edge. In the early twentieth century, the letters were often interlaced and set in a medallion, usually two to four inches high. Only pure linen cloth could be easily embroidered, fabric made of hemp fibers being too thick. Everyday sheets and bottom sheets were simply marked in a corner with red thread, using a straightforward cross-stitch. Pillowcases, when decorated at the corners with fancy white needlework, would be monogrammed in the upper middle or, if conceived in pairs, in opposite upper corners.

Ceremonial tablecloths were monogrammed in the center, unless two monograms were placed symmetrically around the middle so as to avoid being covered by the centerpieces that were so fashionable during the nineteenth and early twentieth centuries. Table napkins were embroidered in the middle when they matched the tablecloth; otherwise they were marked in a corner with red thread in a cross-stitch or in bourdon embroidery. Dish towels were monogrammed in a corner or in the upper center, in red or blue thread depending on the color of the traditional stripe; sometimes they were even embroidered with the words "glasses," "crystal," "dishes," "silver," "pans," "furniture," and "oven," when each type of towel, of differing quality, had a specific use.

Bathroom linen did not escape the craze for personalization. Monograms were generally placed at the top of towels, between the two bands, although they were eventually moved to the bottom where they would be most visible when hung over a towel rack.

Monograms gave birth to a multitude of models and books proposing designs that ranged from simple to highly complex. Apart from the timeless slanted script that the French call *lettres anglaises*, these models reflected the various periods and artistic movements of the twentieth century. Until shortly after the First World War, department store catalogues presented a wide range of designs that could be embroidered by hand or by machine; customers could even send in their own specific design, including crests and arms. In 1914, the catalogue of the bridal department at Les Grands Magasins du Louvre even offered the "extraordinary service" of having complex images woven—views of châteaux, crests, coats of arms, and monograms—no matter how complicated. Customers merely had to send a print or sketch that the store's own designer would copy. Traditionally, the thread used for monograms was white; color did not appear much before 1925. In certain regions of France, notably Béarn, tablecloths and napkins had blue stripes running from one selvage to the other, and would therefore be embroidered in matching thread. All linen garments were also monogrammed, especially handkerchiefs (which, had they not been initialed, would hardly have been worth dropping or leaving behind).

For obvious reasons of identification, all personal items belonging to boarders at schools and other institutions had to be monogrammed in red thread, at least until the invention of machine-embroidered ribbons bearing initials or the entire name, similar to those still used today.

In fact, it was only in the early 1960s that initials and name tags died out in Europe. But the early signs of a revival can perhaps be perceived in the recent timid appearance of monograms that are entirely anonymous. Intertwined initials in the *lettres anglaises* style are ambiguous enough to be read as desired, whether embroidered on bath towels or engraved on glasses. Currently, there is a certain renewal of interest in having personal monograms, and many stores now offer to hand- or machine-embroider items. The Porthault firm estimates that 15 to 20% of its European sales are embroidered, a figure that drops slightly on orders from the United States.

Although sheets are the most commonly monogrammed items, initials are also placed on tablecloths and napkins. The height of refinement on pure linen is hand-embroidery using chain stitch, Beauvais stitch or bourdon embroidery. On cotton, bourdon or Cornely

The style chosen for a monogram often reflects the prevailing fashions of an entire epoch. This hand-woven, salmon pink batiste sheet was adorned with an embroidered crown and Art Deco appliqué monogram in matching tones. It was made by Porthault for Edward VIII, the future duke of Windsor.

machine-stitching is to be preferred. A "laundry mark," which is a sort of identification number, is stitched onto bottom sheets in white or, more conventionally, red thread. The down comforters (or "duvets") from northern climes have become popular everywhere and are now also embroidered, generally centered twelve inches from the top edge. As mentioned above, table-cloths—even when round—usually take two mono-grams, placed a symmetrical distance from the middle.

Dancing nuns— this choreography in black and white takes place regularly at the Trappist convent of Chambarand, when the nuns stretch and fold their sheets after washing.

THE WORLD OF LINEN MAIDS

Although extensively practiced in the nineteenth century, the profession of linen maid is now a thing of the past. When the trade first emerged and became organized during the thirteenth century, it was not exclusively feminine. In 1292, the tax registers record that the linen drapers' and linen maids' guild duly paid its tallage (or tax) and enjoyed certain royal privileges.

At stately residences, even kitchen linen is subject to strict rules of care, observed by the linen maid with all the requisite attention. Once ironed, it must be checked, counted and folded, then stacked at the bottom of the pile in order to maintain the rotation cycle (right).

Napkins, normally square and now much smaller than before, are marked on the upper left-hand corner, visible when folded in a triangle. To add a fancy touch to dish towels, they can be directly embroidered on the colored stripe using contrasting white thread.

For six hundred years—prior to the invention of the sewing machine— stitching, hemming, and mono-gramming an incalculable number of items ranging from medieval diaper cloth and sheets to the last enor-mous trousseaux executed by hand, required billions of tiny stitches patiently aligned one after another by trousseau specialists whose only tools were a needle, pointed little scissors, and an engraved thimble.

Prior to launching his last crusade, Saint Louis, who ruled France from 1226 to 1270 as Louis IX, even allowed the poorest linen maids to display their mer-chandise along the wall of the Innocents' Cemetery, later dubbed rue de la Lingerie.

The guild received its statutes much later, in 1485. In 1572, the various trades associated with linen goods were gathered into one guild, under the name of "linen and hemp goods dealers." The text of the new statutes was quite similar to those of other guilds, except for an additional clause concerning morality. No other document of the same type contains such a clause, which stipulated that "no girl or woman of shamed or

In the Netherlands, both aristocratic and bourgeois residences have large linen rooms just below the attic. This well-ordered room (left) in Duivenvoorde Castle has an ingenious system of moveable rods over which the laundry can be hung prior to folding. The furnishings are painted "fly blue," a color reputed to keep flies away. Miniature examples of such linen rooms can be seen in the famous dollhouses displayed in the Rijksmuseum and Frans Hals Museum, both in Amsterdam.

blameworthy body" could join the guild. This exclusion can probably be explained by the fact that nobles, judges, and "gentlefolk" of the day sent their daughters to board with linen maids so that they could "learn to sew, behave genteelly, and avoid idleness," for idleness, as everyone knew, was the mother of all vice. Newer statutes in 1643 insisted further on the "proper life, good morals and Catholic religion" required of apprentices. The four-year apprenticeship was followed by two years of employment as a shop girl, although married women were not allowed beyond the apprentice stage. In recognition of Louis IX's protection of the poorest linen maids, he was made the patron saint of their guild, along with Saint Veronica.

History has recorded the names of many linen drapers who supplied kings and other royalty—Jean la Violette, Guillemette la Pomme, Jeanne la Briaise and Robinette la Couturière. In the early sixteenth century, one such supplier by the name of Jehanne Cauchonne, was most certainly overwhelmed with work from Louise of Savoy, the duchess of Angoulême and mother of François I, known for her extravagant expenditures on fine linen.

In addition to household linen, drapers also made garments. On both types of product they would add "needlepoints", guipure (or coarse lace) and finer lace (still known as Flemish trim), until a royal decree outlawed lace decoration. Linen drapers nevertheless flouted the ban, selling lace at ever-inflated prices, prompting Cardinal Richelieu to complain several times in 1636 of feeble policing in Paris.

In the seventeenth and eighteenth centuries, linen drapers' shops were located in the arcades of the notoriously racy Palais Royal, so that *noguettes,* as linen maids were known in France, had a difficult time with men on the prowl. In a rather stereotyped way, linen maids had a reputation for being "bawdy." Nineteenth-century reality turned out to be even more trying as their lifestyle became a good deal harsher. The wages of domestic linen maids were low, because convents and women's institutions also churned out quality embroidered goods, creating stiff competition. In Beguine convents in Flanders, as well as in many religious schools, boarders conscientiously tugged at their needles right into the 1930s. Alain Defossé described such a scene in his novel set in an Antwerp orphanage.

The linen room at the Rohan Château in Brittany (above) conveys all the care with which aristocratic French families treat their linen. The room still contains a stove for heating irons, and a large ironing table covered with a cloth. Once the linen is impeccably clean, ironed, and folded, it is carefully labeled and stacked in a huge cupboard (left).

"Orders flooded in. Affluent households wanted embroidered collars, damask tablecloths, sheets, and napkins with their own monogram. We put our noses to the white fabric, working silently in a golden pond of light that crawled slowly across the refectory as the afternoon advanced. . . ."

In mid-nineteenth-century Paris, two thirds of linen maids were mere seamstress-embroiderers who toiled at home, that is to say cooped up in minuscule maid's rooms at the top of Haussmann's new stone buildings. They worked on a piece-basis for makers of luxury trousseaux, and were often women who had been "seduced and abandoned." They were henceforth excluded from society, sometimes raising children on their own. In the countryside, for example, a young woman merely had to have "erred" once for her father to banish her from the family home. With the rise of the "white linen civilization," as Michelle Perrot described it, the linen maid population ballooned in the latter part of the century, numbering some seventy thousand in Paris alone by 1870.

Perpetuating the myth, it was assumed that these young women were unable to pass up a man, thereby providing convenient fodder for male fantasies of the day. True enough, linen embroiderers were also recruited from among the ranks of "kept women" and *grisettes* (seamstresses in the garment industry who were "known" for their loose morals). Whatever the case, using a needle with dexterity, huddled tirelessly over such white, personal lingerie, "sketched a sweet if ambivalent figure of femininity" that has always held great fascination for the male imagination, according to Alain Corbin in an article in *La Revue de la Société d'Ethnologie Française*.

FROM PALACES TO PALATIAL HOTELS

Although the guild of linen maids has vanished, the various tasks they performed are still done by modern professionals responsible for maintaining the house-

hold linen in state residences, private manors, and hotels. At Elysée Palace, where France's president resides, there is a linen room lined with cupboards whose massive doors of carved and polished oak are backed with blond wood. The shelves inside contain the linen tended by the maids. Every morning, they prepare a list of the linen required during the day. In order to remove any trace of folding from a chosen tablecloth, it will be ironed again before being laid on the table. After use, the maids "visit" every item before it goes into the wash, so that they can attend to a hem that has come undone, to early signs of wear, or to a flagging stitch of embroidery. If the situation seems more serious, the maids will mend or darn invisibly. If the item has been embroidered, they reproduce the pattern on the tear and then execute it in mirror image so that overall symmetry is maintained. When the linen is returned to them after having been washed, starched, and ironed (the most delicate items folded in pieces of tissue paper, the tablecloths folded accordion-fashion to make it easy to spread them on the table), linen maids check all items one last time and then place them carefully in the cupboards. Neither Elysée Palace nor the palace that houses France's Ministry of Foreign Affairs on Quai d'Orsay has a laundry on the premises. The Elysée linen is laundered in the suburb of Reuil-Malmaison, while that of the Quai d'Orsay is laundered in Houdan. This is a vestige of a tradition that goes back to the seventeenth century, when fine linen was washed and bleached in fields near Mantes-la-Jolie to the west of Paris.

Another tradition, dating from the time of Louis XIV, is also maintained—namely, a hierarchy of bed linen depending on the rank of guests. Strict rules of protocol determine whether the sheets will be of pure linen, linen-and-cotton, or cotton. Linen sheets are decorated with Venice openwork, the others with bourdon embroidery. A few more sophisticated sets, in white or pastel batiste decorated with embroidery or lace inlays, are reserved for extra special guests.

Most stately residences now housing French government offices have their own sets of monogrammed linen. At the Ministry of Foreign Affairs, which plays host to distinguished foreign guests, damask napkins are woven with various initials: AE for Affaires Etrangères, QO for Quai d'Orsay, and RF for République Française.

The Grand Trianon at Versailles was recently renovated and allocated to the Ministry of Foreign Affairs, which houses certain guests there. A whole range of household linen was therefore designed by the Porthault firm. The sheets are made of a soft white cotton satin, with turndowns showing three wide bands of bourdon embroidery that match the color of each room. The terrycloth towels in the bathrooms are all finished with three satin bands.

At Elysée Palace, the bathroom linen is white with a Greek border; the fine bath towels and hand towels are of different diamond weaves. Like all the other linen in the palace, it is marked "PR" (for *Présidence de la République*) followed by the last two digits of the year it was placed in service.

The linen used by employees also respects tradition. In the kitchen of France's presidential palace, "all-purpose" dish towels have red stripes, those used for china have white stripes, and those reserved for glasses are plain. At the Quai d'Orsay, the red bands on dish towels also carry the ministry's official name which reads *Ministère des Affaires Etrangères.*

In Great Britain, a film made by the BBC to celebrate Queen Elizabeth II's fortieth jubilee shows servants getting ready to set the table for a huge dinner at Windsor Castle by polishing all the crystal with cloths of unbleached linen decorated with thin red stripes and a red embroidered "W" in the lower left corner followed by the date of entry into service.

At Buckingham Palace, the queen herself selects a few firms as "purveyors to Her Majesty" of table and bed linen, according to John de Lierre, owner of The White House, a famous shop founded in 1906 that now supplies Prince Charles with linen. Official suppliers are obliged to design original items for the queen every three years.

In all state residences, the choice of table linen is a question of protocol. At Elysée Palace, the tablecloth is always white, with pastel underlays for casual lunches. During state dinners, the cloths are cotton voile embroidered with gold thread, placed on white

damask underlays that, since 1985, have been allowed to hang down to the floor. One such underlay, designed by the Noël firm, is decorated with large stars, while another Noël design is graced with diamond-shapes. For lunches, the embroidery may be colored; the most often used models are the blue "Elseneur" leaf pattern, the green "Acacia" pattern, and the brown "vine leaf" pattern.

Certain old tablecloths are still in use, like the damask cloths called "Marie-Antoinette" and "Rose des Vents," which date from the early twentieth century. Others are so enormous that they no longer suit the new dining etiquette of small round tables seating ten guests. However, two oval tablecloths embroidered with white and gold acanthus leaves, ordered from Porthault by president Vincent Auriol (1947–1954), are still perfectly suited to the oval presidential table, which can seat up to twenty diners. Not all old linen is so lucky; two thirty-seven-yard-long Egyptian cotton tablecloths decorated with gold stars, which were ordered by President René Coty (1954–1958) for a reception in honor of Elizabeth II, hibernate in the cupboard, as does a gigantic lace tablecloth originally used by the Quai d'Orsay for banquets in the Hall of Mirrors at Versailles. Only the immense damask cloths are still occasionally used on long side tables.

For official receptions, gold embroidery is used throughout the world. At the White House in Washington, where Jackie Kennedy had all the household linen replaced in 1962, a Porthault design displays the great seal of the United States in gold bourdon embroidery. The bed linen, on the other hand, was selected from among Porthault's famous fancy prints.

At Elysée Palace, the French president's personal quarters have their own linen, decorated with fancy embroidery or openwork, for private lunches and teas. The presidential linen cupboard also holds the only two major contemporary designs produced by Porthault for private receptions. One tablecloth, ordered by the wife of President Georges Pompidou

Kitchen linen at the Quai d'Orsay, home of France's Ministry of Foreign Affairs, is made of pure linen with classic red bands. The finest dish towels are woven with the full name, Ministère des Affaires Etrangères. Not a single item is laundered or ironed at the ministry—the laundry is sent to the Paris suburb of Houdan.

(1969–1974), has large geometric appliqués against a beige ground, creating a series of orange and brown circles. With its matching china the ensemble constitutes an excellent example of early 1970s decor. The second Porthault creation is more recent, dating from 1991, during François Mitterrand's second term of office. Aptly called "South Pole," it is woven in blue cotton voile, evoking a sky in which stars and constellations are embroidered in yellow-gold. To add to this enchanting atmosphere, the National Porcelain Manufactory in Sèvres produced superb plates of alternating pale blue or orangish-pink ground, decoratively edged with tiny astronauts, stars and constellations.

In tourist hotels, where intense use rules out fragile materials, room and table linen are selected above all for their sturdiness and ease of maintenance. These days, most hotels rent their linen from companies who launder and repair it. Even if a hotel owns the linen it uses, its sheets may still have to meet the requirements of certain automated laundries that insist for technical reasons (notably the calendering process which produces a sheen) on cotton and polyester blends, which have therefore found their way even into grand hotels.

Nevertheless, many hotels use standard white "70-thread per square centimeter" sturdy cotton percale sheets finished with bourdon embroidery.

More sophisticated linen, supplied by firms like Porthault, is found in only the finest of hotels. Travelers must spend a weekend at luxury establishments such as the Raphaël Hotel in Munich or the Mamounia in Marrakech to enjoy cotton satin sheets silky to the touch but ten times more expensive than ordinary sheets. As for champagne-colored sheets, so vulnerable to launderers' bluing techniques, they can be found only in exclusive hotels such as the Fitz Roy at the French ski resort of Val Thorens. Pure linen sheets are encountered only in certain small, charming hotels that stand out from the crowd, such as the Moulin Hotel in Mougins or the Château de Bagnols near Lyon. Some palatial hotels, nevertheless, inquire of loyal customers' preferences in order to provide special linen in just the right color or fabric. Finally, in all grand hotels, the bed is most often covered with a spread made of cotton piqué.

Bathroom linen is normally divided into thick terrycloth towels and thinner towels of honeycomb or Jacquard diamond weaves, probably the oldest weaves

Every grand hotel in the world has its own logo woven or embroidered on its linen, whether used at the table, in the bathroom or in the bedroom. The logo for the Castello dei Cesari Hotel in Milan was woven in colored damask by the famous Italian specialist, Frette (above). Everything is precious at the Hôtel Ritz in Paris, so linen receives a great deal of attention from the staff. Stacks of colored damask-weave tablecloths and napkins are carefully counted and bundled in the laundry room. As an ultimate mark of luxury, all the bath linen, including terrycloth bathrobes, are embroidered with the hotel logo in gold thread of sturdy lurex (right).

A heated towel rack is one of the most delightful refinements offered by certain hotels. A soft towel that is also warm to the touch produces an unforgettable caress—as can be experienced at the Hotel Trois Couronnes in Vevey, where terrycloth towels are woven with the establishment's complete name (right).

still in use. These traditional honeycomb towels are usually finished at each end with a Greek border, while the terrycloth towels are woven with a twisted thread to give the loops a fuller and slightly coiled effect. Hotel towels are almost always white, or very occasionally a pastel color—fancier colors and designs are reserved for pool use.

Linen, regardless of the hotel's standing, always bears the establishment's name or logo, which inevitably triggers the acquisitive reflex of souvenir-seeking guests. The "standard" signature on traditional towels is the full name of the hotel repeated along the bands woven on the warp. The name may either be white-on-white or woven in one color. The name or logo might also be rendered as a Jacquard print placed above the Greek border. On terrycloth, the name may stand out in loops against the ground weave. If the towel has a band between the two selvages, this may also take the signature woven in white or in color.

What really makes a hotel distinguished, however, is the use of embroidery. Thanks to modern machines, towels and bathrobes can be mechanically embroidered in an infinite range of colors, including gold (lurex), thereby displaying the names and logos of grand hotels throughout the world.

Tradition still holds sway in kitchens. Dish towels are cut from well-known standard cotton or cotton-blend cloth with red or blue stripes. Glasses, however, are always dried with pure linen, especially in the bars of grand hotels, because it makes glasses sparkle and sheds no unsightly lint.

In restaurants, tablecloths are for the most part highly conventional and woven in natural fibers even though the demand for synthetic fabrics is unfortunately increasing every year. They are usually white or pastel, in a checked or dotted Jacquard weave with Greek border. Certain traditional and somewhat more sophisticated weaves can still be found, like the dot-and-ribbon, flowered-check, wisteria, rose, Venice and Trianon patterns. All this widely used table linen is poetically referred to by French professionals as "satin band satin," that is to say framed by a satin band. Such linen may be personalized with a "woven insert" logo.

When the tablecloth is of pure linen or of a linen-and-cotton blend, it may be embellished with a "granite" or "pebble" ground. These textures generate changing highlights for the silver placed on tables at hotels such as the Ritz, the Plaza-Athenée, or the Carlton in Paris. The hotel's symbol or initials are then woven into the center of the tablecloth, unless they figure as a pattern woven all through the cloth, as in the satin tablecloths used at the Troisgros Restaurant in Roanne.

In order to provide a more original touch, some restaurants opt for multicolored Jacquard patterns with flowers or geometric shapes. Porthault designs in such fabrics now grace tables at the Pic and Trianon Palace restaurants. Fashionable prints are generally reserved for glamorous shaded terraces or for the cloths placed on breakfast trays. They are made of cretonne, a somewhat rustic cloth that suits the summery tables of interior gardens in city hotels or, even better, the countryside that comes right up to the door of gourmet restaurants in rural France.

Finally, restaurant owners also like to adorn their tables with traditional linen that is typical of the region. In Alsace, wonderful old-fashioned prints with somewhat naïve flowers continue to be produced by a famous firm in Ribeauvillé, Manufacture d'Impressions sur Etoffes, whose tablecloths and napkins can be found in many an Alsatian wine bar. These cloths have even come to symbolize the region, as does the banded linen found in the Basque country, brought back into fashion by the Jean Vier factory and now widely used throughout France and Spain.

Grand seaside hotels blessed with sun and sand know how much pleasure guests get from sliding into fine white sheets that have been freshly washed, ironed, and delivered by the hotel's linen maids, as in this hotel located in Anguilla, British West Indies (right).

True luxury and refinement in grand hotels always starts in the linen room. Les Prés d'Eugénie, a hotel at the French resort of Eugénie-les-Bains, sets an example of distinguished care and attention to detail (right).

SOAP
OPERA

*L*à-bas dans le pré plein de marguerites
Comme un grand billard mangé par les mites
On voit un tableau sans pareil
Un fil qui brille au soleil
Et puis au milieu des poteaux qui penchent
Tendue sur le fil la lessive blanche . . .

There's a meadow where daisies poke holes
Through a carpet of green as it rolls
Past the wonderful sight
Of laundry so white
On a clothesline stretched tight
'Twixt two valiant but struggling poles . . .

Thus French singer Charles Trenet sang of the days when meadows were dotted with "clotheslines stretched tight" to hold heavy linen or linen-and-cotton sheets. Once taken off the line, two women would pull the sheets taut with all their strength before folding them once lengthwise, then in half again and again. The folded sheets would finally be placed in a large wicker basket with handles. Those were the days when the week was organized around washing day, ironing day, and mending day, and when tradition dictated that upper middle-class homes employ a washer-woman, a linen maid, and a sewing maid, each coming to the house on her appointed day.

Superstition also played a role. People were careful to avoid choosing Friday as the weekly washing day since it was associated with the death of Christ, and thus was one of the many days of the year considered unpropitious for performing the rite of laundering.

FROM WASHBOARD
TO WASHING MACHINE

These days, laundry goes into a machine in the morning and, at the touch of a button or two, is clean and dry by noon. It is hardly surprising that the concept of a special washing day has fallen out of use, especially since the chore is often slotted into the free time available to the mistress of the house. "Doing the laundry" is

The charms of yesteryear included doing the laundry at a fine stone washhouse bathed in the soft light of southern France, using a bar of traditional Marseille soap, a scrub brush, and washboard (preceding double page, left).

Another image from the past is this postcard illustration of a laundry maid carrying linen on her back in a wicker basket, circa 1900 (preceding page).

no longer the trial of strength that it was for centuries, when it was done only once or twice a year, or at best, each change of season. The women in France charged with the task of *la buée* ("the laundry") may well have prosaically dubbed it *la suée* ("the sweat"). This tedious task has a long history, almost as long as that of linen itself. Present-day readers are hereby invited to set the buttons on their modern machine, add some magic powder that inevitably washes "whites even whiter," and pull up a chair for the story.

The opening chapter was idyllic, according to one of the earliest literary accounts, Homer's description of Nausicaa and her attendants in book VI of *The Odyssey*. The goddess Athena advised Nausicaa to do her laundry at a particular place by a stream where she would encounter Odysseus.

"And when they came to the beautiful stream of the river, where there were plentiful places to wash and much lovely water flowed forth to clean what had got very dirty, there they unharnessed the mules from the chariot. . . . They took the clothes in their hands, carried them to the black water, and trod them in pits, swiftly vying with one another. But when they had washed and cleaned all the dirty clothes, they spread them in a row on the strand where especially the ocean washed pebbles up along the shore. They bathed and anointed themselves richly with olive oil. Then they had their dinner along the banks of the river and wait-ed for the clothes to dry in the gleam of the sun."

Long before Homer composed this delightful scene, doing the laundry had been an age-old occupa-tion. Around 4000 B.C., the Egyptians were already making soap from natural sodium car-bonate mixed with fat, and sim-ilar methods were apparently used in India and China. What-ever the case, the fact is that both Indians and Chinese still have a worldwide reputation as launderers.

The Bible gives a "recipe" for soap made from sodium carbonate and potassium, for washing the sacred linen whose whiteness became the

The washhouse has always been a woman's realm, inspiring artists to produce graceful images like this eighteenth-century engraving of Italian washerwomen (below). The woman on the right is scrubbing the laundry, the one on the left is about to carry it off to be rinsed, and the one in the background is smoothing and hanging it. Alchemy of sun, grass and wind. Drying and bleaching laundry—called "grassing"— was long a speciality of the Dutch countryside. The grass had to be clean, and the laundry had to be regularly moistened so that the drying would last several days in order to produce a brilliant white. Such a scene (right) was painted by Pieter Bruegel (circa 1520–1569) in a detail from Flemish Market and Washhouse (Prado, Madrid).

well-known Judeo-Christian symbol of purity. In ancient Rome, chalk was used to clean and degrease fabrics. According to Pliny, the best chalk for making white cloth sparkle came from Umbria. Fumigation with sulfur was another method, used right up to the eighteenth century. Every region had its own recipe. The Gauls reportedly made black soap from tallow mixed with ash, whereas the Teutons were already unwitting ecologists in their use of a natural cleansing agent, namely the stem and root of the saponaria plant, which lathered like soap when crushed in water.

Real soap, however—made from various combinations of alkalis, potassium and sodium salts, and fatty substances—did not become a relatively common product until the twelfth century. Quality significantly improved when potassium and caustic soda replaced the use of ash, and when olive oil was used instead of animal fat. Historians generally date this breakthrough to around 1300; the appearance of scented bars of soap did not occur until 1579, in Venice, Genoa, Malaga, Alicante and Marseille, cities which produced or imported olive oil in quantities sufficient to encourage the manufacture of soap. Traditional Marseille soap, the quintessential French soap still sold today, contains at least 72% olive oil and uses scents from aromatic plants that grow in the dry countryside nearby. Yet the first really pure soap marketed on a retail basis—wrapped in parchment paper and a cardboard box—was an American invention, manufactured by the Lever Company in 1888 under the name "Sunlight."

The second chapter in the story of soap is strangely linked to war, and might be titled, "How to postpone the moment of battle." It occurred in 1297, in the countryside around Lille, when the Flemish city was under siege by French troops. *La Chronique Normande* recorded that the king's daughters had placed "cloths from the household of the king and queen in the field, then spread the washing along La Maladerie near the [city] gate. . . ." When Le Roux de Fauquemont and his knights wanted to leave the building to do battle with

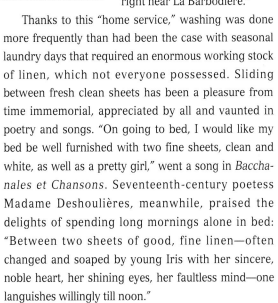

the French, they had to remain inside "till the folk on foot had gathered in the wash."

In order to avoid postponing battle, they might simply have given the laundry to a professional launderer—the tax rolls of 1292 list forty-three. In 1261, the household of King Louis IX (Saint Louis) included a keeper of the household linen and a laundry maid, plus a special "laundress to the king" who washed the monarch's personal clothing. In the Flemish city of Bruges, launderers made their appearance in the register of trades in 1387.

People with servants had their laundry washed at home. The tale *Nuits Facétieuses de Straparole* includes a passage in which a maid is advised, "'Better wait for another day because it is raining'—and hence the chambermaid was prevented from washing our shirts, sheets and other linen. . . ." In towns, when laundry was done at home, strolling merchants would sell the ash used for soap, the finest quality ash coming from oak. Merchants would cry, "ash for laundry maids . . . ash for laundry maids . . . six francs a bushel . . . on Rue Saint-Marceau . . . right near La Barbodière."

Thanks to this "home service," washing was done more frequently than had been the case with seasonal laundry days that required an enormous working stock of linen, which not everyone possessed. Sliding between fresh clean sheets has been a pleasure from time immemorial, appreciated by all and vaunted in poetry and songs. "On going to bed, I would like my bed be well furnished with two fine sheets, clean and white, as well as a pretty girl," went a song in *Bacchanales et Chansons*. Seventeenth-century poetess Madame Deshoulières, meanwhile, praised the delights of spending long mornings alone in bed: "Between two sheets of good, fine linen—often changed and soaped by young Iris with her sincere, noble heart, her shining eyes, her faultless mind—one languishes willingly till noon."

The "soaping" of a traditional semi-annual wash tolerated no such indolence, for it represented a quite

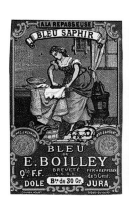

In Europe, laundry day was once what it still is in many parts of the world—a special time of female companionship. Women would meet at the washhouse, often accompanied by their youngest children, where they could chat freely, sharing joys, sorrows, and the local news. In this respect, washing machines will never be able to replace riverbanks like that of the Meuse, pictured here in the early twentieth century (above), nor public washhouses like that of Metz (below). In such public washhouses in large cities, professional washerwomen as well as private housewives would rent a spot along with all the equipment needed to do the laundry.

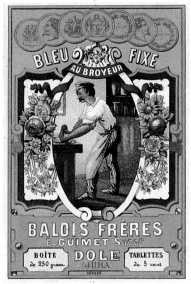

colossal task requiring several days. The operation began indoors with the soaking and scrubbing stages and finished outdoors with a rinse in running water. The sequence remained basically unchanged until 1850 or so, when washing machines first began to make their appearance in cities.

The initial "pre-soak" was done in running water. Then came the "cold soak": a large piece of cloth was placed at the bottom of an earthenware vessel or metal-hooped wood basin (which dates back to at least Roman times), on top of which went the dirty laundry with the finest items at the bottom and the coarsest things on the top. Water was then regularly poured in while the whole mass was trampled underfoot. When the water that overflowed was clear, the "hot soak" could begin. Another cloth was placed over the laundry, and sifted ash from oak or other types of wood mixed with natural sodium carbonates, extracted from saponaria plants found along the shores of the Mediterranean, plus ash from wine lees, was spread over the cloth. Boiling water was then poured continuously over the ash mixture from a large wooden ladle, and the active ingredients would go to work on the laundry. The

water that was drained from the tub would be collected and reused, the whole process lasting from twelve to fifteen hours.

After this slow "chemical" stage, the laundry was transported on carts to a river or washhouse for the second, outdoor, stage. There, women armed with brushes and beaters would finish the scrubbing process. "Finish off the linen" might be closer to the mark, according to eighteenth-century Paris chronicler Louis-Sébastien Mercier. In his *Tableau de Paris*, written between 1782 and 1788, he noted that "there is no city where the linen is more worn than in Paris . . . households that are not indigent will provide plenty at meals, but the tablecloth will be coarse and patched. The Parisians' motto is Horrid Linen! This is apparently because it is constantly torn, and they dread the washerwomen's brushes and beaters."

Be that as it may, following this operation, the linen had to be rinsed, wrung, and put out to dry. Drying was done in fields of "high, dense grass" or on clotheslines, or in well-ventilated sheds. In order to lend sparkle to laundry that was less than perfectly white, the following procedure was employed: "The laundry was

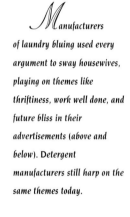

Manufacturers of laundry bluing used every argument to sway housewives, playing on themes like thriftiness, work well done, and future bliss in their advertisements (above and below). Detergent manufacturers still harp on the same themes today.

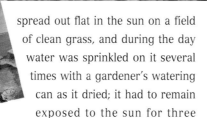

In 1938, the Trois Quartiers department store used the then fashionable image of a Portuguese laundry maid carrying a basket of laundry on her head (below). This poster for the store's white goods display was based on a watercolor by Marino.

spread out flat in the sun on a field of clean grass, and during the day water was sprinkled on it several times with a gardener's watering can as it dried; it had to remain exposed to the sun for three days, it was then folded while still damp and finally ironed." This description from Diderot and d'Alembert's eighteenth-century *Encyclopédie* was derived from methods used at Haarlem in Holland, known for giving a wonderful, bluish whiteness to the laundry that was sometimes attributed to the damp local climate, sometimes to the combined action of sun and moon, sometimes to the quality of the river water, sometimes to the ashes used, indeed sometimes to the use of whey during the rinse. In 1713, Etienne Sabbe wrote a treatise on the subject in which he asserted that the secret was a product called

vedasse, probably from the Dutch term *weed*—for woad or pastel (an indigo-like dye paste made from a decoction of woad twigs)—plus *asse* for ash. The Dutch, moreover, had an important indigo trade and held a monopoly on it for a long time. Bluing, using either indigo or pastel, was first sold in cube or ball form, then in powder, and is still sold in France in the form of a little plastic sphere filled with powder. Indigo had been known in France since Renaissance times, but its importation was outlawed by decree during the reign of Henri IV (1589–1610). Colbert, minister under Louis XIV (1642–1713), eased the restriction under the condition that indigo be diluted to one per cent.

The Dutch reputation was such that early eighteenth-century upper-class French society, perhaps out of snobbery, would hear only of Dutch bleaching methods. The comtesse de Fürstenberg, wrote Saint-Simon, "was prodigal in all sorts of expenditures, and

A white sheet hung out to dry in the sun on a breezy summer day by a graceful laundry maid (left)—a perfect subject for a sensitive artist such as Robert Gemmel Hutchinson (1855–1936).

White sheets dotting the coast like big sails long contributed a poetic touch to the landscape, whether on a pebbly beach in Italy (left) or on a windy moor in Brittany (below).

possessing such perfect lace and so much ornament and linen, bleached only in Holland." The countess was not the only one; to the extent that, during French military campaigns in the Lowlands undertaken by Louis XIV and Louis XV, bundles of linen would be confiscated like so much war booty unless they were dispatched secretly. Ever whiter, ever farther—by the end of the seventeenth century, it was the height of fashion to send one's laundry all the way to the "isles" for bleaching, that is to say to the Caribbean.

During the nineteenth century, the quest for whiteness became obsessive, spurred by concerns for hygiene and disinfection. These concerns were alleviated only with the advances in chemistry that began in the late nineteenth century, first by Chaptal's use of steam and especially Scheele's discovery of the properties of chlorine, then by Termant's work on chloride of lime (bleaching powder), which whitened and purified linen. Finally, the bleaching power of potassium hypochlorate, which became known as Javel water or liquid bleach, was discovered by Berthollet. The real transformation in detergents and washing methods, however, occurred when the natural soda in ash was replaced by artificial sodium carbonate.

Traditional laundering rites were followed in the French countryside right up to the First World War and even afterward, in conjunction with washing machines, according to a few eyewitness accounts from the 1950s. Done at the age-old frequency of two to four times per year, they incarnated, like spring house-cleaning, a cyclic vision of time.

However vague this frequency might be, setting a date was not as easy as it might appear. Numerous religious restrictions eliminated potential wash days. The washing could not be done on 2 February, nor, in principle, during the month of the dead,

nor during Holy Week, nor the day of the procession of Saint Mark, nor the three days preceding Ascension Day, and above all not the day of the Purification of the Virgin or on Assumption Day. Nor could a Friday, which recalled Christ's death, be chosen. The most propitious period lay between 15 August (Assumption Day, corresponding also to the end of harvest activities) and 8 September. Just to complicate this already limited calendar, one had to factor in taboos linked to

Dazzling one's friends with a whiter-than-white wash became a key advertising concept for detergent manufacturers in the early twentieth century (above). It is still used today . . .

A packet of Dior crystal bleach (left). When Claude Berthollet discovered the properties of "Javel water," or chlorine bleach, in the early nineteenth century, he revolutionized washing methods. By disinfecting laundry and leaving clothes impeccably white, bleach was a major improvement on soda that frequently damaged fabrics.

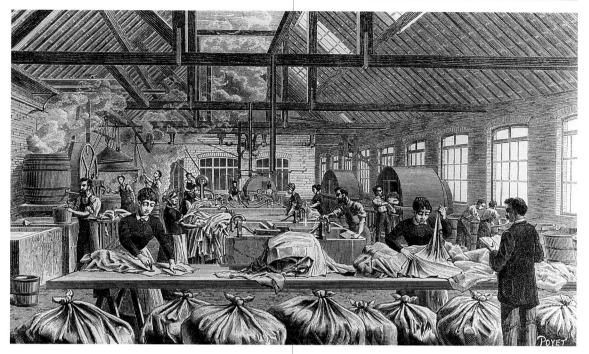

women's menstrual cycles, for they were forbidden to wash "on those days." Nor could it be forgotten that it was better to wait until any chance of frost or rain was past. Ignoring any of these taboos, of course, brought bad luck—common sayings asserted that anyone who flouted these restrictions was "washing her own shroud" or "torturing souls in Purgatory."

In the countryside, wash days entailed the participation of the whole village, providing an opportunity to show off, to display all one's linen to others. Spreading everything out on the field underscored relative abundance, and therefore social position. In cities, where this type of collective laundering was never really possible, laundry was given to professionals to wash. They would come to the house to collect a bundle of laundry, which would be returned clean. The first commercial laundries began this way, and by the nineteenth and twentieth centuries most laundering was done through

such firms, transforming small enterprises into a huge industry. But the industry began to decline during the 1960s, once most homes had installed washing machines. This coincided with the progressive disappearance of linen fabrics in favor of cotton and modern textiles that are easier to maintain and dry much faster. Today, only firms that launder linen for hotels, restaurants and large institutions still exist. Private customers who have no washing machine now go to the launderettes that have replaced the washhouses and laundry rooms of the past.

The earliest organized communities of washerwomen in France date from 1266. In 1351, when the first official statutes were published, women had already been laundering for a long time along the Seine and the Bièvre Rivers that traversed Paris, as well as on the banks of the Gros-Caillou and the port of Grenouillère. It was here, just downstream from Paris, that in the mid-fifteenth century a washerwoman did the laundry daily for the household of the duc de Nemours for a monthly wage of 135 livres; the laundry list included nine tablecloths, forty-eight napkins and clothing for fifty people. In 1623, a washhouse in the form of a boat poetically named *La Sirène* docked near the Pont des Arts in central Paris. *La Sirène* remained in use, after modernization, until it was destroyed by ice floes during the harsh winter of 1830. By the early eighteenth

The first bateau-lavoir, or floating washhouse, was docked along the banks of the Seine in Paris in 1623. There were 422 of them in service by 1886, although their days were numbered. Pictured here (right) is a bateau-lavoir in 1902, moored at the Ile de la Cité in the heart of Paris. If Emile Zola is to be believed, the bateaux-lavoirs were not always the scene of feminine harmony. The famous spanking scene in Zola's novel **L'Assommoir** *inspired this 1878 engraving by Agill (below).*

century, there were eighty-seven of these floating washhouses, or *bateaux-lavoirs*, docked along the Seine, providing space for some 2,000 washerwomen. The various bridges of Paris became hierarchical neighborhoods of linen—the realm of fine linen was located between Pont-Marie and Pont-Royal while, further west, at Gros-Caillou and Grenouillère, coarser cloth was washed. Large firms, having established contracts with distinguished families, would hire washerwomen on a day-to-day basis.

Needless to say, the whole operation was rather insalubrious, especially during low tides (when laundering was theoretically forbidden), and notably in the Hôtel-Dieu and Gros-Caillou neighborhoods where nearby boats housed tripe butchers. As early as 1667, a decree outlawed washhouses along the smaller branch of the Seine, but the city was unable to enforce the law, the washerwomen's potential gain being greater than the sanctions imposed.

Conditions were even worse on the small Bièvre River, where housewives and washerwomen who could not afford the three sous for a place on a boat simply plunked their tubs on the edge of waters reputed to be murky and which dissolved soap poorly. Furthermore, the Bièvre was already polluted by tanners, tawers, and dyers. Over the years, only the poor would still have their laundry

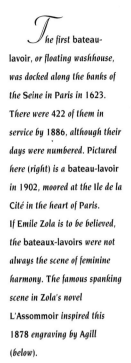

done in Paris. More affluent families sent their laundry to the countryside upstream from Paris, where a large number of laundering companies were established. The laundry would be shuttled back and forth from Paris to the country, where it could dry in meadows. As mentioned above, the court and upper classes in the eighteenth century would send their laundry even further abroad, given the fine and costly nature of their linen. For even country laundries were accused of damaging fabrics by using caustic lime instead of soda (and, later, by using too much chemical bleach that burned holes in cloth and made it rough to the touch).

There were still 94 *bateaux-lavoirs* within Paris itself in the mid-nineteenth century. Then their numbers slowly declined as modern public and private laundries sprang up on the English model, using piped water rather than that of the river. The newer laundries expanded from roughly a hundred in 1852 to 422 in 1886, providing 37,380 paying places for housewives and "piece-work" washerwomen. Payment entitled use of a common hot boiler for the initial wash, a mangle, a steam machine and an open-air drying spot. Each woman had her own compartment with a protective shield to keep her legs dry, a bucket of hot water, soap powder, bluing, and two tubs (one for scrubbing, one for rinsing). These laundries operated under the watchful eye of a manager, since

"*A* row of women stretched along the washboards down each side of the central passage; their arms were bare up to the shoulders. . . And amid the shouting, the rhythmical beating, the swishing of the downpour, amid this storm of noise muffled by the damp ceiling, the steam engine . . . chuffed and snorted away without respite, and its dancing fly-wheel seemed to be regulating the outrageous din." (Emile Zola, L'Assommoir). Photographs from the 1950s, taken inside a public washhouse on rue d'Avron in Paris.

The first washing machines with automatic agitators (right) appeared in the 1920s. Doing the laundry suddenly became child's play—women could not only do their wash at home, they could even do it wearing a blouse and high heels.

A scene from the movie French Cancan (above), directed by Jean Renoir, starring Jean Gabin as the eternal playboy. The situation illustrates the sensuality and mystery with which the male imagination endowed the feminine realm of linen care. The jovial, stocky "Aunt Catherine" (below) was an early twentieth-century example of the advertising archetype of a washerwoman.

customers were not always on their best behavior. It was not until 1930 that the first washing machines were installed, with wooden housings and three-branched agitating rods. In order to prevent items from getting lost or mixed up in the shared boiler, every woman placed her own laundry in a numbered net bag. The same system was used by companies that picked up laundry from private homes. It was not until later in the century that each item would be "tattooed" with an identification number.

The possibility of doing laundry at home was already envisaged in the nineteenth century, with the invention of an object still sometimes found in country attics and basements—a big washtub of galvanized steel with an inner, perforated basket that let water circulate. Right into the 1950s, maids would use this recipient to boil smaller items for hours on the hob or gas stove. Sometimes the laundry would be soaped and scrubbed by a washerwoman who would come to

the house a first time, then return later in the day to rinse it. In towns, where few apartments had laundry rooms, the wash was hung in the kitchen on a special line that could be hoisted to the ceiling. Folding, ironing, and darning were tasks to be done by the all-purpose maid employed by middle-class families that could not afford a special laundry maid. These chores were traditionally done in the early afternoon, before tea was served.

A French maid's handbook published in 1896 stipulated that "washing and laundering should be done on Wednesday, ironing on Thursday, and mending on Friday." In order to educate housewives, a great many "household manuals" were published in the early twentieth century. Women were given advice that reflected the preceding century's overriding concern with disinfecting laundry. In 1917, a time when colored linen was just beginning to appear, one manual discouraged its use with the warning that, although

Artist Paul Mathey (1844–1929) perfectly conveyed the atmosphere of a quiet afternoon in a lower middle-class household in his painting Interior with Woman and Child, circa 1900 (far right). Who, though, is the main subject of this domestic scene? Perhaps it is the somewhat sad boy, who probably wants to drop his hoop and go watch his mother. Or perhaps it is the woman herself, absorbed in her ironing and not wishing to be disturbed.

"attractive and gay," it was hard to care for since it could not be boiled and therefore might be "a vehicle for infectious germs." The handbook added that, for the same reason, towels made of smooth fabric were preferable to terrycloth.

Even today, at the close of the twentieth century, when it is rare for either white or colored clothing to be boiled, eternally symbolic whiteness remains a major selling point for detergents. True enough, claims for whiteness are followed closely by promises of "sparkle and color." Even though the chore of doing the laundry is totally automated, and everything—including drying—happens efficiently behind the portholes of modern appliances, the advertising images that appeal to people are those imprinted on a collective unconscious that dates back to traditional laundry days; in France at least, advertisers still use colorful, stocky characters who would be right at home in a washhouse, scrubbing linen that is then rinsed in clear, running water and hung out to dry in a meadow dotted with daisies, as in Trenet's song.

FROM SMOOTHING TOOLS TO IRONS

The final phase of beautifying linen is ironing, which makes it appear new again, as if by magic. How pleasurable it is to gaze upon and stroke smooth, wrinkle-free fabric that seems unaffected by passing time.

This desire to smoothen cloth is probably as old as weaving itself, which dates from the period when living conditions were sufficiently stable to allow humanity to develop a concern for comfort and appearance. In Neolithic times, fragments of flat bones were used to smoothen cloth. Then people realized that the weight of the tool was a factor, and they began to use polished stones and pieces of hard, smooth wood. Around the year 2000 B.C., the Egyptians, whose tombs reveal the existence of starched loincloths and pleated tunics, added a handle to "smoothing tools" to make it easier to apply greater force.

The Chinese, perhaps motived by the fact that silk wrinkles easily, had already invented a type of iron (in the form of a coal-heated pan) by the time of the Han dynasty, which spanned the years 200 B.C. to A.D. 200. This technique was documented around A.D. 730 by a painting that shows two women smoothing a piece of silk with a finely decorated bronze "pan" filled with coals. In the West, the use of heat did not seem to

occur until the Renaissance. Prior to then, smoothing devices were used; these were especially effective when made of thick glass and given a handle (so that they resembled a glass candlestick). These tools were apparently first used by the Vikings.

It was also in Scandinavia, during the sixteenth century, that Europeans first began using a "calender press." A damp piece of linen would be rolled onto a wooden cylinder that was rocked back-and-forth on the table with the aid of a plank having a carved handle—the rolling action of the cylinder smoothed the wrinkles from the linen.

Hot "irons" appeared in Europe at roughly the time that fashion and flirtation required collars and ruffs with artful pleats. There proliferated a series of instruments strange in shape but perfectly designed to curl a lace collar or to flute a buckram headpiece. These tools would be heated on a miniature oven filled with coals. In the seventeenth century, common use was also made of presses comprising a flat plate on which the carefully folded linen was placed before a second, moveable, plate was screwed on top of it. At the end of the century, as the use of starch became common, "irons" evolved rapidly, acquiring their modern ship's hull shape. The base was henceforth made of solid iron, while size and weight would vary with profession—tailors used a thick, heavy iron weighing ten to eighteen pounds, hatters used a six- or seven-pound iron, whereas laundry maids and housewives would use a more common three-pound iron. A great deal of inventiveness went into keeping irons hot; some irons were hollow so that coals could be placed directly in them, others were trowel-shaped so as to receive a preheated bar of metal.

In the nineteenth century, bases were made of cast iron, an alloy that conducts heat more efficiently and uniformly. Prior to the appearance of electric irons early in the twentieth century, many attempts were made to generate continuous heat by the internal combustion of alcohol, gas, or oil. By 1917, when the Calor Company became the leading maker of electric irons in France, the old irons were being consigned to attics, only to re-emerge decades later to the delight of bargain hunters in antique shops.

Today, the simple electric iron has been replaced by the steam iron. As to rollers and presses, they have long been the sole prerogative of professional launderers. The modern calender is a felt-covered hollow

An electric iron is the only modern touch in this magnificent laundry room (following double page) decorated with wonderful old-fashioned Portuguese tiles known as azulejos, which keep the shaded room cool. The early twentieth-century invention of the electric iron considerably simplified the chore of ironing, which the Chinese apparently developed some two thousand years ago.

cylinder that rolls over a heated metal plate. Laundry fed between the two devices is rolled flat and given a slight sheen. Presses are smaller, and are meeting with some success among private users; laundry is ironed and folded between two heated, felt-covered plates on hinges that can be pressed shut.

Professional ironers, of whom a few still exist in Paris, nevertheless prefer their traditional cast iron equipment. They heat their irons on a small stove with five pads, one for each iron, which they use in turn. Temperature is still gauged by the age-old method of holding the iron close to the cheek or the back of the hand. Professional ironers appreciate old irons for their ideal weight (reducing the risk of unwanted wrinkles), impeccable glide, and perfect "quality of heat" that gives their work an unparalleled finish. Apparently they even save time by using such old-fashioned equipment, since they don't have to pass over the same spot several times to produce perfect results, as is the case with modern steam irons.

Since, in the West, nearly everything surrounding the making and care of linen has been confided exclusively to women, it has been a rich vector of symbolism throughout history, especially during the nineteenth century. Washerwomen, linen maids, and embroiderers belong to a mysterious universe closed to men, stimulating the collective imagination (particularly male fantasies) characteristic of any given period.

Whereas washerwomen may be intimidating, and needlework evokes tenderness, a woman with an iron suggests sensuality. In her damp shop the scent of semi-bared skin mingles with that of warm fabric; the slow, weighty, measured movements of the iron magically restore linen to its original purity and softness. All those personal, lace-trimmed items, embroidered and starched, hang in her stall, imbuing the atmosphere with an erotic power often illustrated in literature and art, notably in a famous series of pastels by Degas.

If washerwomen could be intimidating, it is because they in no way represented the "weaker sex." Hauling sodden hemp and linen laundry all year long

required hefty women with strong arms. It was a short step from there to a reputation as an insolent and battling breed of strike leaders, as described in contemporary novels. In Stendhal's *Lamiel*, the washerwomen shout insults at the doctor as he passes by on horseback, "in a vigorous choir that lasted a full minute." One of them hurled "the little wooden spade with which she beat her laundry," causing the doctor to fall from his horse into the mud pit near the washhouse.

A spanking administered by Gervaise, the heroine of Emile Zola's *L'Assommoir*, was immortalized in the film directed by René Clement. In his novel, Zola described the atmosphere of the washhouse as:

". . . an immense shed . . . supported by cast iron pillars and enclosed by clear glass windows. A wan daylight penetrated the hot steam hanging like a milky fog. Clouds rising here and there spread out and veiled the background in a bluish haze. Everywhere a heavy moisture rained down, laden with the smell of soap, a persistent, stale, dank aroma sharpened at times by a whiff of bleach. A row of women stretched along the washboards down each side of the central passage; their arms were bare up to the shoulders, dresses turned down at the neck, skirts caught up showing their colored stockings and heavy laced boots. They were all banging furiously, laughing, leaning back to bawl through the din, bending forwards into their washtubs, a foul-mouthed, rough, ungainly-looking lot, sopping wet as though they had been rained on, with red, steaming flesh."

Washerwomen were above all worrying, however, because they had the power to read the stories of private lives in soiled linen. In the microcosm of small French villages, the washhouse was perceived as a place of rumor-mongering, of letting off steam, where hags were reputed to be witches and abortionists. Yet historian Michelle Perrot recently described washhouses as convivial places full of friendly smiles and laughter, where beauty tips were swapped and where

Certain traditional tradespeople in Europe have never abandoned the professional techniques that have stood them in good stead. This woman (right) is a specialist in ironing fine linen, and she still heats her irons of cast iron on a stove, testing their temperature on a small piece of cloth. Irons made of traditional cast iron are appreciated for their weight and good heat distribution, which is superior to today's electric steam irons.

Non-steam or "dry" electric irons (right) can give results as good as those produced by traditional cast iron ones on condition that the laundry be correctly moistened. It must also be properly folded— for dish towels, three times lengthwise, then three times widthwise. Photograph by Frank Kollar, 1937.

A highly functional laundry room in Belgium (right) endowed with late nineteenth-century equipment. In the foreground on the right can be seen the stove for heating irons, behind which stands the large ironing table. Once ironed, the laundry is draped over hangers to cool before being folded.

the sense of female solidarity was certainly as strong as the traditional image of clashing "harpies."

In any case, the world of linen care was totally alien to men and, as sociologist Alain Corbin has pointed out, it contributed in the nineteenth and early twentieth centuries to "the dichotomy of sexual roles, of which it represents one of the most potent symbols." Today's couples must now confront the issue of how the household laundry is to be managed, how tasks are to be shared in ways acceptable to the two individuals involved. In extreme cases, each one simply washes what he or she has dirtied; sometimes, even when women are happy to hand over the "chore," they retain an unconscious reticence about relinquishing the expertise they have monopolized for generations.

Once ironed, linen is a delight to sight and touch, but it still lacks something essential—a unique fragrance that is not only pleasant but enables one to intuit, eyes shut, exactly where one is.

FRAGRANT LINEN

Nothing could be more wonderful than sliding into bed between clean, fresh sheets that were dried in the sun and still retain the scent of soft grass and open air. In the words of Baudelaire, "We shall have lightly scented beds . . . " Fragrant memories are etched into

minds and remain intact years later, like laundered sheets carefully stored on the shelves of a perfumed linen cupboard. The sense of smell—"that rare sense of singularities," according to the poet-philosopher Michel Serres—has a long memory.

As poet Colette Wartz wrote in *Paroles Pour L'Autre*, "Order. Harmony. A cupboard stacked with sheets, lavender in the linen. . . ." Clean, carefully folded, sweet-smelling household linen is a pleasure discovered long ago. Back in the Middle Ages, linen packed tightly in chests was scented with flower petals or sachets of fragrances. In 1348, poet Olivier de La Haye penned the following advice: "store sheets, where they lay, in aromatic things." In 1383, Charles VI's chamberlain scrupulously noted in the royal accounts that he himself bought "vine shoots, roses and lavender to place in the king's linen, in the chests of the table linen chamber." A valet to Charles VI's wife Isabeau of Bavaria bought an ell of satin to make "pouches for containing violet powder."

Throughout the centuries, the scent of linen in chests and closets reflected the olfactory mode of each period. Thus in the early fifteenth century, for example, the favorites were melilot (also known as "sweet clover") and rose. Rose, for that matter, never went out of fashion, even when heavier scents of animal origin, like amber, musk, and civet became popular. Toward

A packet of Rémy & Co.'s famous rice starch —"guaranteed pure"—which can still be found in France today (below). It continues to give the same fine results, assuming one has the patience to prepare it. People began starching clothes during the Renaissance, to add body to ruffs and fine linen at neck and wrists.

The visual and tactile delights of fresh linen were soon joined by olfactory pleasures. Fragrance was first added by placing flower petals in linen chests, and later by perfuming rinse water. This flower-scented bluing (above) dates from the early twentieth century and is a forerunner of today's scented fabric softeners.

the end of the Renaissance, the poet Ronsard's third *Eclogue* had already alluded to the growing fashion for linen chests of "fine-smelling amber." The use of such animal scents became widespread in the seventeenth century, a period when people seldom washed.

By the late eighteenth century, with the timid emergence of a new sense of personal hygiene and the discovery of "nature," heady scents began to decline in favor of lighter, plant-based fragrances—ever-present rose, violet, thyme, lavender, and rosemary. Parisian women even planted these flowers and herbs on their window sills. Everything was intoxicatingly perfumed, from linen to candles, scent-filled baskets, and even the surrounding air, thanks to potpourris. (This fashion has been revived recently, and specialists now offer clients custom-made blends of fragrances).

In the eighteenth century, the French strewed chests and drawers with what they called *sachets d'Angleterre*. These so-called English sachets were pouches of Florentine taffeta or silk (since broadcloth was thought to alter scents) filled with a cotton stuffing drenched in perfume or fragrant powders. Throughout the reign of Louis XIV, people even wore "miniature scent holders" and "acorns" under their clothes.

The use of plant fragrances was raised to the status of a social code by the French court, and it persisted throughout the nineteenth and into the twentieth cen-

turies, when lavender became the classic scent used in the linen closet that Bachelard described as "that unique cupboard, with its unique smell, which is the signature of intimacy." Bouquets of lavender, often with a personal touch added, were knotted with a silk ribbon, hung between two shelves or placed in small sachets slid between the folds of sheets, lending the linen a scent "neither completely different, nor completely the same." Sachets would be stitched in an imaginative variety of fabrics and shapes, or else purchased ready-made of printed cretonne in the markets of Provence where lavender is grown.

Good homemakers even established a rota in the use of bedsheets, not only to avoid always employing the same ones, but also to use those that had been sufficiently "lavendered." These days, although some homemakers continue to use sachets, it is above all detergent manufacturers who have taken over the task of perfuming laundry. Plant fragrances remain a key frame of reference, even if there is nothing natural about the synthetic scents used in fabric softeners so evocatively labeled "Springtime Freshness" or "Lavender Scent," not to mention "Forest Fragrance" or "Fresh Meadow Scent."

Nowadays, smelling an "amazing garden" in a terrycloth bath towel, as evoked by the Charles Trenet song, requires more than "a little imagination."

Linen pouches full of dried flowers (left) have been perfuming chests and cupboards since the Middle Ages. Favored fragrances have changed with fashion, from rose to violet to rosemary. Lavender did not become sole queen of the linen cupboard until the late eighteenth century. Only bed linen is perfumed, however; tablecloths and napkins are, in theory, never scented.

THE THREAD
OF THE TALE

Following the thread of the tale of linen from its origins to the present is no straightforward matter. Linen sticks so close to human lives—from swaddling clothes to shroud, from table napkins to lingerie—that its interlocking fibers retain a hidden trace of every contact. Linen bears silent witness to the private side of life.

In the rumpled disorder of sheets impregnated with bodily scents, as well as on a towel imperceptibly imprinted with the outline of a face, a napkin marked with lipstick, or a fine batiste handkerchief drenched with tears of joy or pain, linen records the carnal part of history that humanity has always tried to hide, even erase. Linen takes on this role all the more happily, since it is able to recover its initial purity and whiteness, like magic, with each washing.

Luckily, the thread of the story also runs through the public linen that has been employed at sacred and secular celebrations from time immemorial. Festive linen, by its very showiness, is magnificently decorated, whether destined for altar or banquet table, ritual ablutions or dinner napkins, the maternity bed or funeral bier. This "ceremonial" linen was fortunately considered worthy of description and depiction, and has therefore survived to this day.

For in trying to recount the origins of linen and fabrics, the storyteller confronts the irreparable damage done by time. Textiles are the most perishable of materials, and so from the Neolithic Age (when archaeologists think mankind first began to weave flax and hemp) to the end of the Middle Ages, the history of fabrics is recorded on just a few shreds of cloth whose exact features are difficult to determine.

Some of the holes in this history can be darned with extensive pictorial material, accompanied by certain written sources, dating back to ancient times. Whether religious, poetic or historical, the first allusions to fabric are found in the eighth century B.C. in Homer's *Iliad* and *Odyssey*, in the writings of the Greek historian Herodotus from around 450 B.C., and in the Old Testament (particularly in Genesis and Exodus, the first two books of the Pentateuch). Although Egypt is generally credited with the earliest mastery of the techniques of growing and weaving flax, historians are nearly certain that widespread use of household and personal linen emerged with the Greek and Roman civilizations. Frescoes, pottery, and bas-reliefs sometimes depict tablecloths, small, richly decorated towels, and large pieces of cloth that accompanied the ritual of hot public baths.

However, information concerning the private linen actually owned by individuals is available only from the thirteenth century onwards, thanks to the first compilation of the somewhat grim documents known as death inventories.

This source inevitably provides an incomplete picture, yet it permits an assessment of the quantity and type of items found in the linen chests of medieval kings and nobility, and later of the rich bourgeoisie. For it should be obvious that only the linen of the rich was preserved. That belonging to the poor—scant, dirty, worn, and generally made of hemp—did not last long enough to be bequeathed.

The inventories carefully describe every piece of linen, scrupulously noting the origin and quality of the cloth, its size, decorative weave or embroidery, and finishing touches. Even items with tears or holes were listed, attesting to the importance linen was given in terms of family assets.

From the Middle Ages to the end of the nineteenth century, the most commonly used fiber was flax, followed by a significant amount of the less costly hemp. Prior to the development of very fine linen fabrics and damask weaves, silk (still rare in the West) was used for the most refined sheets, tablecloths and hand towels, which were decorated with embroidered threads of silk, gold, or silver. During the Renaissance, a new lifestyle emerged, and the concept of taste developed by the Italians suddenly conferred new value on certain possessions. As the aristocracy became more sedentary and built splendid palaces furnished for the first time with richly sculpted chests, cupboards, tables, and beds, there arose a demand for luxury goods in all spheres of daily life, especially in the realm of household linen. It was also during this period that weavers began developing ever finer

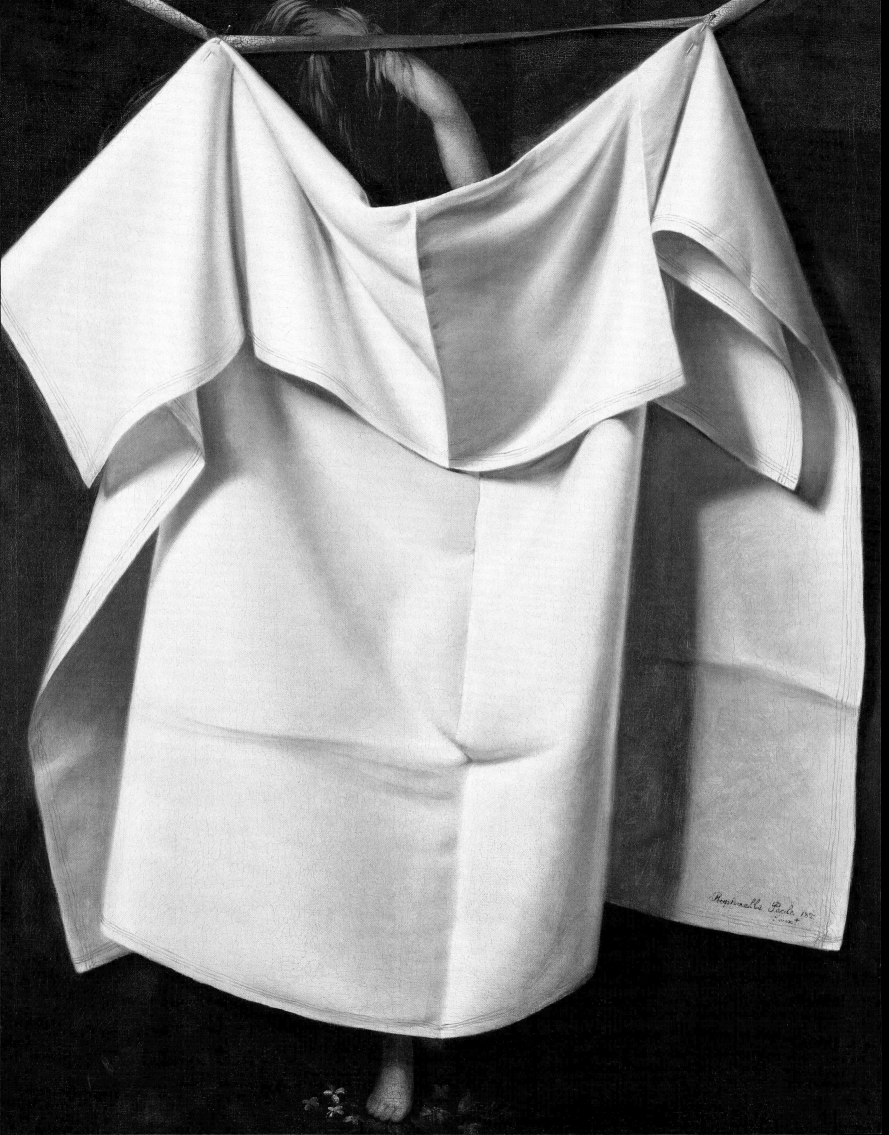

cloth, leading to the emergence of *linomple*, a batiste-type linen used for bed sheets and undergarments. Soon looms began producing patterned weaves, and finally there appeared the wonderful figured (or storied) damask weave that decorated tablecloths and napkins for several centuries. (For a comprehensive discussion of figured damask, please refer to the glossary). All that was lacking from linen's story was the enchanting airiness of lace.

Household linen, like clothing, subsequently attained unmatched heights of luxury throughout the aristocracy. But it should be pointed out that these were highly exceptional items reserved for the ostentation required by "court society." Twentieth-century

else. Suddenly, in the space of fifty years, the industrial revolution made cotton cloth, embroidery and lace available to all, since everything could be manufactured mechanically. This led to the spectacular success of large department stores with well-stocked bridal departments. Zola provided an extremely detailed account of this expansion in his realistic novel *The Ladies' Paradise*. He based the novel on the then recently opened Au Bon Marché department store in Paris.

After the Second World War, inexpensive and easy-to-care-for cotton dethroned linen once and for all—only to be forced into an alliance with synthetic fibers by the late 1960s. Thus household linen, for centuries a cherished possession, a mark of wealth to be

*he white cloths on the table and sideboard were a standard part of Renaissance depictions of classical antiquity. This fresco, titled **The Repast**, adorns an inner gallery of the Palazzo Te, the wonderful mannerist summer palace of the Gonzaga family, dukes of Mantua.*

readers, however, will be struck less by the richness of material than by the colossal quantity of sheets, tablecloths, towels, and napkins contained in death inventories, the only possible explanation being that linen was laundered only once every year or two. Moreover, the lists often include unused linen and ells of cloth kept in reserve. During the latter half of the nineteenth century, in fact, trousseaux were so huge that they were often not used until the following generation, mothers bequeathing to daughters barely used household linen, and so on down the line.

At the end of the eighteenth century, the first balls of cotton began rolling toward English manufacturers, provoking what is known as the "cotton explosion." The plant had been known in the West since the time of Herodotus, but unlike flax, hemp and even silk, it could not be cultivated in temperate climates. This probably constituted a key historical obstacle to the development of cotton fabrics—for centuries, no one thought of processing a plant that grew somewhere

carefully maintained, became an interchangeable product, inexpensive and common.

People no longer took the trouble to mend worn spots, they simply threw linen away when it grew old. Even in good condition, linen became a victim of fashion. Traditional family linen was either disposed of or left to moulder in the attic, from which some has recently reappeared to the great joy of antique linen dealers and connoisseurs at flea markets.

Now that Western society is reaffirming traditional values associated with home and family, women seem once again responsive to a love of fine linen that withered during the early women's movement and the social upheavals of the early 1970s.

So, recounting the history of linen is not only a delightful excuse to "spin a tale," it also provides fascinating insight into the social rites governing the use of linen throughout history, in the context of life's basic, everyday acts—eating, sleeping, and washing—to which household linen is indissolubly linked.

FROM LINEN SHEETS TO COTTON PRINTS

Site of indolence, reverie and especially of love, a bed covered with "dawn-white sheets," in the words of French singer Léo Ferré, can sometimes incarnate poetic sensuality. A stanza from the poem "To the Infinite" by Paul Eluard reads:

"Myself cool or warm
From time to time I was her bed
Her white sheets her soiled sheets
And her intimate pleasure."

Another Eluard poem, which is entitled "To Marc Chagall," evokes the image of white linen on a bed

through the use of a subtle metaphor in the last stanza:

"And in an underground of snow
The opulent vine designs
A face with lips of moon
That has never slept at night."

The crinkle of body-scented sheets, the pleasures of sight, touch, hearing, and smell are described by Michel Serres in a text on the five senses as "waking in a bath of skin and bed . . . the sheets an extension of skin, the body filling folds and soft pockets."

The bed is also the site of sleep and dreams, that ultimate repair of privacy, described by sociologist Pascal Dibie as "the sleeping third of humanity's history." Decorating the bed has therefore been a special concern for thousands of years.

The bed, simultaneously familiar and symbolic, is a site where destiny as spun by the Three Fates is constantly replayed, as though that destiny had long ago been woven into the very stuff that sheets are made of.

Site of birth and of final rest, beds are dressed throughout life's stages in appropriate apparel—the nuptial sheet exposed after the wedding night, the magnificent maternity bedding used to show off newborns, and mourning drapes to shroud the deceased are so many witnesses to the symbolic relationships linking textiles to humankind.

The search for comfort seems to have begun with the making of good bedding such as blankets of doeskin and rabbit fur stitched together. True well-being was not really attained, however, until the invention of the bed as a piece of furniture. The first attempts apparently date back to urban Mesopotamian civilizations, which used wooden-framed wicker structures.

Little is known of what textiles were employed, except that the Egyptians used a semicircular neck-rest carved from alabaster or sycamore which was softened by a small cushion, and that the Greeks used little pillows for head and feet. Homer does not have much to say on the subject in the *Iliad* or the *Odyssey*, since descriptions of the beds of Circe, Calypso and Nausicaa have more to do with sensuality than with fabrics. And when the exhausted Odysseus falls asleep under twin olive trees sprung from the same trunk, he pulls up a covering . . . of leaves! Nor do biblical passages offer much information—one learns merely that Holphern awaits Judith in bed with his head on a pillow, and that King Solomon's bed is "paved with love for the daughters of Jerusalem."

Curiosity is better satisfied concerning the Romans—they slept on a small padded mattress and covered themselves with another mattress of the same size or with a sheet of fine woolen material.

Birth, another fresco in the Palazzo Te, features stacked pillows and linen for both mother and child.

Throughout the Middle Ages, from roughly A.D. 500 to 1000, beds were very rudimentary pieces of furniture. When a family moved, the bed frame (when there was one) would be left in place and another would be built in the new residence. Its primary feature was its size—enormous—and the fact that it was shared. A bed would be between five-and-a-half and eleven feet wide, so that up to ten people could sleep in it. Although separated by sex, all the members of a household, including servants, would sleep and dream together in the nude, in the same room if not in the same bed. Putting taut sheets on these immense beds necessitated the use of long poles called "bed sticks."

As the centuries went by, with the building of magnificent palaces and the rise of what Norbert Elias called the "civilization of mores," everyday acts became subject to modesty. People henceforth slept in a private room which also became a space for daytime activities, given that it was carefully furnished to make it comfortable for reading, writing, working, and praying. Eventually, visitors could be received into bedrooms, and once the room became invested with this social function, beds were not only no longer hidden, but actually became the focus of attention through their lavish appearance—a practice which lasted at least until the late eighteenth century.

Historians date the beginning of the aesthetic career of beds as a distinct piece of furniture to the twelfth century, when the French vocabulary concerning bedding also emerged, remaining almost unchanged to this day. Prior to putting on the sheets, all of the bedding had to be put in place. It usually was comprised of a pallet stuffed with straw or dried leaves, on which was placed a wool mattress (provided one had the wherewithal). On top of that went another small, softer sort of mattress called a *couste* or *couette* (from the Old French *cuilta*, giving the English word "quilt"). It would be made either of ticking, or of wool or silk fustian, and was usually filled with chaff, feathers, or down. In countries that traded with ships arriving from the Orient, the *couette* would sometimes be stuffed with balls of cotton.

Only then came the sheet or, better, pair of sheets.

(Starting around 1322, an undersheet of fustian would be slipped between *couette* and bottom sheet). The finest sheets were of linen, most were of hemp, and the poorest woven from tow, scrap hemp, or flax combings. The top sheet was folded back over a broadcloth blanket that fell down the sides of the bed, the most luxurious blankets being fur-lined. Then the whole bed was covered in a quilted, piqué bedspread that would be white or colored depending on the current fashion. To raise the head, a long, flat cushion or bolster ran across the entire width of the bed, on top of which a personal pillow might be placed.

Pillowcases also made their appearance in the twelfth century, and were the object of special attention. As an ultimate refinement, little pillows might be scattered over the bedspread, scented with the fashionable fragrances of musk, amber, and saffron (lavender and violet scents would only become popular much later). In the fifteenth century, sheets were warmed on cold nights with a warming pan, a custom that an anonymous poet recorded as "bed well appointed, room beautiful, sheets warmed to perfection."

Not all beds were so comfortable, however, and poor folk usually had only one sheet, often in shreds, or no sheet at all. Such was the complaint of poor thirteenth-century poet Ruteboeuf—"my ribs felt the pallet, the bed of straw is no bed, and my only bed is straw." Monastic beds in Benedictine abbeys were not much better, for monks had to sleep fully dressed on a narrow mattress of cheap padding, without sheet or *couette*.

For the aristocracy, a bed swiftly became an object of luxury. It was transformed from the simple transportable bed used in the high Middle Ages into a veritable masterpiece of woodwork in the late Middle Ages and Renaissance. Beds were adorned with tall posts of carved wood to hold the "tester" or canopy. During subsequent centuries, this type of structure would give rise to beds dressed with incredible textile coverings that entirely masked the woodwork.

In the early fourteenth century, Clemence of Hungary, queen of Louis X of France and reputedly a great beauty, slept in a bedroom "all made of white *bougueran*." The French *bougueran* is related to the English word "buckram," which at the time referred to rare

cotton fabric. The queen's bed was covered with "a bedspread, a canopy, and pillows, complete with three rugs and twelve checked pillowcases."

This was still not overly luxurious, compared to the late fifteenth century when the wife of the barber to the king could sleep in a bed six-and-a-half feet long and six feet wide with linen sheets, a feather pillow, a *couette* in Flemish ticking, canopy, a backrest, and linen bedcurtains. Far more ostentatious, however, was a rich Venetian woman of the sixteenth century who slept in a bed noteworthy for its "cream-white canopy adorned with lace, and a gold-embroidered silk bedspread over delightfully scented bedding."

The high point was reached during the reign of Louis XIV, when wooden bedframes were buried under yards and yards of fabric. Figured silk, damask, brocade and lace were draped over and around the canopy like a frieze, while matching bed curtains, panels and wall hangings eventually invaded the entire bedroom.

The first references to bed linen appear during the Merovingian dynasty of Frankish kings (A.D. 500 to 751). The king, who still tended to change his residence regularly, established special offices to coordinate everyday affairs during his peregrinations. He notably instructed his steward and chamberlains to count, superintend, maintain, and distribute the bedding. Unfortunately, we know nothing about this bedding. This gap in the history of bed linen can be partly explained by the fact that bed sheets remained in the private sphere, unlike tablecloths that were always associated with public celebrations.

Although medieval "bed manners" can be gleaned from the rich literature and imagery of the period, it is above all death inventories that provide insight into the evolution of bed linen over the centuries. These lists carefully described the origin and quality of cloths, along with their size (measured in "breadths") and even how worn they were, using concepts like "adequate," "feeble," "bad," "nasty," and "old."

These lists never used the modern French term for sheet, *drap*, preferring the word related to *linceul*, today reserved for shroud, which might strike modern readers as strange. The funereal connotations of the original term perhaps arose from the fact that while rich people were buried in coffins, the poor wrapped their dead in a piece of cloth which, because it was large and common, could serve as a shroud, that is to say, sheet. In English the dual purpose is reflected in the archaic term "winding sheet." Be that as it may, the term *linceul* in French was in no way ambiguous at the time, as demonstrated in a verse by Clément Marot, the famous poet and valet to François I: "Drink delicious wines then later, between two shrouds [*linceulx*] rest thy head." *Linceul* would continue to be used this way into the first half of the seventeenth century.

Except for the earliest sheets of fine wool used by the Romans and by certain nuns whose religious vows entailed the use of woolen sheets up to the end of the seventeenth century, sheets were generally made from linen or hemp. Historians, citing the fact that the founding of the hemp-weavers guild long predated that of linen-weavers, believe that hemp was far more common than linen until the late fourteenth century. At all times, however, there has been an exclusive group of rich nobles who preferred silk sheets, as noted by the twelfth-century poetess Marie de France. Her verses, or lays, were dedicated to Henry II of England; one of them reads: "Opening a chest, she took out a piece of silk, which she put on her lord's bed." In the sixteenth century, François I was enamored of silk satin sheets, and Brantôme's licentious anecdotes of court life recount how a prince has his ladies and courtesans sleep "in sheets of taut black taffeta, completely naked, so that the whiteness and fragility of their flesh appeared at its best in the evening, and gave greater frolic."

In the hierarchy of textiles, linen and hemp cloth were followed by fabrics made from tow and canvas, theoretically aimed at modest folk. The finest linen fabrics were always identified by their place of origin. In the fifteenth century, the accounts of René of Anjou, the celebrated poet-king, mention the purchase of "LXXXII [82] rods of linen from Hainault to make sheets to cover the beds" and for "the garden household, thirty-one sheets of hemp, each of two breadths." Two centuries later, bourgeois gentlemen like André Barbedor and Jean Jouan, in the county of Artois,

were recorded as owning "large pillows and sheets of flax combings." The term "bourgeois cloth" was even used in France for tough textiles that required time and successive launderings before they became soft to the touch. That perhaps explains a fifteenth-century French saying that vaunted "bread cooked at midnight, confessor's wine, canon's sleep, and semi-worn sheets." Certain French kings, however, notably Charles V, were not adverse to the rough feel of so-called bourgeois fabrics.

It was only in the second half of the fifteenth century that batiste-like *linomple* and other fine textiles from Holland arrived in France, becoming the symbol of ultimate luxury and the cloth of kings for nearly three centuries. But what is really striking about the inventories of possessions, from the Renaissance period onwards, is the quantity of household linen, in particular the number of sheets. This number would grow in time, peaking during the reign of Louis XIV. In the fifteenth century, Catherine de Rohan owned 128 sheets of either linen or hemp, and the countess of Angoulême at her château in Madée also had 128, of which 122 were of linen and hemp. A 1601 inventory of the Hardwick Hall possessions of Elizabeth, countess of Shrewsbury, included six trunkfuls of linen that contained not only 94 sheets of linen, Holland, or cambric, but also 650 yards of uncut lengths of linen for making up additional items. Members of the lesser English gentry, such as Robert Hesketh, Esq., owned an impressive variety of linen; an inventory of his manor house at Rufford on his death in 1620 detailed such items as "xvi [16] paire of flaxen sheets & pillowbeares [cases] & a Napkine" valued at "viii[li]" (eight "livres" or pounds). "Mrs. Heskeths Clossett" also contained "x paire of newe Canvasse sheets, xi more paire of flaxen sheets . . . vi paire of flaxen sheets & v paire of Canvasse sheets" for a total of 48 pairs of sheets in that "closet" alone.

Such figures pale into insignificance alongside the hundreds of sheets contained in the trousseau of Anne, duchess of Brittany (1477–1514), who was married to two kings of France, first of all to Charles VIII, and then upon his death to Louis XII. Her daughter, Claude of France, who also became queen of France as the wife of François I, collected ells of *linomple* so that her seamstresses could stitch sheets softer to the skin. Louise of Savoy, mother of François I, was so unable to control her passion for fine linen, that after her death her son had to pick up the colossal tab.

All wealthy women of the day indulged in the pleasure of fine fabrics, which is understandable since people still slept in the nude at that time. The ladies of the French court in the sixteenth century drifted off to sleep in *linomple*, from Henri II's wife Catherine de Medici to his favorite, Diane de Poitiers, and from Louise of Lorraine, wife of Henri III, to Gabrielle d'Estrées, the adored favorite of France's first Bourbon ruler Henri IV.

Louis XIV's mother Anne of Austria (1601–1666), queen of Louis XIII, used only batiste for her sheets; this, moreover, was about the time that the word *linomple* disappeared from use. Madame de Motteville, Anne's lady-in-waiting, recounted in her memoirs how intransigent the queen could be regarding the quality of the fabric. "It was difficult to find batiste fine enough for her sheets and blouses, and before she would use them, they had to be soaked several times to make them softer." This led Anne's trusted advisor, Cardinal Mazarin, who was in the habit of joking with the queen on the matter, to comment ironically that if she went to hell, her only torture would be to sleep in sheets of fine Holland linen.

It is worth remembering that, apart from the time Louis XIV ordered 1,237 ells of standard quality batiste from Gilbert Lemarchand on 7 October 1674, French royal sheets were always made of fine Dutch cloth. In 1687, the king's chamberlain purchased "four pairs of sheets of Holland cloth, of four breadths." This tradition was respected until economy measures obliged Louis XVI to order sheets of "semi-Holland" quality. The king's personal garments nevertheless continued to be embroidered with his coat of arms, as were those of all French aristocrats until the fall of the *ancien régime*. It is hard, then, to know exactly

what to make of the following anecdote recounted by the king's valet, Pierre de la Porte: "Although the king was given twelve pairs of sheets and two dressing gowns every year, I saw him use six pairs for three years running, so worn that several times I found his legs sticking through them." This royal surprise makes one wonder about the sheets used by the vast majority of the population. For though it appears that even poor people had owned at least one sheet since medieval times, it is not hard to imagine the state of that sheet toward the end of the owner's lifetime.

Throughout the eighteenth century, all levels of society continued to hoard bed sheets. Madame de Verru, in her Meudon residence, owned 258. The linen cupboards at La Rochefoucauld's château contained 347 sheets of Paris cloth, while the Château de Verteuil had 72 in Holland and tow cloth. A provincial noble, meanwhile, had 103 sheets for his family and 40 for servants, while a bourgeois gentleman boasted 108. In 1753, the daughter of a farmer had 112 sheets of hemp and linen, and a provincial lawyer and judge named Adrien Delahante had 40 sheets in use, 54 in reserve, 125 ells of extra cloth, and 24 pillowcases!

Ever since the Middle Ages, pillows have been the object of extravagance. One of Marie de France's twelfth-century lays, *Milun*, describes how parents "laid the child in a little cradle, wrapped in a white linen cloth; beneath his head they placed a fine pillow." Texts usually described pillowcases minutely, whether they be in fine linen batiste, in silk, embroidered with gold or variegated silk thread, with openwork, or tied with colorful silk ribbons stitched with pearls.

Anne of Brittany liked to have her pillowcases made from silk taffeta. Margaret of Austria preferred them "decorated in gold and silk thread." Charlotte of Savoy had a secret, rose-scented chest in which she locked away "two embroidered pillowcases, hand towels in Holland cloth, eight bed sheets of Holland cloth, bed sheets of cotton, two embroidered towels in *linomple* and two sheets of *linomple*, each one made of six cloths and six ells wide." At the time of Charlotte's death in 1483, these items were worth a considerable sum.

Starting in 1580 and continuing into the eighteenth century, pillowcases were above all decorated with lace. Three inventories of French royal furnishings, carried out between 1673 and 1697, described pillowcases "in Holland cloth decorated with Flemish lace and two pillows covered in white-striped dimity from India, adorned with Flemish lace." In 1721, another inventory now at the National Archives in Paris noted that the widow Brion, a linen draper, delivered to the favorite of Louis XIV, Madame de Montpensier "eight pillowcases in demi-Holland cloth, very fine, adorned with Mechlin lace with brides and thread tie."

After 1750, however, lace began to disappear, while muslin came into fashion. Bedclothing and personal linen were henceforth usually given muslin decoration. There is a 1769 order from the Château de Choisy for "eighteen pillowcases decorated with muslin, of which six in semi-Holland cloth." On 21 August 1789, the house of the famous singer Sophie Arnould was burgled, depriving her of pillows "decorated with muslin." Was this substitution of muslin for lace a question of fashion, or did it stem from the same economy measures that led to royal linen being made of "semi-Holland" instead of "Holland" cloth?

Like pillowcases, bedspreads have always been ornate. During the early Renaissance, fashion in Venice dictated that they be of gold-embroidered silk. In France around 1525, they were *piqué*, (or quilted). Pierre le Gendre owned at least four, "one quilted in diamonds surrounded by boughs, another in chevrons and diamonds, [another] in hemp with fleur-de-lys in the corners and a rose in the middle, [and] the most precious, in diamond-quilted linen, of three breadths and two-and-a-half ells wide." Starting in the fifteenth century, bedspreads would also be decorated with techniques known as *reticella* and *punto in aria* (Venetian lace), and finally in all major types of needlepoint lace. In fact, during the seventeenth century, such magnificent details were taken to excess. Ruffles and lace not only graced collars, cuffs and shoes, but also every item of household linen. In the month of July 1639, in celebration of the birth of Louis XIV, the heir to the French throne, Pope Urban VII sent "four sheets of [linen from] Cambrai adorned with Flemish lace and seams stitched in precious thread." In her correspondence, later in the century, the Princess Palatine, Louis XIV's sister-in-law, described in detail her

lace used, cost being directly related to its size; in those days, acquiring lace could swallow up as much capital as a palatial mansion to put them in!

Descriptions of decoration on sheets are far rarer than for pillowcases or bedspreads, even in royal inventories. The French royal furnishings inventory of 1681 listed only two magnificent bed sheets "of a single piece, painted all over with a frieze of five flowers in the middle and in the four corners." Obviously, "paint-

This fine bedspread of Venetian point lace in linen thread, now at the Musée des Arts Décoratifs in Paris, dates from the early seventeenth century and depicts the animals of the Creation.
The two figures flanking the fountain in the lower right are wearing sleeved garments fashionable during the time of Catherine de Medici.

daughter's wedding gifts and trousseau with its abundant "linen decorated in lace with the arms and initials of the couple . . . she has 20,000 ecus' worth of linen, lace, and needlepoint, all very fine and in great quantity, filling four huge chests."

In December 1639, a decree by the French parliament attempted to curb such excesses by forbidding in the future the addition of decorations such as "braid, lace, or needlepoints to sheets." But, like all edicts that hoped to put a brake on unbridled extravagance in clothing and linen, this one was widely ignored and had no more success than its predecessors. Another decree nevertheless tried to legally limit the width of

ed" here means decorated with a needle, probably using a flat satin-stitch and colored thread. This same inventory lists a few sheets made of cotton, an innovation that would not become commonplace until two centuries later.

Descriptions of sheets thus have to be sought elsewhere—in personal accounts or diaries, and in the memoirs that became fashionable in the sixteenth century. These magnificent sheets were nevertheless saved for special occasions—childbirth, the "churching" of a woman after giving birth, convalescence, and death. The famous tale of *Tristan and Iseult*, composed around 1150, described how Tristan's lifeless body was taken from the bed, placed on velvet, and then covered with an embroidered sheet. In 1559, King Henri II was laid out after his death on a ceremonial bed covered with "a large sheet of fine Holland cloth to the quantity of thirty-five Paris ells, whose four corners fell down to the edges of the podium."

Ceremonial sheets were always invested with a social function. They were relatively few in number, compared to the stacks of sheets duly described in pri-

spread by an extra length and were of such fine Reims cloth that they were valued at 300 francs. Over the cover of gold cloth was another large sheet of linen as fine as silk, all of a piece without seam, which is a new-found thing to do, and at very great cost."

Many accounts attest to the grandeur attained by "churching" sheets displayed by the seventeenth-century bourgeoisie. An Englishman passing through Paris wrote with amazement how one lady received

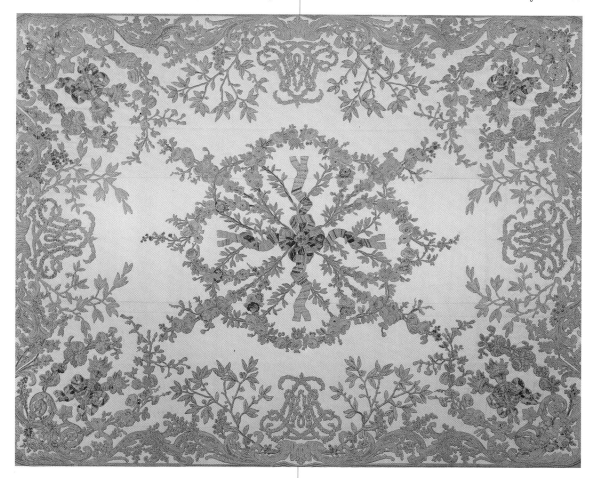

vate inventories, notably that of the French crown. But such sheets were a good pretext for costly display whenever visitors were received at one's bedside, which was fairly common in the seventeenth century. Back in the early fifteenth century the celebrated writer Christine de Pisan had already complained to the queen of the extravagance of the practice of having ceremonial sheets. One wonders what Pisan would have made of the following description of the ceremonial bedclothing of a bourgeois woman celebrating childbirth: "The big, fine bed was curtained with much handsome adornment and rugs all around, endowed with great decorated sheets that hung below the bed-

visitors from her sumptuously adorned and perfumed bed, while a French commentator marveled at a woman "on an Antique bed, painted gold, blue and ochre." Some churching sheets are mentioned, by chance, in inventories; a Château de Turenne list includes two ceremonial sheets of five breadths each, the first of "Holland cloth, with four bands of white gauze decorated in black silk and silver roses," and the second of "Holland cloth with nine bands of white gauze decorated with crimson and gold silk."

The great cost of these sheets, apart from the quality of the cloth and the possible use of embroidery or lace insertions, lay in the fact that despite their grand

This extraordinary bedspread once belonged to Marie-Antoinette and can still be seen at the Versailles Château. The raised-point embroidery is done in gold and colored thread. The queen's intricately entwined initials can be seen on every side.

size they had only one seam which ran through the center. The height of luxury was to have a sheet made from a single piece of cloth. Weaving such sheets required the construction of very wide looms, and so they were quite rare and always considered to be items of extreme value.

Right into the early twentieth century, seamless

Rural sheets tended to be narrower than city sheets, measuring three or four ells wide in the country as against five or six ells wide in town. They were often made from hemp, tow, or mixed fibers. Pure linen remained the privilege of wealthy families. Thanks to department stores and their sales catalogues, we have a fairly precise idea of the types of linen used in those

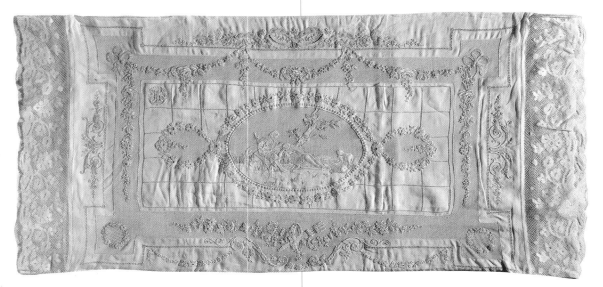

linen sheets that were sold in exclusive boutiques were known in French as *draps de maîtres*, or "masters' sheets." It is hard to believe that sheets with several seams were still the most common throughout the nineteenth century, and that those with a single seam were available until the 1930s. When the cloth around the central seam of the sheet would begin to wear, it could be unstitched, turned, and sewn up again along the intact edges, a technique known in English as "sides-to-middle."

During the nineteenth century, the linen in homes piled ever higher. A rich town-dweller's trousseau at the turn of the twentieth century might include 96 sheets for family use and 60 sheets for servants. But the growing stacks of linen were not only found in the cities, they were also accumulating in country cupboards. Some historians see this oversupply as a way of absorbing local production of flax and hemp, for want of broader markets.

days, at least by the urban population. From the beginning of the twentieth century and onwards, catalogues have replaced death inventories as primary documentation on the choice of fabrics and decoration.

Up to the early 1920s, sheets with no middle seam were made of fine linen or even cambric (so appreciated by Anne of Austria). Decoration remained highly classic, and consisted of fancy white-on-white needlework, openwork, lace insertions (even double insertions), or flounces of Venice and Valenciennes lace. Fashions were launched for "Richelieu lace," "Colbert embroidery," and *broderie anglaise* with ribbon-loops of knotted pale blue or pink satin. Pillowcases respected a tradition of refined adornment that went back to near-medieval times, being made of batiste with flounces, cutwork or scalloped borders, fancy needlework at the four corners, and monograms centered at the top or in the middle. The pillowcases, however, did not necessarily match the sheets. At the

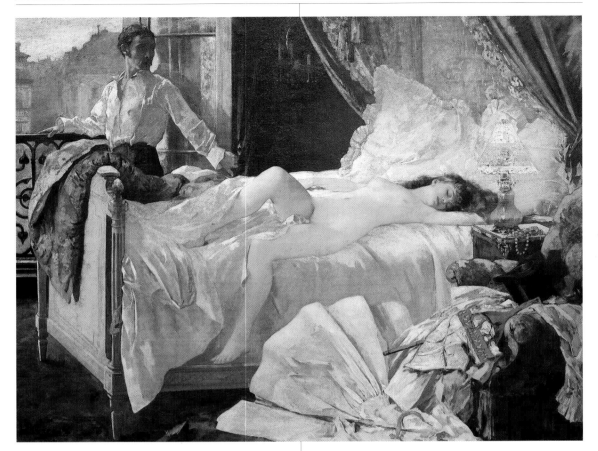

Climbing into a bed this soft, fluffy, and white could only be compared to sleeping on a cloud (right). The immaculate sheets and pillowcases are hemmed with lace, the quilted bedspread is of silk satin. Illustration from a catalogue issued by La Grande Maison de Blanc, 1938.

One of the most sensual depictions of a bedroom scene in the history of French painting, this canvas (above) demonstrates that sheets are never more beautiful than when rumpled at the feet of a delightfully shameless body—fabric and skin, muslin and hair are wedded in shared sensuality. Rolla, by Gervex (1852–1929), sparked a scandal when it was first exhibited in 1878.

A long, lazy morning in bed is made all the more comfortable by an embroidered satin quilt, as suggested by this ad for Clark's embroidery thread (below).

same time, silk sheets and pillowcases also retained a solid following, having had enthusiasts for centuries.

Beginning in the lavish 1920s with the arrival of Art Deco style, several major fashion designers created lines of household linen for the first time. The houses of both Worth and Lanvin employed sophisticated fabrics such as crêpe de Chine and silk satin to soften winter nights, or sheer batistes and linen lawns to freshen summer ones. Fashionable decoration at that time often included a series of inlays, either of lace, of the same fabric, or of a different fabric (satin on batiste, for example), and were generally pastel in color, the whole effect sometimes being enhanced by embroidery. The revolutionary innovation of bed linen in the 1930s began on the American continent, with the use of colors and prints; conventional Europe clung to the eternal symbolism of white

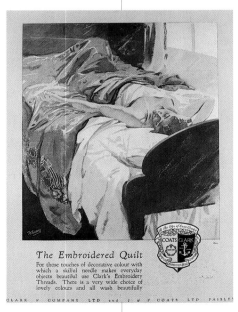

The Embroidered Quilt
For those touches of decorative colour with which a skilful needle makes everyday objects beautiful use Clark's Embroidery Threads. There is a very wide choice of lovely colours and all wash beautifully

CLARK & COMPANY LTD and J & P COATS LTD PAISLEY

(revived in the late nineteenth century by the symbolist movement around Stéphane Mallarmé) and only adopted this innovation several decades later.

It is therefore amusing, these days, to flip through specialized publications such as *Le Figaro Artistique* of 1931, where it was asserted that crêpe de Chine sheets are "barbaric nocturnal finery" and that a nightgown and peignoir in jade green silk are "things sullied by eccentricity." On the other hand, *Le Figaro Artistique* loudly applauded "the latest thing in good taste: matching sets, with consequences more far-reaching than first appeared, because they create an atmosphere of order and moderation that pervades one's very existence."

There then followed a detailed description of matching sheets, pillowcases, nightgowns, bed jackets, and negligees, all "coordinated" in crêpe de Chine

with rose-pink inlays, and fine openwork batiste adorned with wonderful Mechlin lace.

Even if the story of bedding is now written largely in terms of cotton, color, and prints, truly sophisticated refinement still calls for linen, crêpe de Chine, and fine cotton satin with embroidery and lace. Except for the fact that the number of sheets has dropped drastically, beds still get made in much the same way as they have been for centuries. Habits formerly typical of one country, however, are more easily adopted by others, leading to the internationalization of Scandinavian down comforters, of multiple little throw pillows, of tiny neck bolsters, and of large, convenient bedspreads that produce a swiftly-made and neat-looking bed.

FROM DIAPER CLOTHS TO PLACE MATS

Although tablecloths and napkins were occasionally used at banquets in ancient times, it was only when people began regularly eating at a table that they systematically covered it with a cloth and, a bit later, started routinely to use napkins. Throughout antiquity, meals were eaten while stretched out on couches or beds, and it was not until the Middle Ages that the sitting position was adopted in the West. Today, the position is becoming even more vertical as humanity, ever more pressed for time, eats standing up, indeed while walking, at any time of day.

It was during the Merovingian dynasty, between A.D. 500 and 700, that people began "sitting down" to a meal, as demonstrated by the existence of certain chairs; but the practice only became truly common with the advent of feudal society. Until the late Middle Ages, tables consisted of planks placed on trestles, covered with long "diaper cloths" (the generic term used for any piece of table or personal linen), as illustrated by a wealth of contemporary imagery. The medieval lifestyle was still marked by a certain nomadic spirit, and such inexpensive "tables" could be left behind when place of residence changed. Planks and trestles would simply be rebuilt elsewhere. The table of the feudal lord and his family would then be "set" in the main

room of the castle, where the diners would sit on benches, all on the same side of the table. These modest furnishings could then be removed when not in use.

The table was seen as a distinct piece of furniture only with the building of the magnificent Italian Renaissance residences that also required permanent cupboards and beds. It was not until the end of the eighteenth century, however, that tables used solely for meals made their appearance, thanks to the fashion for intimate dinners launched by Louis XV in his private apartments at Versailles. Finally, starting with Louis XVI, an entire room, along with specialized furnishings, was set aside for dining.

Guests invited to dinner by rich Assyrians around the year 700 B.C., when Assyrian civilization was at its height, would have noted the fringed cloth covering the table on which slaves placed the dishes. This was not common practice in ancient times, and even under the Roman emperor, Diocletian, in the first century A.D., there was still no word for tablecloth. They simply used the term *gausape*, which referred to a woolen cloth that was shaggy on one side and could be used as a tablecloth, napkin, hand towel, bed sheet, or even as a fabric for making certain garments.

Right into the late Middle Ages, tablecloths were used only for feasts and banquets, not on an everyday basis. Such cloths, like all ancient linen, were embroidered with gold and colored thread and in general had fringed edges, possibly the easiest and prettiest way to "finish" a hem.

It was probably during the fifth century, according to mosaics discovered at Ravenna, that the first tablecloths were used for liturgical repasts. It was also at this time that the "mantle" or *mantelium*, which originally meant "hand-cloth" or towel, began to signify tablecloth. A century later, the Order of Saint Benedict decreed that any brother arriving late to table would have to eat alone, with neither tablecloth nor wine. In France at roughly the same time, the poet Venance Fortunat addressed a sort of prose poem to Queen Radegond in which he described a banquet that would seem to provide reliable testimony of the everyday

This fifteenth-century painting (right), The Marriage of Cana by Giovan Pietro da Cemmo (1474–1504), illustrates a typical late medieval table—a plank is set on trestles, guests are seated along one side, and the tablecloth is decorated with dark blue bands. (Church of the Annunciation, Borno).

In the seventeenth century, it was the custom to "break" the smooth surface of a tablecloth by ironing creases into it, in accordion or checkerboard patterns. This provided added texture, as seen in the painting (right) by Francisco Zurburán (1598–1664), Saint Hugh in the Refectory. The "broken" tablecloth is one of the few decorative elements of the austere setting.

Both ends of this fringed tablecloth are decorated with a wide, dark blue band woven with stylized dragons. In Italy, this type of work is often associated with the city of Perugia. This detail is part of the huge semicircular table of the **Last Supper** *by Domenico Ghirlandaio (1449–1494) which hangs in the Ognissanti monastery of Florence.*

usage of tablecloths—"on the ground were strewn so many flowers it was like walking on a meadow . . . the table alone offered more roses than an entire field. This was the tablecloth that ordinarily covered it, it was all roses. . . ."

The ritual of covering the table with a white cloth perhaps evolved from the sacred meal only, then to any monastic repast, and later to secular use. Whatever the case, the practice became more widespread during the late Middle Ages, and by the twelfth century it was practically universal in Italy and France. Perhaps that was because simple plank-and-trestle tables needed to be hidden from sight, unlike ancient tables of fine, richly worked wood. From that point onward, tablecloths began to assume social and aesthetic importance.

In the twelfth and thirteenth centuries, a new literary genre known as "courtly romance" recounted not only fine tales of chivalry, but also attested to evolving daily habits. References to tablecloths appear everywhere, as in the *Roman de Renart*: ". . . and then cloths were laid on the seated tables, also were salts and bread." The *Roman de Guillaume le Faucon* even more specifically described

". . . the low seated tables, and the white cloths set, and afterward the dishes brought." In 1396, Froissart, in his *Chronicles*, recounted the wedding of Isabelle of France and Richard II of England. "The dinner over, being quite brief, the cloths were removed, the tables taken down, and wine and spices were taken. . . ." Several decades later, tablecloths were no longer the sole prerogative of the aristocracy, and their use spread to the middle classes and tradesmen.

Such use is attested to by popular plays or "farces"; one hero vigorously exclaims, "Zounds! Lay the cloth! I'm bloody mad with hunger!" Another character states that "Women should cover the table and place honorable linen on't." Even innkeepers covered tables with a white "diaper cloth" that, it appears, the poet

François Villon would not hesitate to use as a handkerchief—and he was probably no exception.

The quality of material and decoration is known through the inventories that have survived from the late Middle Ages in Italy and France. Tablecloths were described as being fringed at both ends, and enriched by multicolored embroidery with silk thread. They might also have two woven stripes, colored red or black, running from one selvage to another, a detail still found on tablecloths made in the French Béarn region and the Basque country.

Silk was also used and represented the height of refinement in the art of dining. In 1380, King Charles V owned several silk tablecloths described as follows: "two tablecloths of white silk with stripes, another silky one with band of sea-green silk and gold stripes, and three others, one of silk violet and green, the other sea-green and red," and the last "decorated with roses and eagles." The inventory of the extremely rich Jean, duke of Berry, included a very large tablecloth of "five-and-a-half ells of silk with gold stripes and vermilion silk, the two ends banded with fancy work in gold and silk." This same list cites a rarity in the form of "a tablecloth of nettles, with fancy needlework in cotton [representing] birds, beasts and leaves." The design became classic and continued to be woven in linen damask for centuries.

Before the appearance of damask, certain weaves produced small geometric patterns. Such cloth was said to be "decorated." The first samples probably came from the Orient, and had a "grain" or "check" of varying size, usually named accordingly. The duke of Berry, for example, owned a piece of diaper cloth in a "wheat" weave. But the one seen reproduced most often in contemporary imagery, and which is still made today, consists of large or small diamond patterns known as "Venetian-style lozenge, large and small." In the early fifteenth century, small flower patterns were specifically mentioned in the linen inventories of Charlotte of Savoy and Catherine de Rohan. This weave constituted the most original table linen prior to the invention—in Flanders—of "Damascus weave," that is to say a type of "storied" or figured damask that incorporated magnificent representational images.

However, even if this type of linen was seen only on princely tables, it is not too risky to assert that by the fifteenth century the linen chests of all houses contained at least one tablecloth. The only difference, other than quantity, was the quality of fabric and the decoration. "The tables were promptly set up, then covered with precious cloths," recounted Rabelais all too succinctly in *Pantagruel* during the supper for Queen Quinte-Essence. But whether it be a banquet given by François I in honor of the most beautiful ladies of Bordeaux, or a simple repast, once the meal was over and "cloths removed, hands washed, thanks given, the tables, trestles, and stools were taken away and people began to dance," according to sixteenth-century chronicler Noël du Fail. It was not to dance, however, that Mary Stuart, Queen of Scots, ordered the cloth "lifted" from her table in 1587—it was so she could reread and alter her testament as the moment of execution approached.

Even though no description has been found, that fateful cloth was surely in "Damascus weave." For figured damask was the linen of kings during the Renaissance and for two hundred years thereafter. Only the economy measures initiated during the reign of Louis XV and pursued under Louis XVI (the pomp and wars of the previous century having depleted the royal resources) triggered a decline in orders for this special weave for the personal apartments of the king and queen. They were forced to settle for decorative linen of lesser expense.

Figured damask illustrated timeless subjects such as religious themes, coats of arms, hunting and nature scenes, flowers and fruit. Other, more specific themes, commemorated important events like royal weddings, coronations, and great battles.

Nevertheless, despite the absolute reign of damask, there were magnificent exceptions. Thanks to an engraving ascribed to Pierre-Paul Sevin at around 1680, there is an image of a white tablecloth richly decorated in lace on the occasion of a banquet given at the Quirinal by Pope Urban VIII for Queen Christina of Sweden. Another exception was the infatuation for calico prints in the early eighteenth century; although forbidden by decree, these tablecloths briefly swept through fashionable society. In 1700, *Le Mercure* reported that a celebration given by Monsieur le Prince on behalf of the duchess of Burgundy boasted tables covered with rich calico prints, notably one on the sideboard that had borders of gold and colored decoration. Apart from this isolated vogue, however, white damask cloths remained the norm for a long time indeed. Around 1750, tablecloths were even embroidered in white to imitate damask.

The use of tablecloths was so much a part of habit by the early eighteenth century that when, in the summer of 1704, Louis XIV offered a light meal to the king and queen of England, served directly on tables set up in the gardens, a member of the king's retinue, one Dangeau, thought it so extraordinary that it merited mention in his court diary.

For by the early seventeenth century there was no lack of tablecloths, not only among princes and nobles, but also among the more modest classes. The linen cupboard of Molière's mother, Marie Cressé, wife of a tapestry maker named Poquelin, displayed no fewer than forty. A certain Charles Benoît, notary public, owned seventy-two. Some wealthy merchants even had enormous tablecloths that were large enough to accommodate seventy guests. Other tablecloths represented incredible extravagance, like the one ordered by a merchant from the Faubourg Saint-Antoine

Five centuries later, these cloths are an echo of medieval "runners" (narrow napkins that ran the length of the table). Of pure, lozenge-weave linen damask with blue bands and hand-knotted fringe, they are used as place mats, and are produced by the Jean-Vier company.

neighborhood, whose accounts of 1779 reveal that a cloth of finest Bengal cotton cost him the sum of four thousand five hundred livres.

Hoarding tablecloths was obviously a sign of wealth, yet ample supplies were also required by the long period between annual or biannual washing days. A contemporary treatise on good taste stipulated that "one never uses [table linen] twice in a row, unless one wants to be sparing or unclean," making it clear that hoarding tablecloths and napkins was not an obsession afflicting our ancestors, but fulfilled a real need. Especially once it is remembered that people ate with their fingers until nearly the end of the seventeenth century; not everyone was as dexterous as Louis XIV who, refusing to adopt a fork, ate with three fingers yet reportedly never stained the cloth.

Certain scathing writers of the day, in fact, left some unappetizing portraits of their contemporaries. There was not only La Bruyère and his famous character sketches, but also Tallemant des Réaux who, in his *Historiettes,* named names when describing foul eating habits, accompanied by instructive illustrations of "hands smeared up to the elbows, tablecloths dirtier than dishcloths and rags, the ends of the tablecloth used to wipe sweat from the brow." And, "if the occasion arises, they even wipe their noses with the aforementioned tablecloth." The nobles in questions were perhaps ignorant of the numerous treatises on manners that had appeared since the Middle Ages.

At the dawn of the nineteenth century, even though people ate less messily, trousseaux still included a great number of tablecloths. Damask slowly lost its supremacy, but white remained traditional. This led to a renewed taste for white-on-white needlework, satin-stitch embroidery, buttonhole stitch-

ing and openwork. In the mid-nineteenth century, sophisticated etiquette permitted for the first time—and only at lunch—a white tablecloth embroidered with colored thread, usually red. During France's Second Empire (1852-1870), table settings became more feminine. Lace insertions and mesh came back into fashion, along with embroidered gauzy fabrics like cotton muslin, organdy, and lawn. Then, during the Victorian era, there was also a rage for elegant tea services, since sipping tea had become fashionable. More innovation came in the early years of the twentieth century with the appearance of place mats. According to a 1906 manual of etiquette, it was henceforth acceptable to slide a small rectangle of cloth under each place, the function of which was not to indicate social rank (as had been the case in the Middle Ages), but simply to keep the tablecloth clean.

These days, unfortunately, place mats in France reflect all the ills of modern materials yet are frequently employed instead of a tablecloth for daily meals. In the United States, on the other hand, where place mats have long been used even for refined dining, they come in batiste and organdy, often decorated with embroidery or inlays and always accompanied by a matching napkin. Since American tables are often made of much less fragile materials than those found in Europe, Americans are perhaps more willing to put their place mats straight on the table. This may explain European hesitations over the use of place mats, even though one need merely slip a pad between place mat and table to prevent damage.

Today, tablecloths remain the norm for all official dinners and at restaurants. At home, a tablecloth is the symbol of a special, serene moment, a "patch of whiteness" like some island refuge amid a sea of daily worries,

This detail (left) from a painting by Frans Hals (1580–1666) features a magnificent figured damask tablecloth. One of the representational figures can be seen in the lower right.

A tablecloth ironed into the checkerboard pattern typical of the first half of the seventeenth century is evident in this engraving named Taste *by Abraham Bosse (above) from a series which illustrates each of the five senses.*

In a habit that began in the Middle Ages, the corners of a long tablecloth were sometimes knotted so that it did not trail on the floor, as seen in this engraving (left) by P. Jazet, Between Two Victories, 1879.

according to writer René Cazelles, who feels that "everything can breathe again [when] the tablecloth is white."

Although the basic act of spreading a carefully ironed cloth over a table has changed little since the Middle Ages, the way the cloth is arranged has evolved. Medieval planks and trestles being narrow, places were set along one side only, and the tablecloth fell to the floor on the diners' side. Fifteenth-century trousseaux, such as that of Marie, duchess of Burgundy, included diaper cloths called "runners" that were often identical in length and decoration to the tablecloth, which they were designed to protect. A long, narrow runner would be placed over the tablecloth so that diners could wipe their hands on it and thus spare the tablecloth. Italian inventories at roughly the same period also began listing *guarda nappi*, or "cloth protectors"— narrow pieces of cloth two meters long, sometimes embroidered at both ends, generally stored in chests in multiples of six. Another way of placing the cloth on the table involved folding it completely back on itself to form a double layer. "Doubles" were still being used in 1625, placed over an undercloth that constituted yet another layer. For a banquet at Fontainebleau Château, the table was dressed with "an ordinary tablecloth first, then a second very fine damask tablecloth, folded in two and allowed to fall to the ground, thus forming tablecloth and carpet at the same time, to cover the table." Certain paintings show that when tablecloths fell to the floor, they were occasionally knotted at the corners to prevent them from trailing on the ground.

Apart from the decorative function of tablecloths, they also gave rise to highly symbolic rules of etiquette. In feudal French society, *partager la nappe* ("share the tablecloth") meant complete equality between the guests. If a noble dined with servants, he might share the table but never the cloth. If the cloth covered the entire table, a small diaper cloth would be placed before the lord to indicate hierarchy. When a prince wanted to honor his guests, he shared his tablecloth, but if one guest ranked higher, a small (and often very precious) cloth would be placed under his "trencher" (wooden board). A late fourteenth-century chronicler, Olivier de la Marche, noted in his account of Charles the Bold's household that there was also "another cloth which covers the place occupied by the duke."

In similar vein, any infraction of the laws of chivalry would be punished and made public by forbidding the culprit to share the tablecloth with his peers. For serious violations, the tablecloth would actually be cut, this symbolic act representing the greatest shame that could be inflicted.

In later centuries, the tablecloth was not cut, but rather was pulled toward oneself or turned over, which also became a way to inflict an insult. Madame de Motteville recounted how, during the seventeenth-century revolt of French nobility known as the Fronde, the duc de Beaufort went with many companions to an inn owned by a certain Renart in order to insult the

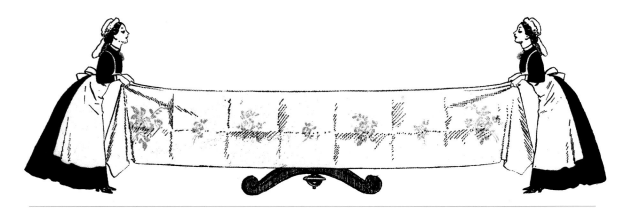

duc de Candale who was dining there: ". . . and so saying, he lifted the table-cloth like a pope and overturned dishes of fine food that Bautru will never eat."

TABLE NAPKINS

Unfolding a napkin prior to starting a meal is one of a multitude of automatic everyday acts that have been performed by Europeans for nearly six hundred years. On certain occasions, however, when the fold is artful and the fabric refined, fingers experience renewed delight in delicate textures and crisp starch, prior to placing the napkin on the lap in anticipation of a delicious holiday dinner.

It might be thought that napkins were widely used in ancient Rome and Greece, given the many accounts of banquets in those days. Yet this was apparently not the case. Athenian texts refer to a *gausape*—a fine piece of wool that was shaggy on one side and smooth on the other—but it is not certain that the cloth was employed at the table. The Spartans, although known for their rough manners, used a sort of dough cut into small pieces called *apomagdalies*; by rolling and kneading the dough in their hands they wiped them clean.

It was in Rome that napkins were first used. There were actually two types of small napkins with distinct uses. The *sudarium*, ancestor to the modern pocket handkerchief, was used to wipe perspiration from the face, whereas the *mappa* was used at the table. Guests brought their own *mappa* to dinner parties, and at the end of the meal the host might invite them to take leftovers home in it. By the end of the Roman Empire, *mappae* had become so luxurious and so coveted that people no longer carried one for fear of theft. The most magnificent *mappae* were made from fine linen or silk, embroidered with gold thread, painted or woven with scintillating colors.

In Rome the *mappa* was tossed into the arena to signal the start of the games. It is even reported that Nero threw his own *mappa* from his Domus Aurea (Golden Residence) where he dined, in order to quiet the clamor of spectators and start the combat.

According to tradition, table napkins, as they are known today, date back to the 1422 coronation of Charles VII in Reims, France. These napkins were presented to the king by the city of Reims, already highly reputed for the quality of its cloth. The use of napkins at court perhaps slightly predates this event; since, to serve the infant king his porridge, the royal linen office had ordered half a dozen napkins to place before him.

The use of a napkin folded lengthwise over the arm of the person serving goes back to the Middle Ages, a time when *écuyers-servants* (squires of the body) wore a napkin on their shoulder as a mark of their rank. In 1739, the duke of Luynes noted that at the court of Louis XV, the *gentilshommes-servants* (gentlemen in waiting) henceforth wore it on the arm, only to drop it altogether later.

Throughout the Middle Ages (until roughly 1642), the term *touaille* was used in French for the modern word *serviette*, or table napkin. Like "diaper cloth" in English, this word designated finished pieces of fabric of varying sizes that might be used in various ways—as tablecloth, napkin, or towel.

Touaille, derived from the Frankish word *thwahlio*, is related to English "towel" and German *Tuch*. But this Germanic etymology may dovetail with a Latin root, *torus*, indicating the place where one ate, that is to say the couch, leading to the Italian term *touaglia*. Medieval *touailles* were placed over reading stands to protect manuscripts (and later, books) and on credenzas that displayed silver. They were also used as altar cloths, wrapped around bread, and placed over valuable cushions or pillows to protect them. Women even draped *touailles* around their heads. Given the multiple

"I am not from Paris, and would not know how to give worthy praise to the cloths with lace insertions and openwork that fashion slides under baskets of strawberries and slices of lemon to serve as tablecloths and napkins," wrote Colette with false modesty in a catalogue for La Grande Maison de Blanc. This very Parisian table setting was photographed in 1928 (right).

uses to which they were put and the various sizes and qualities they came in, *touailles*, or diaper cloths, were found in every personal inventory. Subsequently, the meaning of the term evolved and is now restricted to the loops of cloth suspended from a roller and used to dry hands. Since "napkins" were more limited in number than tablecloths, it can be supposed that guests did not systematically use them at the table; they could always wipe their hands on the tablecloth, which fell down around their knees.

with bands of dark blue or black, and were used to wipe the mouth and fingers during light refreshment taken standing up. The accounts of Charles V's Grand Treasurer include several cloths with their dimensions—four ells long (over four yards). This huge size can be explained by the way the cloth was used—it was hung on the wall in double thickness, or else it was folded in two and draped over a wooden roller set rather high on the wall, not unlike today's standard towel-rack. *Touailles* that hung from the walls in this

Up until the seventeenth century, napkins were very large and were often shared by two guests. This detail from the Last Supper by Dieric Bouts (1415–1475) is one of the rare visual proofs of the collective use of napkins (Saint Peter's Church, Louvain).

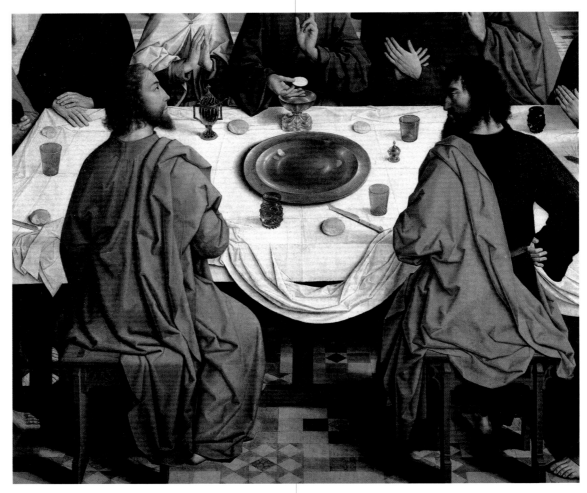

Highly precious *touailles* are listed in all of the inventories of kings and nobles. As early as 1380, Charles V had some silk and fine linen cloths "striped with silk thread down the length, of white and of black," as well as another decorated with "three wide stripes all gold and strewn with white roses." At his Chancellerie in Bourges, Charles VII owned "a *touaille* bordered with a half-ell of silk fringe, with the shield of Monseigneur in the middle," and "a heraldic *touaille* with the four evangelists in the four corners."

Some diaper cloths were larger but less costly,

way were then listed in the inventory as *serviettes de collation*, or "refreshment towels."

Many contemporary treatises on housekeeping and hospitality described this tradition of serving a collation, a light refreshment consisting of fresh and candied fruit and other sweetmeats taken shortly after the meal or even in between meals. Such texts offer advice like: "To honor strangers, in the room after large meals, [place] irreproachably white *touailles* with which the mouth is to be wiped when the lid of the sweetmeat dish has been taken off."

This custom was overtaken by the fashion for individual napkins, and if a noble like Timoléon de la Baulme still used the collective diaper cloth in 1676 it was certainly because he lived in rural Ardèche, far from the French court. For trousseaux had included napkins for quite some time, although their numbers remained modest—two dozen at the residence of Marguerite, countess of Clèves, and a mere dozen at Charles VI's pantler's office (six in Reims weave, six in Venice weave).

But as the fashion spread, the number of individual napkins grew. In 1497, Catherine de Rohan, countess of Angoulême, possessed twenty-three dozen matching napkins, and eighty unmatching, inventoried (like the rest of the household linen) according to a very precise hierarchy of fabrics: first the finest decorative weaves, then Venetian-style weave, and finally "common" or plain weave. Luxuriously decorated napkins were still considered exceptional items—so one wonders whether a delightful cloth "dotted with flowers braided in thread of gold and violet silk" was really used as a table napkin, or as a towel for cleansing the hands before a meal.

During the sixteenth century, napkins became a common part of table settings in France and England, as confirmed by numerous anecdotes and poems in addition to inventories like that of Elizabeth of Shrewsbury, who in 1601 owned twenty-seven dozen napkins. In 1620 Robert Hesketh, Esq. possessed forty-three "dyap [diaper] Napkins" in addition to half a dozen "dyap table Cloaths."

Other accounts provide indirect evidence of the general use of napkins—a chamberlain to Henri IV named Pierre de l'Etoile (1546–1611) recounted an amusing anecdote of how the duke of Guise, on sitting down to dinner, found a note underneath his napkin in which it was written that he "be on guard, people [were] on the point of playing a nasty trick."

Sixteenth-century jurist and chronicler Noël du Fail explained that a napkin took the place of people absent from the table. Napkins became so common in France that by the end of the century, they were even being used in prisons.

Strangely enough, Italians, who led the West in the use of forks and other refinements, continued to wipe their hands and mouth on the tablecloth, or else to eat very neatly with no mess—as did the Germans, who apparently earned a reputation for their cleanliness.

Catherine de Medici was nevertheless won over to the French habit, for in 1589 her "tablecloth chamber" included fourteen dozen napkins in either "plain" or lozenge-weave damask. In his famous *Essays*, Montaigne declared in peremptory fashion that he could manage "without a tablecloth, but German-style without white napkin, only very inconveniently," and added, "my fingers become messier than theirs and those of the Italians, and I regret that we did not adopt a procedure that I saw begun in imitation of kings: that napkins were changed like plates." This "procedure," however, shocked Artus Thomas, author of *L'Isle des Hermaphrodites*, who was outraged that during a single meal the napkins "were changed with each course, indeed more often, as soon as something dirty was seen on them."

Beginning with the reign of Louis XIII in 1610, the use of napkins became general among the upper strata of society and quickly spread downward. This amazed an English traveler, the agronomist Arthur Young, who noted in an account of his eighteenth-century voyage that a French carpenter had his own fork and napkin, and that a serving wench at an inn placed a clean napkin in front of every diner, including on the kitchen table used by the poorest of travelers.

Just prior to the French Revolution, the standard size of table napkins was approximately 45 by 35 inches. They were always in white damask, but did not yet match the tablecloth. It was only in 1742 that the idea of a matching table service first emerged. "Twelve napkins, a large tablecloth and a small one, comprise what is called these days a table service," wrote Savary des Bruslons, as though announcing a great innovation, perhaps following the fashion for private dinners launched by Louis XV, who detested large receptions. Non-matching tablecloths and napkins were still found in trousseaux, alongside matching services, right up to the First World War. Balthazar Claës, the rich Flemish protagonist of a Balzac tale, was said to have possessed exceptional napkins "in the Spanish fashion," that is to say with a fringe.

In the early twentieth century, the height of fashion was to have luncheon napkins in stiff cloth decorated with daring red embroidery, which was often in herringbone stitch; dinner napkins, of course, were still embroidered with white on white, and trimmed in hand-made openwork hems or lace insertions.

These days, napkins are produced in much smaller sizes, standard ones being roughly 24 by 24 inches or 20 by 24 inches, barely large enough to cover the knees. Then again, people no longer knot them around the neck, stick them into a buttonhole, or spread them in front of the whole body.

Every child has been admonished at least once "not to play with your napkin, place it squarely on your lap," or to "discreetly wipe your fingers and mouth before taking a drink." All of these repeated and acquired habits are associated with a good upbringing and are documented in books on etiquette. Such books go back to the Middle Ages, when they were known as treatises on "courtesy" or "civility," instructing children how to sit properly at the table and how to use a napkin. One such piece of advice reads: "Child, 'tis a shameful thing, if you have napkin or cloth, to drink from your tankard with mouth all covered with filth and spittle."

It was the humanist Erasmus who popularized the term "civility" with his treatise on etiquette aimed at children, *De Civilitate Morum Puerilium*, published in Amsterdam in 1530. The book was an instant success, being reprinted thirty times in six years, and ultimately going through 130 reprintings (thirteen of them as late as the eighteenth century).

A translated, plagiarized version appeared in France by 1537. The purpose was to mold the manners and behavior of a young man in refined society, notably in terms of "the outward proprieties of the body," but it was dedicated to a prince who, Erasmus took pains to stress, had no need of such advice.

Although this may have been the most famous treatise on etiquette, it was by no means the first. Similar manuals, often written by monks, had appeared in Germany and Italy since the thirteenth century. In England, *The Babees Book* counseled children to wipe their mouths with a napkin before taking a drink. It is perhaps worth pointing out that even prior to the advent of napkins, the mouth was always wiped—with the back of the hand, the end of a shirt sleeve, with bread or, as mentioned above, with the tablecloth. Moreover, as late as 1729 a French treatise was obliged to point out that "it is ungentlemanly to use a napkin for wiping the face or scraping the teeth, and a most vulgar error to wipe one's nose with it."

As table manners became more established, taboos regarding the use of napkins became more numerous.

Today, napkins are only pressed to the lips and only with the tips of the fingers, at that.

By the early eighteenth century, individual place settings, complete with knives and forks, were the rule, so much so that nothing could be handled anymore with the fingers. Antoine de Courtin, in his *Nouveau Traité de Civilité*, indicated that "an indecency to be avoided is to frequently wipe one's hands on one's napkin, and to dirty it like some dishcloth, so that it renders ill those who see it brought to the mouth." Certain more "permissive" schools of etiquette, however, advocated first wiping the hands with a piece of bread (to be left discreetly beside the plate) in order to spare the napkin somewhat.

Whereas there was never any doubt as to the use to which a napkin should be put, exactly where it was to be placed sparked an erratic little dance between shoulder, arm, and chest until it finally came to rest, once and for all, on the lap (where it had been in the Middle Ages when shared by two diners, as seen in a mid-fifteenth-century painting, the *Last Supper* by Dieric Bouts). Erasmus, in the sixteenth century, advised that "if napkins are distributed, yours should be placed on the left shoulder or arm; goblet and knife go to the right, bread to the left."

When Renaissance fashion obliged men to wear ruffled collars, it simultaneously prompted them to knot a napkin around their necks. Once this eccentric clothing vogue had passed, the napkin went into the collar to protect the lace on shirtfronts. The place of the napkin continued to shift regularly.

The court of Louis XVI and the fastidious Marie-Antoinette already found it appropriate to place their napkins across their laps, yet a 1774 treatise advised spreading it so that it "covered the front of the body down to the knees, starting from below the collar and not tucked into said collar." Indeed, it had long been attached to the chest with a pin or tucked into a buttonhole, a practice that would continue into the middle of the nineteenth century. A 1786 anecdote of a conversation on the subject, between the poet-abbot Jacques Delille and another abbot named Cosson, is highly revealing:

"And what do you do first of all with your napkin, on sitting down at the table?"

"With my napkin, I do like everyone—I spread it

A good illustration of the use of table linen in aristocratic residences of eighteenth-century France is offered in this detail (right) from Two Epicureans *by* Robert Le Vrac, *alias* Tournières (1667–1752). *The tablecloth is ironed in checkerboard creases, and the casually draped napkin is large—generally 36 inches long by 30 inches wide at the end of the century.*

out and attach it to my buttonhole."

"Well, my friend, you are the only one to do so—it should not be spread out, but left on one's knees."

Although "court society" in the late eighteenth century ultimately imposed many rules of etiquette, notably in terms of table manners, it never matched the level of "quasi-holy" refinement attained in the second half of the nineteenth century, when everything was highly codified, such as the arrangement not only of glasses and tableware, but also of napkins, which had to be placed on the lap—but only half open. A rule of decorum dating back to 1729 was followed, in which "the person of highest rank in the company should unfold his napkin first, all others waiting till he has done so before they unfold theirs. When all of those present are social equals, all unfold together, with no ceremony." This etiquette is still followed today, for that matter. Another tradition which has changed little since the second half of the eighteenth century is the place of the napkin on the table—it is usually set on the plate, sometimes with bread nested underneath. Otherwise, it may be placed to the side, next to the knife.

This early nineteenth-century napkin of somewhat heavy linen is woven in a small lozenge, or petite Venise, pattern. The initials are embroidered in matching thread.

Every occasion calls for its own napkins—small ones have accompanied the rite of sipping coffee and hot chocolate ever since these drinks appeared at the court of Louis XIV. At that time, the China trade brought "fabric of silk, pieces of which are separated and divided into lengthwise sections to make napkins." In France, therefore, such napkins were called either "China napkins" or "coffee napkins." They were of course in damask weave, often with a weft of silk and adorned with fringe. Occasionally, as described in a 1678 text, they were of chintz or calico, exotic fabrics appropriate to equally exotic beverages.

Tea napkins came into use somewhat later, for although tea was known as early as 1635 in Amsterdam, London, and Paris, it was longer in becoming a popular beverage. Today, seventeenth- and eighteenth-century tea napkins have become collector's items, especially those with embroidered monograms, which are extremely rare. Finally, the twentieth-century American social innovation of the cocktail party (a stand-up affair, much like late medieval "collations" discussed above) calls for individual napkins that are conveniently tiny.

Today, table settings may be infinitely varied, according to personal inspiration. In contrast, during the Middle Ages and even in Renaissance times, the only objects placed on the tablecloth prior to the food itself were the trencher (wooden cutting board), salt, and sometimes knives. Goblets and glasses waited on a sideboard. It took much imagination to enliven such a sparse setting. Since the tablecloth was practically the only decorative feature, it was given greater volume by being folded at regular intervals with one or several flat creases. Artus Thomas described this effect in *L'Isle des Hermaphrodites*:

"The magnificent tablecloth of a most delightfully damasked linen was folded in such a way that it strongly resembled a wavy stream stirred by a gentle breeze; for among the several small creases, many bubbles could be seen. . . ."

Early seventeenth-century engravings, meanwhile, suggest that there was a vogue for "breaking" tablecloths into square or rectangular patterns during ironing, to add relief to the flat surface by catching the light at various angles.

FROM SHIRTFRONT TO CENTERPIECE

Once napkins appeared on the table, they quickly became a decorative feature. The art of skillfully folding napkins was all the rage in the seventeenth century, when favorite subjects for these cloth sculptures included animal, fruit, and geometric forms.

Each napkin could take on a different shape and, if various accounts are to be believed, the overall effect

The riotous nature of certain eighteenth-century repasts explains why napkins needed to be so large. Etiquette was relaxed and mattered little when amusement was to be had. Napkins could be casually tucked under a collar or slipped through a buttonhole (right), as seen in this painting by Nicolas Lancret (1690-1743), The Ham Dinner (Chantilly Museum).
The table was not yet the temple of strict propriety that it would become in the nineteenth century.

must have been magical. Thus in 1600, for the engagement of Marie de Medici and Henri IV of France, the table was "covered with a hunt scene containing all manner of animals and large trees, partly made from sugar and folded linen."

A 1611 text by Guillaume de Rebreviettes poetically described how the plates at a banquet were "lined up around the edge, each with cut bread covered with napkins disguised as several types of fruits and birds." This vogue lasted throughout the seventeenth century, so that a contemporary commentator like Tallemant des Réaux could recount how he had seen "countless times a deaf and dumb man, quite presentable and quite clean, fold linen admirably into all sorts of animals."

In 1685, near Porte Saint-Martin in Paris, a certain Monsieur Vautier was known for his mastery at ironing, goffering, and folding tablecloths and napkins. Numerous treatises explaining the art were published, and certain "masters" became famous, like Mathias Giegher (who published a 1639 treatise in Padua, Itay), Pierre David (author of a manual that explained twen-

ty-seven different ways of folding napkins), a German named Härtsdörfer, and the Englishman Giles Rose.

The most complete work of this sort was nevertheless the 1680 cookbook published in Lyon, *L'Ecole des Ragoûts*, which devoted an entire chapter to the most complicated and amazing folds. In a comic list worthy of French poet Jacques Prévert, a napkin could be disguised as "a melon, a cantaloupe, a double-scalloped shell, an ox trotter, a cock, a pheasant, a hen nesting in a bush, a capon, two chickens in pâté, four partridges, a pigeon nesting in a basket, a turkey, a tortoise, a dog with collar, a suckling pig, a hare, two rabbits, a pike, a carp, a turbot, a cross of the Holy Spirit, a cross of Lorraine, an artichoke, or a swan."

Often the folded linen would be stitched and adorned with animal heads of painted porcelain or wood, which meant that it was obviously designed only for decorative use.

During the reign of Louis XIV, whose every gesture became the object of an elaborate ceremony, "the king's napkin was properly goffered and folded in small squares." It covered both the plate and the

Napkins were very large up to the end of the eighteenth century, when they slowly began to diminish in size down to their present 18 by 24 inches. The limited dimensions of twentieth-century napkins are evident from the cover of this 1929 catalogue issued by the Frette company (above).
A fine wreath of leaves adorned the linen damask napkins designed by the Frette firm for the Hôtel Belle Venise in the early nineteenth century (right).

Plumed hat, high-necked tucker, long gloves, and fan characterize this society lady (whether high or low), as seen by Gervex at the Aux Ambassadeurs restaurant (right), circa 1900. She seems to be awaiting a gentleman who has not yet come to shake out the napkin typically folded in a "bishop's miter."

The art of folding napkins attained the height of sophistication in the seventeenth century. No figure seemed too complicated for professional folders, who supplied flowers, fruit, and animals by the dozen for grand occasions. Numerous treatises were published so that domestic servants could learn to fold napkins themselves.

A page from the 1639 treatise by Mathias Giegher, which explains how to fold "all sorts of animals" (right).

This swan (below) was produced by scrupulously following the instructions given in a 1680 cookbook by Jacques Canier, L'Ecole des Ragoûts.

caddinet (royal tray) that held the king's bread, spoon, fork, and knife. Underneath that, two officers had first spread a tablecloth, covered by a large napkin half of which dropped down one side of the table only to be folded up back over the entire setting. The bread was always presented in a folded napkin, placed on a gold plate.

In the eighteenth century, place settings were less showy and napkins less artfully folded. Geometric shapes became more common, for not only did they make it easier to nestle the bread between two folds, but they also avoided too much crumpling of fabric, out of consideration for guests.

This habit persisted throughout the following century, as amply attested by various literary descriptions of bourgeois table etiquette. Gustave Flaubert, in his novel *Madame Bovary*, describes the intricate decoration of the table dressed for a festive dinner at the Château de Vaubyessard. With incredible sensuality, he evokes the magical atmosphere that so impressed Emma

Bovary the moment she entered the dining room:

"Here the air was warm and fragrant; the scent of flowers and fine linen mingled with the odor of cooked meats and truffles. Candle flames cast long gleams on rounded silver dish-covers; the clouded facets of the cut glass shone palely; there was a row of bouquets all down the table; and on the wide-bordered plates the napkins stood like bishops' mitres, each with an oval-shaped roll between its folds."

Today, simple geometric shapes are common, especially in hotels and restaurants, and at official dinners, where concern for hygiene strives to minimize handling. In hotel schools, students are taught to fold napkins using tweezers or wearing white cotton gloves.

In general, professional restaurateurs recommend the simple necktie shape when folding light and soft fabrics, whereas heavier fabrics that "break" well when folded can be shaped into wave,

The simplicity of the "necktie" fold is elegantly appropriate to this English-style place setting on a linen tablecloth decorated with Venetian drawnwork (right).

diamond, point, or double-scroll patterns.

FROM DIAPER CLOTH TO TERRY TOWELING

Although acts of personal hygiene have always been associated with bath linen, the items most commonly found in today's bathroom are barely a hundred years old—bath towels, bath sheets, and terrycloth bathrobes. Indeed, from the Renaissance to the end of the eighteenth century, water hardly even entered the picture. The only towels that survived therefore were those for washing the face, hands and feet plus, to a lesser extent, the frilly cloths that draped dressing tables. In order to understand the reason, it is necessary to briefly retrace the history of washing through the ages.

From ancient Greece and Rome to the end of the Middle Ages, despite a long tradition of public baths, there was never any explicit reference to something equivalent to today's bath towel. Instead, people used large pieces of cloth of no specific name or quality.

Prior to the nineteenth century, few items of linen were reserved exclusively for washing and drying the body. The cloth in this anonymous Flemish still life (left), dated 1480, has typical blue bands at both ends and could be used either at the table or for ablutions.

There is visual documentation from the reign of Constantine (306–337) showing Roman use of large sheets wrapped around the body, as well as small towels placed on the face to absorb perspiration. Some historians consider these towels to be forerunners of the modern handkerchief.

In 1292, town criers strolled through the streets of Paris extolling the virtues of bathhouses, both steam and tub types; prices would vary according to category and might include a meal and a bed. The city ran twenty-six bathhouses, and the profession was organized into a guild.

But the height of fashion was to have a bath "drawn" at home. That is why certain estate inventories contain some linen specifically related to bathing. The 1328 inventory of Clemence of Hungary, wife of Louis X of France, included "bathtub sheets," or pieces of cloth used to line the tub in order to make it more comfortable. The court of Burgundy also apparently employed a type of bathtub sheet whose dimensions

In the Middle Ages, before a "dread of water" gripped the West for two centuries, people bathed in wooden tubs, as illustrated by this miniature from the Book of Hours of the Blessed Virgin Mary (above). Linen bathtub sheets protected the bather from splinters; they continued to be used as late as 1920, when enameled bathtubs became standard.
In the fifteenth century, washing was often done with basins of water and hand towels decorated with traditional dark blue bands. Such towels are being brought to Saint Anne and the infant Virgin in the painting Birth of the Virgin (left) in Prato Cathedral, by Paolo Uccello (1396–1475).

were carefully recorded—five to six breadths wide, five to six ells long.

Isabeau of Bavaria even had her bathtub transported from castle to castle. Bathing was not just an aristocratic privilege or habit, however, and by 1500 it was common among all classes, as well attested in France, Italy, Saxony, Bohemia, and Germany, despite a certain disapproval from monastic quarters.

During the Renaissance, baths became less and less frequent, for two main reasons. First of all, there was a growing moral intolerance of public bathhouses,

slight incommodities to our health for having abandoned this custom." A newborn babe, after the first hasty wash, would generally have to wait seven years before taking another bath!

Starting in the sixteenth century—and especially in the seventeenth century—hygiene was measured by another standard, namely that of appearance as assessed by sight and smell. Water had no place in a courtier's washing habits. The diaper cloth or towel was no longer used to dry a gleaming body, but just to rub the visible parts, that is face and hands. References

and secondly there was a growing distrust of water. Starting in the sixteenth century, immersion in water actually acquired a bad reputation. Water was increasingly thought to favor epidemics, notably the plague, by entering the body and weakening bodily organs. The level of scientific knowledge was such that people were still unaware that human skin is practically waterproof.

Thus baths—and, by the same token, bath linen—vanished for several centuries. The writer and moralist Montaigne deplored this situation since he felt that "in general, bathing is healthy" and that "we incur some

were even made to a "washing cloth." The use of perfume became an indispensable part of this art of appearance—clothes chests were scented and sachets of aromatic fragrances were worn on the body, under arms, around the hips, in the folds of dresses and the lapels of doublets.

Cleanliness henceforth focused on undergarments—and how often they were changed. The "whitest and sweetest" personal linen took the place of soap, and in court society it was changed almost every day. An account of the way the Princess Palatine "washed" after a trip taken in the middle of summer

Dry washing finally went out of fashion in the second half of the seventeenth century. The pleasures of water were rediscovered—people would lounge in baths perfumed with oils, then dry themselves briskly with clean linen straight from the scented cupboard.

A linen manufacturer used this 1906 illustration by Marchetti as an advertising image.

of the year 1705 is a perfect illustration of this attitude. Having arrived at the royal château at Marly, she reported that she "even had to wash her face, covered with a gray mask, so much dust there had been." As to the rest of her body, the princess simply changed her underblouse and put on another dress. At a time when the fountains of Versailles Château were spraying forth vast quantities of water, practically none of it was used for washing.

It wasn't until the middle of the eighteenth century that special rooms were built at Versailles to accommodate bathtubs. Louis XVI was the first French king to have a complete bathroom installed, an innovation that was designed following English examples.

Concerning bath linen, a 1765 inventory from the Amilly Château included a large and small cloth of muslin and lace to cover a dresser, and another embroidered with floating bouquets, as well as bath linen decorated with point d'Angleterre embroidery and Alençon lace. These, however, were bathtub sheets, which were used to line the sometimes rough surface of the tub, and covers, which were placed on top of the bathtub when it was not in use.

In any case, water remained rare and costly for most people, and their *cabinet de toilette*—a small room for washing and dressing—had no running water. In Paris, water was carried upstairs by wooden-clogged carriers with two buckets. Starting around 1820, lucky owners of a tub could also have bathwater delivered, but emptying the tub meant using a pump and tubes that dribbled water onto the pavement for an hour and a half. In such conditions, people did not wash much at home, and public and private bathhouses once again opened their doors. The most luxurious were located on the fashionable grand boulevards in Paris, and provided towels and bathrobes delightfully warmed on a stove.

It was not until roughly 1880, when real "bathrooms" with running water slowly appeared in upper-class buildings, that specific bath linen began to be developed. Cotton, and later terry toweling, then entered the scene and revolutionized bath towels. "Bathing gowns" were also made obsolete by modern habits: hot water straight from the faucet put an end to the need to have servants in attendance. The bathroom thus became a totally private place, where nudity did not have to be hidden since there was no one to see it (even though puritanical Catholics considered it inde-cent to look at one's own body). Bathtub sheets, however, were still listed in department store catalogues as late as 1913, for not all tubs were enameled or made of porcelain.

It was only during the 1920s and 1930s that the discipline of cleanliness evolved into the pleasure of washing, a pleasure which was still reserved for the upper classes in Europe, where bathrooms did not become the rule for the lower classes until the 1950s.

Now that the cult of body care has been added to the pleasure of washing, bathrooms have become a special place for relaxation, even sensuality. They are decorated with the same care as other rooms in the house, and are nearly always endowed with wonderfully soft linen.

Cloths that we would now call hand towels have always existed for ritual ablutions involving hands, feet, and face. In the West they were used that way—and only that way—for hundreds of years. Such ablutions still exist in Islamic countries, at the entry to mosques and before meals, where diners are brought swan-necked ewers of water for rinsing hands. In the Far East, hot damp towels, elegantly rolled, are offered at the beginning and end of meals, while in the West good breeding demands that hands be washed in the bathroom prior to sitting down at the table.

What we now call a bath towel was given many other names according to the era in which it was being used. As mentioned above, multi-purpose cloths were called *gausapes* during the Roman Empire and *touailles* during the Middle Ages. Throughout the seventeenth century such towels were not always limited to drying. For a long time they were "washing cloths" in the literal sense of the term since, like a child who "forgets" the soap, most people used only a dampened towel to wash. The skin never dripped with water.

The term "bath towel" did not come into common use until the nineteenth century, when washing was done in bathtubs and showers, and towels were used for drying the whole body. All available documents and images suggest that, prior to then, only hand and face towels were employed.

The ritual washing of hands dates back at least as far as the dawn of the Christian area, as attested by religious texts. The rules of several monastic orders even obliged their members to gather together at the cloister fountain in order to wash their hands before a meal. The Benedictine rule specifically mentions the communal maintenance of the "linen with which brothers dry their hands and feet."

During the medieval period, offering water for washing the hands was a sign of welcome, friendship and courtesy, as described in twelfth-century romances. A lay composed by Marie de France alluded to this ritual: "they gave him water for his hands and a towel to dry them, and they brought him food." In 1396, when Isabelle of France married Richard II of England, the famous chronicler Froissart recounted that prior to the wedding banquet "water for washing was called for, one took the basin, the other the cloth." These cloths were the object of great decorative refinement among kings and nobles; they were usually of "silke" adorned with colored embroidery and finished with knotted fringe.

As to wash basins, the ones owned in 1305 by the count of Flanders, in the service of King Charles V, were made either of silver or of "enamel dotted on the edges with roses and tiny royal crests."

In the Middle Ages, aristocratic children would be taught the basic habits of cleanliness, including the washing of hands before meals (which evolved into the use of a "damp towel" throughout the seventeenth century). But in medieval times the following precepts were stressed: "Honorable child, wash your hands on rising, on dining and on supping, which makes at least three times . . . your hands shall be well washed with cool water in the morning . . . your face and hands shall be washed with water fresh from the well, as cold as you can find it."

The ritual of using a cloth to wipe the hands before eating was already highly elaborate at the court of the Burgundian dukes, as described in detail in the memoirs of Olivier de la Marche. "When a prince wants to wash his hands, the pantler gives the cloth to the first maître d'hôtel, who must give it to the first chamberlain, who gives it at his discretion to someone of greater rank, then renders said cloth to the maître d'hôtel. Once the prince has washed and dried his hands, the maître d'hôtel returns it to the pantler, who puts it back on his shoulder."

A simplified version of this ritual was repeated in all manuals of etiquette from the Middle Ages to the eighteenth century. Erasmus, in his 1530 treatise, explained that the diner should extend his hand so that a page could sprinkle a bit of water on it and then pass

him the towel. Erasmus added that the water could be scented with camomile or rosemary and that, on solemn occasions, the towel should be of silk "decorated with flowers and woven with threads of gold and purple silk, and two ells long."

By the late sixteenth century, Montaigne was noting in the third volume of his *Essays* that:

". . . such habits had become totally integrated into the society of manners [and that] custom has already, without thinking, imprinted its character so strongly on me in certain things . . . that I would be as uncomfortable without my gloves as without my shirt, or without washing at the end of a meal and on rising."

But with the early seventeenth-century rise of what Georges Vigarello called "dry washing," water vanished from the scene, for it was considered too dangerous. Straight water was used as little as possible, and would be purified by the addition of vinegar or alcohol. In 1605, at a time when the use of water was already outmoded, Louis XIII's doctor, Héroard, described a new use of the "washing cloth." This so-called French style of washing involved "twisting" the towel, that is to say wringing the water out of it.

The following anecdote, though not entirely explicit, is nevertheless amusing: "At supper, Monsieur de Montmorency offered the cloth to the Dauphin who took it, saying, 'Well now, I'll wash myself *à la française*,' and then gave the towel a twist. 'You see, that's how you wash *à la française*.'" Somewhat later, Louis XIV would do little more in the morning than wipe his fingers and face with a towel dampened with water mixed with wine spirits which were poured from a magnificent ewer into a small silver saucer.

The ritual of washing one's hands in a basin prior to meals thus gave way to the ceremony of the "moistened napkin." It would seem to have started before the end of Louis XIII's reign in 1643. The preliminary ablutions at a banquet offered by Louis to the papal legate were recorded by a chronicler named Di Posso: "As soon as they were both on the dais, they were given damp napkins to wash their hands, the count of Soissons handing it to the king, and Monsieur de Beaumont to the cardinal."

It was at Louis XIV's court, however, that this protocol became scrupulously defined and choreographed. The moistened towel was brought forward

Decoratively woven and fringed bath linen provides a sensual setting for the nude body in The Bather, *by J.A.D. Ingres (1780–1867).*

between two gold plates by the "officer of the day" and given to the maître d'hôtel, who gave it to the king after having had the officer of the goblet test it by taking it in his hands. At the end of the meal, another towel was brought by the ranking prince of the blood or legitimized prince, or in their absence by the presiding gentleman, in the latter's capacity as "gentleman carver." The ceremony was almost as solemn and elaborate for the heir to the French throne and royal siblings, but the plates used to hold the napkins were made only of silver or silver-gilt rather than gold.

A detail as charming as it is rare—the classic red-and-white monogram is held in the beak of a swallow embroidered in red thread (right). This fine diapered linen towel with its hand-knotted fringe is from the early twentieth century. Playtime is over, dinner is ready—inciting children to wash hands and face dates back to classical antiquity. A twentieth-century version can be seen here in a catalogue illustration from Printemps department store (below).

The damp towel with which a person's hands had been wiped could never remain in the hands of someone of higher rank. At the end of the *ancien régime*, the ceremony became simpler, and then was dropped during the French Revolution. Napoleon brought it back into fashion, with one small change—it was the grand chamberlain himself who moistened the emperor's fingers with the towel, with no preliminary testing. Finally, the ritual declined until it was totally forgotten. The only vestige today is the practice of washing one's hands before meals.

Modern habits require absorbent fabric for drying the body after a bath or shower. Prior to the nineteenth century, however, towels were made of linen and did not need to be so absorbent, given the minimal amount of water used. Certain weaves have nevertheless been used since the Middle Ages to lend greater density to the material. These include huckaback, honeycomb, lozenge, and diamond Jacquard weaves.

But the late nineteenth-century invention of terry toweling revolutionized bathing. With the little loops on the warp threads of the fabric making it soft and absorbent, cotton terry toweling steadily conquered all bathrooms. As a new fabric, it incarnated new habits of cleanliness.

An idea of what bathroom linen was like before the advent of terry toweling can be had by leafing through department store catalogues dating from the 1880s. Linen is described and illustrated down to the tiniest detail; special "white goods" issues even included swatches of cloth glued to the page, so that various types of honeycomb, huckaback, lozenge, and diamond weaves could be compared, not to mention "pebble grain" textures and the plain, but very fine, linen used for expensive towels. Linen towels in truly exceptional trousseaux would not only be monogrammed but also decorated with lace insertions, Richelieu-work, openwork, and long, knotted fringes.

Examples of such linen dating from the 1920s and 1930s still belong to certain families, collectors, and specialized antique dealers. These days, connoisseurs can purchase similar items made from pure linen, linen-and-cotton blends, or cotton, finished with satin stitching or an appliqué border and, in the most sophisticated range, hand-crafted openwork or knotted fringe. These fine towels are more or less appreciated depending on local custom—the Italians, English, Belgians, and Germans are more enthusiastic than the French, whereas the Americans do not like them at all, given the national penchant for terry toweling that has inspired the extensive range of remarkable products made by prestigious firms such as Dan River, Wamsutta, and Fieldcrest.

The little loops on terry toweling were an inspired invention of the late nineteenth century. Forming these loops depended on the ingenious idea of incorporating an additional thread during weaving; a second weft thread was added to the foundation using a roller that moves up to eight times faster than the main thread. This produces an

The soft absorbency of honeycomb weave linen is coming back into fashion in a range of white, beige, and ecru tones. At right, by Catherine Memmi. Pure linen was the queen of bathroom fabrics until the end of the nineteenth century. These three monogrammed towels (below) in fringed honeycomb and diamond weaves were advertised in a catalogue issued by Les Grands Magasins du Louvre.

This handsome cotton bath set (right) of matching hand towels and bath towels has a knotted fringe and fine checkerboard weave produced by alternating smooth sections with fluffy sections (typical of the towels used in steam baths in Turkey). The embroidery of stylized roses is done in gold and silver thread.

A magnificent hand towel (below) in plain linen is adorned with rich openwork and Venetian reticella lace insertions. It was featured in the 1918 Printemps catalogue.

With their bands of dark blue decoration and knotted fringes, these towels (right) are nearly replicas of medieval models. Some of them have an alternating mat-and-glossy cotton weave. To prevent the fringe from getting tangled in the wash, the towels should be placed inside a pillowcase before going into the machine.

excess of thread between the taut warp threads, forming a loop that alternates with the normal weft. The greater the number of threads per square inch the greater the number of loops, and the better the quality of the pile. The length of the loops can also be varied, of course. The denser the pile, the more luxurious the towel. That is the reason why professionals refer to weights, which for towels are usually 350 to 450 grams per square meter, rising to 550 grams. Beyond that point, the fabric becomes stiff—only carpets have a density of 750 or 850 grams per square meter.

When the pile is cropped close, it becomes known as "velour toweling," which is subsequently less absorbent. That is why printed bath towels, which are often of velour because it renders the print better, tend to retain the loops on the back. The loops enhance dry cotton's natural capacity to absorb 30% of its weight in water, unlike linen which absorbs best when already damp.

A certain amount of terry toweling in pure linen is nevertheless produced for men's bath linen, because it presents a denser, and what is thus considered more "masculine," appearance. The same results can be produced with cotton by using twisted thread or up to 8% of polyester fibers, a technique that is used primarily by manufacturers in the United States.

According to one specialist, the finest terry toweling is produced from beautiful, long-fibered cotton, not necessarily combed nor too fine. In Western Europe, two countries have made this fabric their specialty both in terms of quality and quantity—Turkey and Portugal.

Terry toweling has clearly reached a degree of perfection in thickness and softness that was absent at the beginning of the century. Back then, loops were slack, the fabric limp, and designs very limited. Large check patterns were the rule, with stripes of several colors.

Starting in the 1920s, Art Deco designs were woven with pastel colors on a white foundation, appearing positive on one side and negative on the other. Little by little, fringe went out of fashion. Beginning in the 1950s, printed towels, along with sheets and tablecloths, began to appeal to women, and by the late 1960s solid, bright colors came into favor.

In 1922, a sales catalogue for Les Galeries Modernes expressed the timeless qualities generally sought in a towel, regardless of taste or period:

"The bath towel, veritable handmaiden to feminine beauty, must be strong enough to stimulate the circulation of blood under the skin, yet soft enough to avoid irritating the skin. It should be velvety enough to absorb the coolness of water and dense enough so that a fragrance lightly sprinkled over it will not evaporate too quickly."

COTTON
LINEN
AND SILK

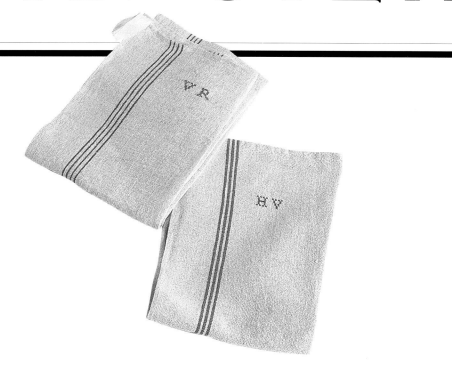

French philosopher Michel Serres wrote in *Les Cinq Sens* (The Five Senses): "Prior to form, prior to color or hue, the material must be touched. Skin, pillowcase, smooth or rough. . . .prior to the gaze, the grain."

Fabrics appeal to the sense of touch. Hemp is reputed to be coarse, linen cool yet alive, cotton soft and warm, silk smooth and velvety. The universal language of fabrics has been spoken at all times, in all places, among every group of people, regardless of the raw material available to them. Fabrics are present every moment of the day and night; they witness life's most intimate scenes, thereby weaving a very special relationship with each individual. As Patrice Hugues wrote in *Le Langage du Tissu*, "Between day and night, between dream and reality, a large part of ourselves is played out in fabrics."

Fabrics cover and warm. Touching and feeling them is reassuring, as children demonstrate when they choose bits of soft, often ragged material to clutch and stroke as they fall asleep.

The invention of fabrics dates from the dawn of civilization, probably as a result of braiding plant fibers to make nets, ropes, baskets, and wicker objects. The actual weaving of fabrics appeared nearly everywhere in the world during, or just prior to, the third millennium B.C. But of the approximately seven hundred fibrous plants that could have been spun into thread, only half a dozen were commonly employed: cotton, flax, hemp, jute, sisal, and ramie. Ramie, or "China grass," was used to make the "Canton batiste" that figures in the medieval inventory of the duke of Berry in the form of "a cloth of [China] grass decorated with several fancy animals, birds, and leaves made of cotton." Victor Hugo, in *Les Misérables*, testified to its continued use in the nineteenth century: "When China grass becomes old, it has filaments and fibers like hemp and flax. The cloth woven from it is like hemp." Some surprising plants have provided textile fibers at times, including trees

Pl.293. Chanvre cultivé. Cannabis sativa L.

such as willow and linden. In North America, a muslin cloth was produced from the agave plant and Indians in the West were skilled in the weaving of cedar fibers.

The current vogue for ecology has led to attempts to revive the use of hemp and ramie in the production of fabrics with new textures, especially for the making of tablecloths. And, thanks to extremely sophisticated technology for processing and spinning fibers, new yarns are being obtained from alcepiad (a plant similar to ramie), from raphia mixed with silk, from banana trees (the Japanese have produced a hemp-like fiber) and from pineapples (yielding a fabric not unlike raw silk). "Madagascar floss," a fiber used early in the twentieth century is even making a comeback. This fine, yet tough, material is still being woven by tenant farmers on the island of Madagascar.

For centuries, however, the standard plants used for household linen were hemp and flax, until cotton (pure or blended with synthetic fibers) finally took the lead.

Silk, on the other hand, has always been an exclusive, legendary fabric that has had both supporters and detractors, given its very special feel against the skin—hot and fluid, like running water. Silk is nevertheless the fabric used for producing the most spectacular bed sheets and covers, whether of satin or crêpe de Chine.

HEMP AND FLAX

While recent fashion has tried to re-establish hemp's pedigree, the plant is no longer grown in Europe for textile purposes, although hemp fibers are still used for manufacturing paper pulp and hemp seed serves as livestock fodder. Coarse dish towels, bath linen, and bed sheets, which were rough on the skin, disappeared from bridal trousseaux long ago. That explains why even specialist boutiques offer very little antique household linen made from hemp.

The first use of hemp probably dates all the way back to the third millennium B.C., somewhere in central Asia. Despite its notorious reputation for coarseness, Herodotus noted that skillful Scythians and Thracians in the fifth century B.C. were able to weave fine cloth from hemp:

"Someone without great experience would not recognize whether they were of hemp or linen, and whoever has not yet seen hemp cloth would think the garments were of linen."

In medieval Europe, hemp was used to make underclothing and household linen, as well as rope (ropemaking was the only trade that lepers in Brittany were allowed to practice).

Brownish-gray in color, thicker and coarser than linen when new, hemp cloth was often preferred by religious communities and, due to its much lower cost, by the poor. An anecdote asserts that Marie de Medici kept two hemp blouses among her magnificently rich trousseau—perhaps for doing penance. However, anyone lucky enough to touch a length of aged, well-used hemp cloth is amazed by the extreme softness and substantial drape of the fabric, which is similar to that of heavy flannel.

Throughout history hemp was used more widely in the countryside than in towns, since every farm had its field of hemp (and perhaps another of flax) designed to meet daily household fabric requirements and to supply part of the daughters' bridal trousseaux. In 1920, French novelist Colette evoked the widespread use of hemp cloth in a text for a sales catalogue issued by La Grande Maison de Blanc:

"On garden tables or round Empire tea tables, depending on the season, a cross-stitched hemp tablecloth—that was spun at home, woven at the neighbors' house and embroidered at school—would make white, scallion-mottled cheese seem even whiter. . . ."

In Europe, hemp was once grown from the Baltic region in the north down to southern Italy, that is between roughly the same latitudes as flax, the plant used to make linen cloth. The two plants were among the first used to produce textiles in human history—flax was already being grown in Iraq and Egypt in the sixth millennium B.C. In Europe its fibers were being woven as early as the Neolithic period at lakeside dwellings in present-day Switzerland, according to remnants of cloth analyzed by radiocarbon and thermoluminescent dating techniques. Yet the origin of weaving linen is more poetically explained in terms of divine inspiration, than in the sterile language of science. The Egyptians attributed the invention of linen to the goddess Isis, the Romans to Minerva, and the Lydians to Arachne. In Teutonic mythology, it was the earth-goddess Hilda who taught mankind how to grow flax and weave linen. Biblical tradition holds that flax found in Caucasia had been brought from the central Asian plateaux by Gomer, son of Japhet and grandson of Noah.

First harvested in the regions of Caucasia and Mesopotamia, flax was acclimated by the Egyptians, who developed an annual variety. Right up to the time of the crusades, the pharaohs' flax was considered superior to that grown in Western Europe, where tireless Phoenician traders had introduced it long before.

Thanks to this extraordinary raw material, Egyptians were able to produce a very fine fabric known as lawn as early as the fourth millennium B.C., despite their use of an extremely rudimentary horizontal loom without shuttle. Even eighteenth-century machines could do no better! Pieces of Egyptian cloth were not very long, however, because weavers had not yet thought of winding the warp yarn on a roller as they wove. Only a few exceptional items, designed to wrap royal mummies, attained the length of six yards.

Stem and flower of **Linum usitatissimum**, *otherwise known as flax. The stem of the flax plant yields thirty to forty bundles of fibers used to produce textiles.*

In most countries where it is grown, flax is harvested in mid-July. Although 90% of the world's flax harvest is produced in Russia and the Baltic countries, the finest flax is grown in the Pays de Caux region of France, seen here (right). When harvested, flax is pulled up rather than cut, in order to keep the stalks as long as possible. It is then bound in bundles for processing (below).

Paintings in the ancient cliff tombs at Beni Hassan, Egypt, along with the cave paintings of Elkab, reveal how ancient Egyptians grew, harvested, processed, spun, and wove flax into linen.

In his history of Cambyses, king of Persia, Herodotus reported:

"The Egyptians have established customs and laws that generally differ from those observed by the rest of humanity. In Egypt, it is the women who go to the market and trade, men who stay home and weave. Everywhere else, the weft is worked from bottom to top, whereas they do it from top to bottom!"

Production swiftly evolved from a domestic activity to an industry that became synonymous with national wealth. The royal manufactories were manned by slaves whose uniform for thousands of years was a short skirt of coarse linen. Production must have required a great number of slaves, given that a mummified body called for 270 meters of cloth (fully 900 for a pharaoh).

Once woven, linen was moistened and beaten with sticks on polished stone to soften it and remove the crispness produced by the wheat starch used in spinning.

Twelve hundred years before Jesus Christ, Moses brought Egyptian know-how to the Promised Land. The numerous references to linen in the Bible include a description of Solomon's temple, in which the ark of the covenant is said to be kept behind a large screen of gold-embroidered linen.

The Greeks naturally dressed in the fleece provided by their numerous flocks of sheep. Homer recounts how Odysseus, during one of his voyages, brought back women from Egypt who knew how to spin and weave linen. According to Aristophanes, fashionable Greek women used linen to make a sort of tiny handkerchief.

In Rome, flax had the bad reputation of exhausting the soil. It was nevertheless grown on the supposedly rich lands of the Po River plain, in Campania and Etruria. Linen was originally worn only by priests; patricians initially considered this fine-textured cloth to be

The subtle intensity of the violet-blue flax flowers in the Pays de Caux region (right) is a sign of the finest fibers. Other varieties of flax display pinkish-white flowers, but produce poorer quality fibers.

too feminine, but they later made it fashionable. It was during the Roman Empire that flax began to be planted on a broad scale. Advisors were brought from Egypt, and fields of flax sprouted in Germany, Belgium, and Gaul (where Druids dressed in linen when they gathered sacred mistletoe). Pliny waxed ecstatic over the fine cloth woven in Cahors; it was "white as wool" and was imported by the Romans for making mattresses and bedding. Pliny also extolled Spanish weaves from Tarragona and Ampurias, whose dazzling whiteness he attributed to the quality of the water used for retting (or soaking) the flax.

The fall of the Roman Empire and subsequent barbarian invasions partially ruined flax cultivation. Only

became widespread in France up until 1337, when the turmoil of the Hundred Years' War began. During the period of expansion, blue-flowered flax could be seen growing nearly everywhere—around Paris, in the Anjou region, in Brittany. Linen was also imported from Flanders, where the first linen trade fair took place at Courtrai. In 1180, when Isabelle of Hainault, the future wife of King Philippe Auguste, was about to make an entrance into Courtrai, the townspeople bedecked the streets with linen cloth and demonstrated the various stages of growing, spinning and weaving. It was around this time that wealthy nobles began constituting hoards of cloth, launching the long and passionate history of household linen.

the Saracens managed to rebuild an industry, selling their fabrics thanks to a maritime trade that dispatched ships as far as India and China, returning with cargoes of spices, cotton, and silk. Once relative peace was restored, the emergence of new nations favored the growth of cities and trade. European civilizations recovered a certain sense of well-being, and naturally turned again to linen. Flax was sown once more, looms were set up and linen production boomed at the expense of wool.

In 760, Charlemagne founded Bruges, which became the future capital of linen cultivation, thanks to nearby monks who had kept the tradition of flax growing and processing alive. Another Flemish town, Ypres, was founded in 960 and quickly became famous for its production of table linen. Also around this time, domestic spinning and weaving reappeared.

Starting in the twelfth century, linen cultivation

In the thirteenth century, Baptiste of Cambrai invented the wonderfully fine, tightly woven cloth that is still called "batiste" (the weave that Anne of Austria, mother of Louis XIV, so adored in the seventeenth century). Soon, however, the finest batiste was being made in Reims. Reims linen was so splendid that in the late fourteenth century, a piece of it served as the ransom sent by Charles VI to the sultan of Turkey in exchange for a noble prisoner. War nevertheless ravaged France throughout the next century, and fields of flax became battlefields. When peace finally returned, French and Flemish linen production was slow to revive. It was not until the reign of Henri IV (1589–1610) that cities like Lille and Arras became export centers.

Holy Roman Emperor Charles V is reported to have said, "I do not have to worry about Flanders so long as there are fields for growing flax, fingers to spin it, and hands to weave it." Yet it was his own son, Philip II of Spain, who would destroy the Flemish linen industry through a policy of religious persecution. Protestant weavers fled Flanders by the thousands, moving to France and especially to England and Ireland.

Religious intolerance produced the same effect in France when the Edict of Nantes was revoked in 1685. Roughly six hundred thousand French Protestants, called Huguenots, fled the country, crippling not only linen production, but also the lace and silk industries. They set up shop in Germany, Holland, England, Ireland, and Switzerland (where the finest lawn was being produced as early as the Middle Ages). Everywhere that Protestant weavers went, they spurred linen production, and certain countries have continued to nurture this expertise—the finest cloth in Europe is still woven in Switzerland and Ireland.

The earliest colonists on the American continent followed the traditions they had always observed in Europe. Every farmer, therefore, planted a field of flax

and his daughters learned to spin and weave. It was not until the arrival of eighteenth-century immigrants, including many Huguenots, that flax was planted on a more extensive level and quality linen began to be produced. But it was just at this point that cotton started its inexorable rise, forever throttling the future of American linen. In France, on the other hand, the close of the eighteenth century confirmed the primacy of flax—over 700,000 acres of it were planted at a time when weaving was still a fairly artisanal activity. Nearly every farm possessed at least one weaving loom until the late nineteenth century, when competition from cotton fabrics and department store linen forever silenced the home loom's rhythmic click.

FROM SLENDER STALK TO SHEER LAWN

The word "linen" is derived from the Latin *Linum usitatissimum*, the botanical name that Linnaeus gave to flax. The plant has striking blue flowers and gives a

his flax grower (below) from the Pas-de-Calais region of France, around 1935, could contemplate his crop with satisfaction—the stems are long, straight and fine, most likely with the uniform yellow color that indicates top quality.

he word "cloth" is perhaps never more evocative than when applied to the plain, loosely woven linen or linen-and-hemp cloths, often decorated with a simple red band, that long served as dish towels and dust cloths (right). More than any other fabric, linen has a natural feel, thanks to a texture and grain that recall the plant from which it is produced. That impression of naturalness is reinforced when linen is unbleached, as seen in this harmonious composition of ecru cloths in a wicker basket (following double page). All are modern except for the monogrammed napkin, which dates from the late eighteenth or early nineteenth century.

fine textile fiber from which the best linen is made. The highest quality flax is still grown, as of yore, in Egypt and surrounding areas. But the most common, so-called Riga variety produces a coarser and less abundant yet highly sturdy fiber when cultivated in northwest Russia and the Baltic countries, a region that now produces 90% of the world's flax harvest. Quality improves, however, as the fields move further south, to Saxony, Silesia, Bohemia, and southern Poland. Even finer flax is grown in Sweden, Ireland, along the North Sea and English Channel, and especially in Belgium. The warmer French climate in the Artois and Somme provinces is also highly propitious, whereas the absolutely finest French flax is grown in the Pays de Caux area of Normandy. Merely growing flax requires a great deal of attention; when added to the various processes needed to prepare it for spinning, and the complications in weaving due to the yarn's lack of elasticity, it quickly becomes clear why linen faces an insurmountable economic handicap compared to cotton, which is simpler and cheaper to produce.

Linen has therefore become the exclusive domain of the wealthy or of certain connoisseurs, and is not well known to the general public. Even when women are familiar with linen, they complain about how wrinkled it gets and how hard it is to iron. The remedy is simple, however: the linen must be damp when ironed, and the iron must be extremely hot (not necessarily heavy nor a steam iron).

Linen's positive qualities, on the other hand, are unmatched. The parallel arrangement of its basic fibers produces a very sturdy cloth that will give twenty years of use. Since it is highly absorbent, linen is also perfect for dish towels. Thanks to its insulating qualities, a linen sheet produces an impression of coolness ideal for summer nights, unlike cotton which "heats up." Stronger wet than dry, linen stands up to countless washings without shagging and grows imperceptibly softer through the years.

Yet pure linen no longer has many admirers who

are willing to overlook its inconvenience in order to benefit from its incomparable feel. Linen is a subtle mixture of firmness and suppleness, giving an austere softness that feels wonderful whether smoothed or crumpled. From the sturdiest linen fabric to the airiest batiste and sheerest lawn, its milky whiteness and ivory highlights seduce the eye. Batiste and lawn are made from only the finest yarn, which distinguishes them from standard linen. This yarn comes from the longest, top quality fibers that measure about four feet. It is spun while damp so that it can be stretched to a maximum, giving a metric count of 80 to 100 for lawn, or slightly thicker—around 60—for batiste. If lawn is almost as diaphanous as muslin, however, that is above all the result of its weave, which is looser than batiste.

Bed sheets of lawn are so soft and light that the effect is that of being caressed by an imperceptible breeze; only the most ethereal lace and finest white needlework are light enough to adorn such sheets. Batiste, which is denser and less transparent, produces sheets and tablecloths that are particularly suited to colored embroidery and appliqués. Batiste also takes a full range of pastel dyes and is perhaps the most subtle type of linen, thanks to a naturally glossy and slightly starchy feel combined with an impression of sensual fragility due to its fineness.

But regardless of whether flax is to be transformed into coarse, thickly woven cloth or into unbelievably sheer lawn, once the plant has been harvested it has to undergo the same series of odd-sounding operations.

RETTING AND SCUTCHING

The first step in extracting useful fibers from flax is called retting. Formerly, after the stems were harvested, they were spread in semicircles and left in the damp morning dew for three to five days until they whitened. The pale stalks were then bound into little bundles wrapped in a protective layer of straw before

In Cholet, France—a traditional textile center known as "the handkerchief capital of the world"—automation has never been allowed to undermine old-fashioned quality. The mechanical loom (above) is weaving bolts of linen for dish towels. The shuttles of white yarn, comprising the weft, are automatically sent across the warp yarns.

The perforated cards used in a Jacquard loom (center) encode the pattern to be woven. Certain more modern machines use computer disks, but can only execute small repetitive patterns.

As the cloth is progressively woven by the machine, it falls into accordion-like piles (below), from which dish towels will be cut and hemmed.

The warp yarns are wound on these huge spindles (right), since the length of the yarn determines the length of the piece to be woven.

All photographs were taken in the Alexandre Turpault factory, the oldest and largest firm in Cholet. Founded in 1847, the company makes handkerchiefs and household linen in cotton, in linen, and in blends of the two.

being submerged in a stream of running water, taking care to see that they touched neither the bottom nor the banks. Depending on the temperature, retting would last eight to twelve days.

Traditionally, the best water came from the Lys River in Flanders, which largely made the reputation of Courtrai linen. French linen was always dependent on this Flemish river and its canals, and suffered on several occasions from the vagaries of Franco-Belgian politics.

These days, retting is accelerated by immersing the stalks in concrete vats full of hot water. When the stems are sufficiently pale, they are rinsed with running water and dried in the open air. The bundles are then spread in a field in cones called "chapels." These chapels are left to stand until the stalks take on a fine, even color.

The retted flax—"the chrysalis of snow-white linen," as described by Marguerite Yourcenar in *Archives du Nord* —is then ready for scutching, This stage entails beating the stalks to separate the textile fibers from the woody parts. Formerly, scutchers beat the flax with a wooden knife until the fibers were completely free of the stalk. The fibers were then scraped with an iron knife prior to being handed over to the spinners. These days, the operation is mechanized. Once the fine fibers have been separated from the tow (coarse, broken fibers), the flax is ready for spinning. Flax that has been scutched looks like long blond hair, an analogy that did not escape poets and composers including Goethe and Debussy (who composed a prelude for the "girl with flaxen hair").

SPINNING AND WEAVING

The prehistoric technology of spinning remained unchanged for millennia, until spinning mills were set up in the last third of the eighteenth century. The only major advance in home spinning occurred with the development of spinning wheels, around 1520. Long

Recalling old player pianos, these rolls of perforated cards are essential to the process of weaving damask. The cards constitute part of the treasured heritage of the Italian firm Frette, which specializes in damask weaves.

before writing was invented, the art of spinning had already been developed. Sewing needles have been discovered, which date from around 10,000 B.C., with eyes so small that only carefully processed fibers could go through them. It is amazing to think that in rural communities the same age-old gestures were still being repeated, almost unchanged, at the dawn of the twentieth century.

The principally feminine task of spinning had already acquired powerful symbolic meaning in classical times, when spindle and distaff represented life and fertility, and thread symbolized passing time. As Jacques Bril put it is his study on the origins of cloth and spinning, "thread is the concrete essence of time, fabric, and life."

In ancient Greece, the invention of spinning was attributed to the goddess Athena, who held a distaff, symbolizing peace, in her right hand. Much later, the distaff became a symbol of fairy-tale witches. It was also the symbolic gift offered to fiancées in rural nineteenth-century France. These apparently contradictory symbols hinged on preparations for marriage and its consequences. Once the spinning wheel was invented, it too became associated with a whole range of popular imagery evoking fireside serenity accompanied by a rocking, peaceful song. As the wheel turned, so turned time, ineluctable, as expressed in Ronsard's sixteenth-century sonnet addressed to Hélène:

"When you are old, at evening by the fire,
Sitting and spinning in the flickering light,
You will say, marvelling at my songs' delight,
'Ronsard praised my beauty with his lyre.' "

The earliest techniques for spinning were very simple and required no other equipment than the human body. The textile fibers were spread on the ground, and the spinner took one or two fibers in her hand, pulling and twisting them between hand and thigh,

MONZA
STABILIMENTO DI CANDEGGIO

progressively incorporating other fibers, twisting all the while. As the thread lengthened, it would be wound around the fingers; once a large ball was produced, the spinner would start all over again. The spindle was one of the first improvements, giving the fiber a faster and more even twist, followed by the spindle whorl, a sort of ring that served as a counterweight. But it was not until the end of the fourteenth century, when the spinning wheel was invented, that a continuous strand could be spun.

In the late eighteenth century, England pioneered mechanical spinning mills, a phenomenon that would paradoxically speed the ruin of the linen industry in the following century. That was because the manufacture of "dry" linen with equipment invented for cotton yielded a quality inferior to hand-spun, "wet" fibers. And when "wet" spinning was finally invented by Philippe de Girard in 1810, it was too costly to stem the advancing tide of inexpensive cotton.

Today, the spinning of flax fibers must meet extremely precise standards that are a guarantee of quality. It is always done either "dry" or "wet." Only very fine fibers are produced by wet spinning. Spinning involves twisting discontinuous, parallel textile fibers into an unbroken thread of uniform thickness, twist and strength. The yarn, which must contain between forty and fifty fibers at all points, is then classified according to three criteria—fineness, strength and wear.

As with all other fibers, once spun and woven, the fabric must then undergo a beauty treatment.

BLEACHING

Unbleached flax is grayish-beige in tone, which does not accord with the traditional whiteness associated with household linen. So throughout history it has been bleached—formerly after the weaving stage, today just after spinning.

A great deal has been written about bleaching methods, particularly the Dutch process. One of the

The visual poetry of bleaching laundry in a field inspired the lyrical yet realist 1917 painting (left) Bleaching Linen by S. J. Serebrjakowa (1885–1967).

most traditional methods involved moistening—or, better, soaking—a piece of cloth with whey and spreading it in a meadow. Then it was merely a question of waiting for the alchemy of sun, moon, and dew to produce the whiteness so coveted by royalty and lovers of fine linen all across Europe. In Flanders, various shades of white were already a gauge of quality by 1545, and held the same importance as the length and width of the pieces. Although Holland has historically been the leader in bleached linen, the Dutch were not beneath stooping to subterfuge in order to profit from their reputation— in sixteenth-century Haarlem, merchants imported linen from Silesia and Westphalia, then bleached and sold it without mentioning its true place of origin. And in the seventeenth century, they would buy linen in Courtrai and then cut the pieces down to lengths measured in Holland, or Flemish, ells (27 inches instead of 45 or 47). That is how the most highly prized and costly cloth came to be known as "Holland cloth." Obviously, Courtrai weavers took umbrage and tried to set up their own bleaching operations, but they could never match Haarlem's whiteness.

In France, meanwhile, a favorable flax-growing climate in the Vosges and Brittany regions spurred the founding of bleaching firms in Gérardmer and Cholet, where green meadows and damp weather produced an attractive bluish-white hue. This industry still exists today but, as elsewhere, the bleaching is almost always done by purely chemical means. However, linen quality is still partly judged according to its exact shade of white with varying degrees of whiteness that include: pure white, half-white, quarter-white, cream, and finally, washed-out white.

European countries have recently agreed to promote linen, making the general public more aware of its advantages. In France, products made of pure linen are entitled to display the "blue flower" label. New techniques are being sought to minimize wrinkles, cheaper cotton-and-linen blends are being promoted once again, and mixtures of linen and silk or synthetic fibers are appearing on the market (polyester for household linen, viscose, nylon and

stretch fibers for ready-to-wear garments). After a period of materials "so processed that you look in vain for some life in the material," in the words of textile specialist Lee Edelkort, the era of fabrics with a livelier, somewhat dryer feel is about to dawn. Linen would seem to fit the bill. The message has reached recent summer fashion collections, and promising reactions have been detected in the household linen industry.

It is almost tempting to believe historians who point out that, since the Middle Ages, every time lifestyles evolve toward higher standards of domestic comfort and refinement, the linen industry rises from its ashes.

COTTON

Nowadays, it is hard to imagine living without cotton fabrics. Cotton's reassuring softness and adaptability to body temperature makes it seem like a second skin, providing a gentle impression of comfort. A spoiled child, in France at least, is said to have been "raised in cotton."

Even though cotton has been cultivated in India since at least 2000 B.C., the now irreplaceable fabric was not adopted in Europe until the invention of mechanical processing techniques in the late eighteenth and early nineteenth centuries.

The Greek historian Herodotus had already been told of the Indian plant during his voyage to the East around 450 B.C. Herodotus never got as far as India and therefore never saw cotton plants himself, but he reported that "there are trees which grow wild there, the fruit of which is a wool exceeding in beauty and goodness that of sheep. The Indians make their clothes of this tree wool." According to Herodotus, the Egyptians even used cotton more extensively than linen,

although this assertion may be the result of lexical confusion, since the word *byssos* could mean fabric made of flax *or* cotton, somewhat in the same way that "linen" in English has now become a generic term for fabrics used in the household, whether made of flax, cotton, or even synthetic fibers.

Ancient Egyptian fabrics that have been discovered and analyzed, moreover, are almost always made of flax. Cotton was considered to be an exotic luxury, acquired from Syrian traders.

Alexander the Great helped to make the cotton plant more widely known. On returning from his expeditions, Alexander's soldiers recounted that they saw "a wool tree that yields very white, very fine garments." Vestiges of this linguistic confusion still exist in the English term "cotton wool" and in the German word for

sades that cotton became more widely known in Europe. On arriving in Antioch, the crusaders adopted not only the white smocks made in the ancient Egyptian city of Pelusium (on which they would stitch their heraldic emblems) but also the richly colored cotton goods and magnificent silks from Syria and Persia.

After the last crusade, which ended in 1291, merchants remained in contact with the Saracens and organized trade in cotton goods, using Venice as their headquarters. As the mandatory point of passage for

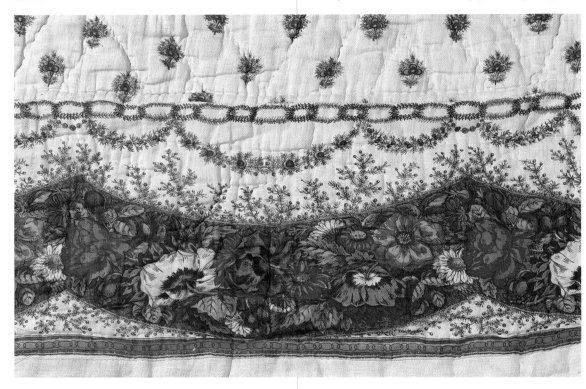

Cotton is mainly associated with softness and fluffiness, yet it can also be beautifully decorated. This magnificent calico print bedspread dates from the late eighteenth century and was manufactured in France. The old continent's classic taste can be detected in the colorful flowered frieze and the tiny patterns against a light ground.

cotton, *Baumwolle*, which literally means "tree-wool."

In Rome, Pliny called cotton *gossypium*, and praised it by asserting that "nothing is to be preferred to its fibers for whiteness and softness." But as they had done with the introduction of linen, Roman men rejected the fabric because its delicateness made it seem too feminine. Patrician ladies, however, enthusiastically draped themselves with this light, fine cloth, which was woven for the first time in Europe on the Greek island of Kos.

In the eighth century, Arab invaders brought cotton garments to Spain. The Spanish word for cotton, *algodon*, is moreover derived from the Arabic *al qutn*. It was in Baghdad, a new stage on the route from the East, that Arabs bought cotton grown in Persia, India, and China, until they began cultivating it locally in Egypt, Algeria, and Baetika. It was not until the cru-

such goods, Venice added a bit of its own prestige to the merchandise making its way north to Italy, Switzerland, and southern Germany. France was less permeable, being trapped in a feudal economic system and later mired in the Hundred Years' War. Despite this trade, cotton fabrics remained rare throughout the Middle Ages, and a gown or bed sheet of cotton would be bequeathed from one generation to the next like the precious object it was.

But it was above all the use of cotton flock as stuffing for the softest of mattresses that lent the fiber its reputation for luxuriousness—cotton promised the most comfortable of nights to those who could afford it.

Venice maintained its monopoly for some two hundred years, channeling the trade in cotton yarns from Aleppo, Damascus and, later, Cyprus. Wars between France and Italy helped spread awareness of these yarns in France, notably in Rouen where weavers made the first French "fustian," a somewhat thick cloth composed of a linen warp with a cotton filling. In Italy and in the city of Bruges, such fabric entailed a cotton-wool mixture, while in Manchester fustian was woven of pure cotton. By the end of the sixteenth century, just when direct trade routes between Europe and India were opening up, various types of weaves appeared in several other cities. In Lyon, Troyes and the Rouen area, a fustian-type linen and cotton twill known as

use in household linen goods was not common until the industrial revolution.

Although India was the cradle of cotton, as well as Europe's main supplier, cotton was already called *si* in the Chinese *Book of Odes* as early as 1000 B.C. But production of cotton in China did not develop until much later, since the social code held that the rich should dress in silk and the poor in wool. A ninth-century attempt to launch the cultivation and weaving of cotton did not meet with much success, for the Chi-

Because of the crusades, India was the West's main supplier of cotton fabrics. The seventeenth-century rage for exotic calico prints, which sparked a European enthusiasm matched only by porcelain from China, reinforced India's market dominance so much that European courts issued protectionist decrees in an attempt to halt imports. India is still a major cotton exporter today (left).

There are 42 different varieties of gossypium, or cotton plant (below). Its white fluffy bolls often caused cotton to be called "tree wool."

basin was developed, while the village of Creton in Normandy pioneered the sturdy fabric that became known as cretonne. Marseille also specialized in a sturdy cotton similar to cretonne, known as *cotonine*.

When Holland, England, and France established their respective East India trading companies, the market for what was then called "painted fabrics" suddenly expanded, as did that for imported "muslins" from Mosul in Iraq. But it was above all thanks to calico prints that cotton finally seduced European courts, and their popularity would never flag despite periodic protectionist measures. The demand created by this fashion craze led to the emergence of a cotton printing industry in Europe during the closing decades of the sixteenth century. The actual weaving of cotton fabrics in Europe did not begin until sometime later, and their

nese believed that the fiber could produce only ordinary fabrics or stuffing—the only advantage being that it was less costly than silk floss. The Chinese would not begin wearing cotton garments for another three centuries, and then only when peasants were practically forced to grow and weave it. China has never looked back, however, and is today a major exporter of cotton.

In Japan—where clothing habits, like most aspects of culture, were imported from China—feudal lords dressed in silk. Each family wove cotton fabrics, however, according to its needs. The cotton industry only began with the fall of the Tokugawa shogunate and the advent of the Meiji era in the late nineteenth century. Yet by the eve of the Second World War, Japan had become the world's leading supplier of cotton goods.

Everywhere that cotton grew naturally, it was recognized as a textile plant—serge-weave cotton

garments of sophisticated production dating from the late thirteenth century have been found in the Upper Zambesi region of Africa. The cotton plants grown there today are still of the same variety, *herbaceum*. In Mexico, the use of cotton probably dates back to the fifth millennium B.C. It is known that the cotton industry was a main source of wealth during the fifteenth-century Aztec empire, when fields totaled over 100,000 acres. In Peru, where a strong cotton tradition still exists today, native Peruvians in the south and on the Pacific coast have been weaving absolutely amazing fabrics since before the Inca period.

In North America, the cotton story could have started over eight thousand years ago, since an extraordinary mesh of cotton, dating from 6000 B.C., has been discovered in what is now the state of Utah. Instead, it required a terrific leap forward in time to the early seventeenth century with the arrival of English colonists in Virginia and the planting of the first major cotton fields—without, as it happens, much success. As late as 1791, only 100 tons of cotton were delivered to London, whereas less than seventy years later, at the outbreak of the American Civil War, over a million tons of United States cotton reached England. In between, of course, there had been an extensive "importation" of black slaves from Africa and the tragic episode of southern plantations written with the blood of slaves and echoed in their poignant songs. Besides this forced labor, other factors that favored increased production at the turn of the century were the invention of the mechanical cotton gin in 1793 by Eli Whitney, and the planting, in 1806, of a superior

variety—Sea Island long-fibered cotton.

The Civil War that started in 1861, however, meant the end of the southern plantations. Five years of terrible war, immortalized in Margaret Mitchell's novel, *Gone with the Wind*, also slowed the British textile machine, despite the purchase of cotton from India (then beginning to develop its own industry) and Egypt (where cotton had been reintroduced between 1820 and 1860 by a Franco-Swiss engineer named Jumel).

Once peace was signed and slavery abolished in the United States, American cotton fields bloomed again, pushing ever further west. The "Cotton Belt" stretched across an area twice as large as the entire country of France. Today, American cotton ranks among the best, although Egyptian cotton is still the most highly prized of all.

In 1987, cotton production on three continents totaled fifteen and a half million tons. Given the historically rapid rise of cotton, one might wonder why Europe waited so long—nearly two thousand years—to discover and adopt it. Historians generally argue that although Europeans knew of cotton, they could not conceive of developing a textile industry around a plant that could not be grown locally. In addition, transportation was slow and unsuited to carrying the full quantities of raw cotton needed for exploitation. But these reasons do not explain everything, and it is no coincidence that the adoption and mass production of cotton followed the development of mechanical techniques for sorting, ginning, preparing, spinning, and weaving cotton. Another reason sometimes advanced, based on the fact that cotton first became

popular in Europe via calico prints, was that the basic uses to which plain cotton might have been put were already covered by flax and hemp, whose cultivation and processing had long ago been mastered.

FROM COTTON BOLLS TO ORGANDY

"The cotton plants of the country, turning back their expanded capsules, looked like white roses," wrote Chateaubriand during his American travels. Some fifty days earlier, those same cotton plants would have flowered for the brief instant of a day, then quickly transformed flowers into fruit. When the bolls finally burst they would have revealed a wonderful bouquet of soft, dazzling white puffs composed of fibers more or less long depending on the variety. It is the length of the fibers that determines the quality of cotton yarn, which is classified into eight grades. The average grade provides the standard against which prices of superior and inferior qualities are set. This system, devised in the late eighteenth century, is still used on commodity exchanges.

Jumel Egyptian cotton produces the longest fibers—roughly seventeen inches long. The ultimate refinement is to comb long-fibered Egyptian cotton using very finely aligned mechanical teeth to obtain the purest fibers. This produces an exceptionally fine yarn—with a "count" of 200—from which muslins and other sheer fabrics, or voiles, are woven. After Egyptian cotton, the second longest fibers are produced by United States cotton. Then, in descending order of quality, comes cotton from India, Pakistan, China, the former USSR, and Africa. The shorter the fibers, the poorer the yarn.

As with pure linen, the feel of various cotton fabrics is a function not only of the fineness of the yarn, but also of the number of threads per square centimeter (or weight per square meter).

Cotton voile and satin are the most sophisticated fabrics for sheets that guarantee sweet dreams. These two completely different weaves both fully exploit the warm feel of cotton produced by its wonderful softness, roundness, and smoothness.

Bed sheets of cotton voile are like a gentle breeze on the skin. Voile is a type of muslin in a fine, open, plain weave, somewhat less transparent than that used for lingerie and other garments. In order to avoid heavy decoration, opalescent cotton voile is usually adorned with lace, fine white or colored embroidery, and flounces that reinforce the sense of airiness.

Satin, in contrast, is opaque, brilliant, and fluid. It is a very tight weave of very fine yarn—its incomparable brilliance comes from the fact that the weft yarns are invisible from the front, thanks to the special "satin weave" technique in which warp yarns are floated over weft yarns or vice-versa.

Satin damasks also make fine tablecloths, although truly exceptional table linen generally exploits the artificial stiffness of organdy and organza, transparent muslins which are given a permanent crispness when the fabric is bleached. Transparent white or colored organdy is a sublime setting for satin-stitch embroidery or appliqués.

Finally, in contrast to this "unbearable lightness" of voile and organdy, the impeccable drape of piqué—whose raised wales are produced by a special weave in which the warp yarn is much finer than the weft yarn—yields tablecloths and bedspreads that are as sharp and gay as summer.

Alongside these famous materials, cotton has also inspired a wide range of fabrics whose names are almost forgotten today. A look at old department store catalogues brings to mind fabrics and weaves like madampolam, calico, shirting, and percale that were used for everyday items in the nineteenth and early twentieth centuries.

Cotton has become the most widely employed natural fiber textile of the twentieth century, largely because it is one of the least expensive choices. It is indeed a generous textile, within reach of every household budget, offering qualities that accord perfectly with a modern lifestyle.

This cotton harvested in Turkey may well be used to weave the terry (or Turkish) toweling for which the country is famous (right).

The big southern cotton plantations, where a few huge fortunes were amassed and countless black slaves were made to suffer, have left their mark on American history. The plantation shown (right), established in the eighteenth century, was photographed by Henri Cartier-Bresson in 1960. The United States is now the world's second largest producer of cotton, after China.

SILK

"The silk department was like one large, romantic bedroom, draped in white on a lover's whim for the nakedness of snow, for a gambol in whiteness. All the milky hues of every part of a beloved body were reproduced there, from velvety lower back to silky thighs and gleaming satin breasts . . . silks and satins stood out against this creamy white ground . . . and there were paduasoys and Sicilian grosgrains, light scarves and silk surahs which ranged from heavy white to Norwegian blond, from transparent white heated by the sun to an Italian or Spanish russet."

Emile Zola's images in his nineteenth-century novel *The Ladies' Paradise* evoke the eternal sensuality and fascination associated with silk. Sweet and warm like the gentle brush of a caress along a body that immediately "feels itself become passive," in the words of early twentieth-century psychiatrist Gatian de Clérambault, silk sheets have always had, perhaps for this unconscious reason, their staunch defenders and stern opponents. For while there is "sometimes desire in the feel of certain materials, sometimes repulsion, and occasionally respect, it just might happen that people prefer to keep a distance from what their eyes admire," observed novelist Hector Bianciotti.

In terms of household linen, silk is employed primarily for bedclothes; it is used only rarely at table, given the delicate care it requires. The weaves usually employed are satin—so smooth and glossy that eye and hand slide along it endlessly—and crêpe de Chine, with its fine, sensuously crinkled surface that begs to be touched.

When adorned with lace insertions, appliqués, or fine silk embroidery, silk sheets can be veritable works of art. Silk became particularly fashionable from the 1930s onwards, when it was considered avant-garde to sleep in black satin sheets. Salmon pink nevertheless remained the favorite color. Silk damask was also appreciated, as were mat crêpe and glossy satin combinations, with Art Deco appliqués. In a more classic mode, extraordinary bedclothing was made by Porthault for Barbara Hutton in the 1950s—pink silk satin faced with old point d'Angleterre lace, with garlands of roses in satin-stitch embroidery, and embroidered tulle inserts of a maiden plucking the roses. Nowadays, sheets of polyester crêpe de Chine and satin can exercise the same attraction, while those in real silk are more simply and sensibly edged with Venetian drawn-thread work. Fashionable colors now include pale pastels, pearl gray, straw yellow, tea rose, peach, or pale blue. Midnight blue and black, of course, have been favorites ever since the days of François I. Damask weaves with moiré effect are highly appreciated in Italy, and are a specialty of the Frette firm, while Marc Porthault sets a more modern tone by printing crêpe with original multicolored designs, complete with matching sets of nightwear.

Silk is a magic substance, its history woven with myths and wondrous tales, including that of its origin. According to legend, it was in the year 2697 B.C. that a Chinese princess discovered the art of weaving silk. Si-Ling-Shi, first wife of Emperor Huang-Ti, who was the founder of the Arts of Architecture and Administration, noticed during her garden walks that a strange caterpillar was spinning its fine cocoon on a mulberry tree. After the butterfly had emerged and flown away, the princess unwound the ball of thread from the abandoned cocoon. Thus was born the art of raising these magic insects and spinning their celebrated yarn which was to become the fabric of the imperial city.

Archaeologists, meanwhile, are categorical in dating the presence of silk back to the Neolithic Age, based on a cocoon found in Chen-Si province, while fragments of silk cloth dating from circa 2800 B.C. confirm knowledge of early weaving and dyeing techniques. In the second millennium B.C., the land of Seres, as the Romans called China, definitely possessed the skills of raising silkworms, gathering cocoons,

The art of cultivating silk began in China five thousand years ago and has not slowed since. Cultivation techniques, indissolubly linked to the life-cycle of the Bombyx mori caterpillar, have changed very little in China. Mulberry leaves—the sole diet of "silkworms"—must be harvested, selecting the tenderest shoots. Cocoons are hand-sorted on trays, and transported on small craft to the market. These images evoke all the poetry of one of humanity's oldest and most wonderful traditions.

smothering the chrysalis inside before it pierced the cover (which would render the thread unusable), and finally softening the cocoon with boiling water in order to unravel the thread. Spinning and weaving were women's work. It was the empress herself who "opened" the silk season; ladies invited to participate had to perform purification rites that included fasting and the eschewal of all luxurious garments, in order that all the force of femininity be concentrated on the cocoons. Silk fabrics were the sole prerogative of the imperial family and of high dignitaries—infractions were punished by death.

Until the third century B.C., China, which lived in almost total isolation, kept secret the art of silk-making. Since the exportation of cocoons, worms and eggs was forbidden, silk remained unknown elsewhere.

It was sometime between 200 B.C. and A.D. 200 that silk finally escaped from China and became an item of exchange. After trade was established with central Asia, it traveled as far as Babylonia and Phoenicia. Rome was the first Western civilization to adopt the use of silk. After 273, when the Middle East trading centers of Petra and Palmyra fell into Roman hands, silk moved down the Ganges and Indus valleys and their estuaries.

Finally, in 526, his majesty the silkworm arrived in Byzantium. From that point on, the mulberry tree slowly spread across the west, from Greece to Sicily, up through Italy into Calabria and Naples. Meanwhile, cities like Lucca, Florence, Sienna and Bologna established silk industries. The Arabs brought it to Spanish towns like Jaén, Grenada, Cordoba, Toledo, and Almeria. By the late thirteenth century, the West's demand for silk fibers was practically met, at which point Italian workshops could produce figured silk fabrics as perfect as those from Damascus.

In 1309, when the papal residence was moved to Avignon in France, silk was already being cultivated near Uzès. The weavers soon produced magnificent silk to satisfy the prelates' needs, but the industry went into a decline in 1377 when the papal seat was transferred back to Rome. Some of the weavers moved on to Lyon, a city that would not make its fortune with silk until nearly two centuries later. In 1536, two men arrived in Lyon from Piedmont, and with privileges granted to them by François I, were able to recruit a considerable number of master weavers within only a few years. In 1603, Henri IV further improved the situation by planting mulberry trees—some sixty thousand of them—anywhere they could be grown.

Lyon then underwent its golden age of silk production, which lasted until the Edict of Nantes was revoked in 1685, leading to the departure of a great number of Protestant weavers. The Regency period and Madame de Pompadour's "reign" led to a resurgent fashion for silk, but then the French court discovered printed calico and cotton muslin, which quickly became all the rage. The French Revolution delivered another blow to the local silk industry, until Napoleon revived it years later. Lyon maintained a flourishing industry throughout the nineteenth century, but in the twentieth, with the progressive mechanization of weaving techniques, workshops and looms in the Lyon region were slowly abandoned. These days, the local industry survives thanks to silk yarn imported mainly from China, but also from Korea, Thailand, Japan, and Brazil. Once silkworm farming declined in France, former silk cottages in the Cévennes region were converted into upscale country homes recognizable by their high walls and small windows. There has recently been a certain revival of Cévennes sericulture, however, in an attempt to link traditional French savoir-faire to modern technology. In what seems to be a sign of success, even the Japanese now visit the village of Saint-Hippolyte-du-Fort in order to learn how silk was traditionally produced!

Although Japan is the world's fourth largest producer of silk today, it was not until the nineteenth century that the country began raising the bombyx worm and adopted Western weaving techniques.

Silk is one of nature's marvels, which is why it is as fascinating as it is beautiful. This mature cocoon contains a single strand of silk thread nearly one kilometer long.

Centuries of tradition informed the skill, expertise, and enthusiasm that went into transforming a silk thread into this eggshell satin bedspread, produced in the 1950s by Porthault (right). The 1913 poster (below), designed by Otto Baumberger for Zurich silk merchant Adolf Grieder, betrays an oriental influence.

Whether from Japan, France, or China, silk has steadily woven itself into the fabric of human life, from the third millennium B.C. to the present day, thanks to a tiny caterpillar known as the mulberry bombyx, or silkworm. Long before mankind developed the silk industry, female butterflies were laying their eggs on black mulberry trees in Asia, and on white mulberry trees in Europe. When the caterpillars, inaccurately called "worms," began to be farmed, they were placed in cocooneries on screens that were regularly supplied with tender green leaves.

Once the eggs have been laid, it takes thirty-three days for a caterpillar to grow from three millimeters to nine centimeters long, increasing in weight by a factor of eight to ten thousand. In order to become a moth, it must then weave a white cocoon composed of over a thousand yards of unbroken thread twisted into a figure eight, in special buildings called cocooneries.

The unraveled silk thread is known as "raw" silk. It must be "thrown" by being twisted and passed through a roller that removes impurities. Only then is the silk dyed and woven. Today, broad widths of fine quality silk crêpe de Chine and satin are manufactured by only two weavers, one in Lyon, and another in Italy. The silk yarn they use is imported from Asia. The demand for silk sheets by clients of a linen firm like Porthault is limited—roughly one out of a thousand customers. Although nature offers mankind silk yarn in a form which permits almost immediate use, it is employed to produce only the most sophisticated of fabrics: precious, satin-smooth silk whose shimmer transcends all decoration, whether lace, embroidery, damask, or print.

This sublime satin sheet (right) is inset with leaves of crimped silk, evoking the softest and lightest of caresses. It was photographed by Frank Kollar for Harper's Bazaar.

SEIDEN·GRIEDER
AM PARADEPLATZ
LES GRANDS MAGASINS DE
SOIERIES ET NOUVEAUTÉS
ADOLF GRIEDER & Cⁱᵉ
ZURICH

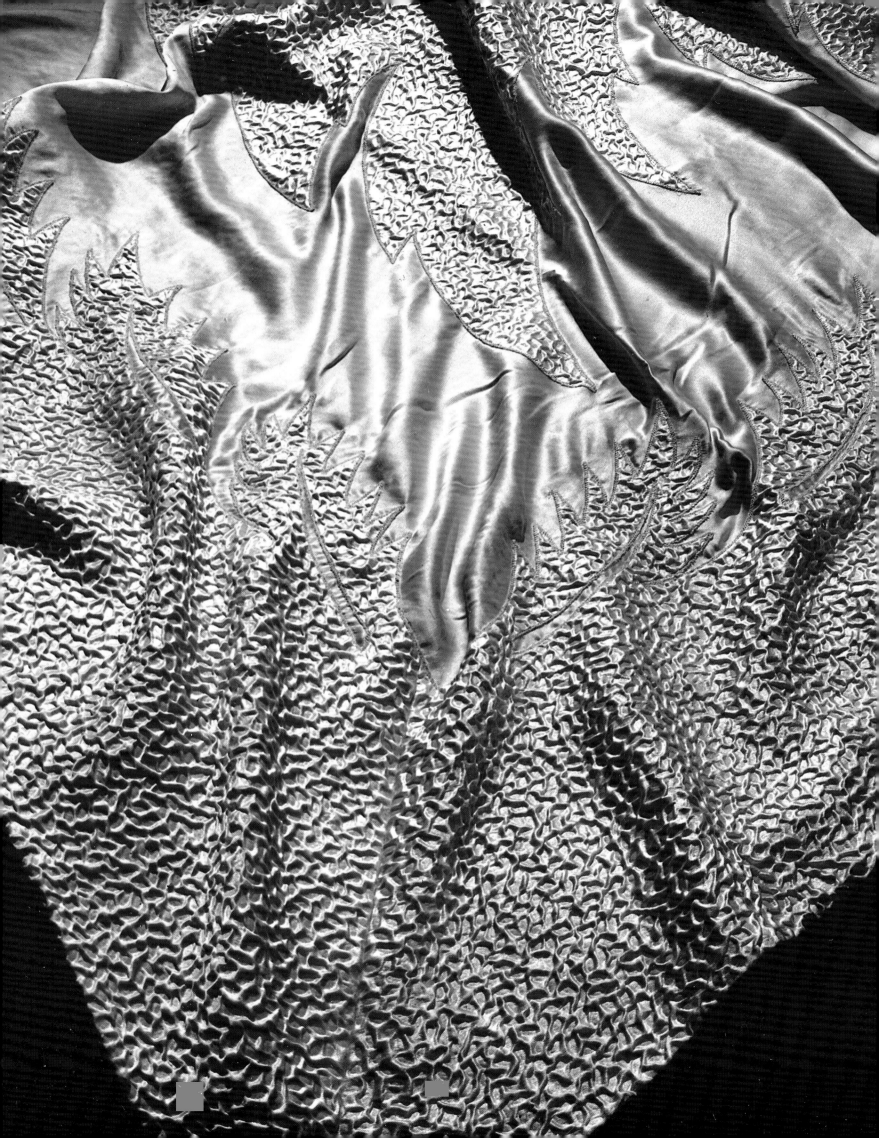

ORNAMENTATION

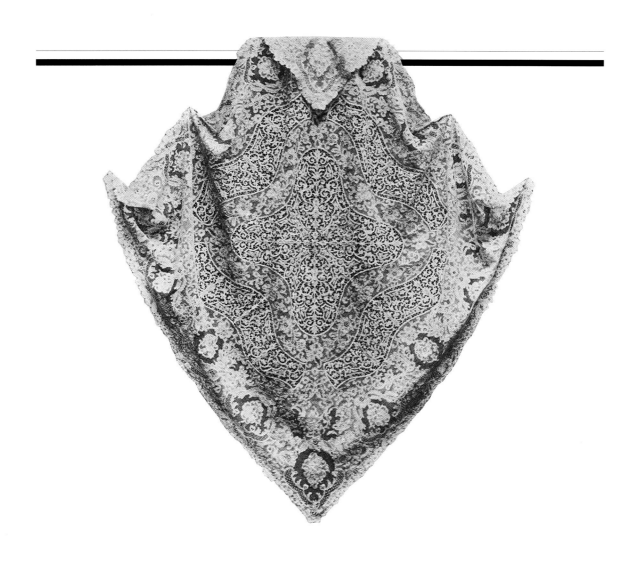

While fabric appeals to the sense of touch, ornamentation stimulates vision, for the eye is attracted by novelty, opulence, inventiveness. The earliest decorative details were probably simple geometric patterns obtained by weaving cloth with a hand shuttle and several yarns of different colors. Then, when it was realized that every imaginable design could be executed with a simple needle and thread, the first embroidery stitches were developed.

Color soon followed. Dyeing was done with substances provided by nature. Goethe asserted in his *Theory of Color* that humans experience innate pleasure on seeing color, that the eye positively needs it—everyone feels exhilaration when the sun suddenly shines on a gray day.

Eventually, several colors were combined in an attempt to print designs, and fabric printing was born. All of the above decorative techniques date back to antiquity and have adorned the fabrics of every civilization in the world. The two most sophisticated decorative inventions, however, emerged in the West as late as the Renaissance. The first was lacework produced solely from interlaced threads, and the second was linen damask which, thanks to a special weaving technique, produced actual monochrome paintings on tablecloths and napkins. With the exception of damask weave, none of these decorative effects were invented specifically for household linen, yet all have graced it at one time or another, depending on fashion. Modern taste is mainly dominated by bright colors and prints, which are both cheerful and stimulating. The fabric designer Primrose Bordier, a pioneer in the use of color for bed linen, has said time and again that "color is life itself!"

EMBROIDERY

All good little girls used to be taught to embroider at least one handkerchief, napkin, or place mat with outline stitches or cross-stitches—"naïve stitches that are the childhood of the art," according to Colette. The results would then be proudly offered to mom on Mother's Day. Some colored thread, a needle, a little dexterity and imagination, and any design became possible!

Embroidery is the world's oldest textile decoration. Originally, it consisted of embroidering strips of cloth that were later attached, or appliquéd, to the main fabric. When thread was used directly on the fabric itself, the various stitches, or methods of embroidering, became known as "points." The oldest visual evidence of embroidery can be seen on Assyrian and Babylonian sculpture that shows both appliqué and direct embroidery. Egyptian paintings, meanwhile, are unclear as to whether embroidery or weaving techniques are being depicted, yet a mummy embalmed during the reign of the pharaoh Ramses III (1198–1168 B.C.) contained fragments of embroidered cloth.

As with the invention of other crafts, embroidery is the source of countless legends. In Greek mythology, Arachne was changed into a spider for wanting to outdo her powerful rival, the goddess Athena, in the art of embroidery. This myth is behind the tradition of parading an enormous embroidered veil in an annual procession in honor of Arachne.

Helen, in the *Iliad*, was described as tracing an embroidery design on a heavy length of cloth "as white as alabaster." It is true that wall-hangings and furniture coverings were embellished with embroidery long before bed sheets were decorated. There are many descriptions of such cloths; Aristotle recounted that the fashion in Sybaris, a city known for flaunting luxury, was to display enormous tapestries "adorned with figures." Later, heavy embroidered cloths decorated Greek peristyles and Roman atriums, and were also used as curtains and bedspreads.

Hebrew tradition ascribes the invention of embroidery to a daughter of Noah. At numerous points in the Bible, linen cloth is described as being decorated with embroidery—Ezekiel has embroidered cloths spread out for holy celebrations; the tent covering the ark of the covenant was woven of embroidered twined linen;

Subtle, delicate floral motifs decorate a tablecloth designed in the 1930s for La Cour Batave (preceding double page, left). It is made of white organdy framed by pink organdy, sprigged and embroidered with satin-stitch sweet peas.

Since its invention during the Renaissance, lace has been the favored decoration for precious linen. This tablecloth in Venetian gros point lace (preceding page) was pictured in a catalogue issued by L. Giraud, a former Paris affiliate of the English firm The White House.

Boughs of mimosa are hand-embroidered in threads of yellow and gold on this pure linen tablecloth (left) proposed by the famous Noël firm, founded in Paris in 1883.

These small guest towels (left) in honeycomb weave with openwork borders, decorated with cross-stitch embroidery, are presently produced in India. Cross-stitch is one of the oldest points known in the history of embroidery.

in Exodus, Moses was instructed to "make the tabernacle with ten curtains of fine twined linen, and blue and purple and scarlet [yarn]; with cherubim skillfully worked shall you make them."

In the first century A.D., Pliny mentioned the Phrygians' art of needle embroidery, involving gold thread magnificently embroidered on cloth, mesh, and cutwork strips. Called *opus auri phrygium*, "Phrygian gold work," in Latin, the phrase became "orphrey" in the Middle Ages, a technical term for gold embroidery. Initially used exclusively for ecclesiastical cloth, gold embroidery eventually became associated with precious royal linen. It is still used today for magnificent ceremonial tablecloths employed during state dinners in countries throughout the world.

Embroidered table linen already existed in Roman times, even if there are few descriptions of it. Roman *mappa*, or table napkins, so luxurious that they became objects of theft, were described in the preceding chapter. Many tablecloths of similar extravagance existed, including the banqueting cloths of Emperor Heliogabalus (A.D. 204-222) which were illustrated with all the dishes that were about to be served! A century later, during the reign of Constantine the Great, tablecloths were decorated with animals and mythological or biblical scenes. When sheer fabrics like muslin (from Mosul), gauze (from Gaza), and silk became available, noble Roman women had their veils embroidered with delicate stitches. In the church of Saint Sophia in Byzantium, fabulous cloths embroidered in gold and silk covered the high altar.

In northern Europe, embroidery was also practiced by Celtic peoples—the term derives, moreover, from the Celtic and Frankish root *brozd*. With Romanization and the spread of the Catholic church, many of the abbey workshops which sprang up at that time began disseminating the arts that had initially been reserved for the house of God. Embroidery thus entered lordly manors, where it became one of the favorite pastimes of "gentle ladies" throughout the Middle Ages.

Etienne Boileau, who authored a thirteenth-century treatise on trades, declared that six years of apprenticeship and three years of journeyman work were required to become a master embroiderer. Kings had their own personal master embroiderers, whose work was so secret and so impatiently awaited that they were sometimes shut up in royal prisons until the commission was finished! Highly reputed embroiderers were recruited from Italy, Sicily, and Flanders. On the eve of the Renaissance, the art of embroidery became very sophisticated, and new points such as split stitching were developed in Italy. Northern European countries, meanwhile, refined their innate sense of harmonious colors. Gradually, embroidery, like painting, came to require the preliminary work of artistic drawing. Famous painters were even recruited—Raphael designed the matching bedclothes and tapestries for the chamber of François I.

Embroidery on medieval tablecloths and hand cloths of silk and linen consisted of garlands of leaves and flowers. This design was repeated time and time again, as evidenced by a 1380 inventory of King Charles V's linen: "five silk cloths, of which two for use as tablecloths, [one] with three large stripes of gold dotted with white roses, and the other of fifteen gold stripes in the manner of leaves, with four bands of purplish-blue silk, violet, and six bands against blue field, worked in gold and silver." An example of sixteenth-century Italian work in the form of a small tablecloth, now in the Musée des Arts Décoratifs in Paris, shows a band approximately six inches wide embroidered with nymphs inside medallions, connected by interlacing leaves and flowers adorned with the heads of women, putti, and animals. The figures were done in chain stitches and seed stitches with multicolored silk thread, while the garlands were done in flat and plain satin stitches and gold thread cordonnet. A true masterpiece of intricacy!

It is unfortunate that no equally detailed description exists of the tablecloth used at the banquet given by François I for Holy Roman Emperor Charles V on Thursday, 1 January 1539. An allusion to it in the king's chronicles simply notes:

"Above the marble table where the emperor and king were supping was a canopy of gold drapery. The cloth that was on this table was adorned all around with the coats of arms of the emperor, the king, my lords and heirs duc d'Orléans and the duc de Vendôme, done in embroidery."

Another more modest method of embroidery, known as cross-stitch , was often employed because it was easier to execute while remaining highly decorative. It was done from a model drawn on graph paper in cross-stitches or running stitches, with Italian or

*E*xtremely fine Italian Renaissance embroidery techniques are amply illustrated by this detail from a tablecloth (above) now at the Musée des Arts Décoratifs. The embroidered band, six inches wide, reproduces entwined garlands of foliage and flowers in gold and colored thread. Small figures are featured in the medallions.
A fine example of Assisi embroidery (below)—cross-stitches complemented by Italian stitches, with the design appearing white against the embroidered ground—can be seen in this detail from Ghirlandaio's Last Supper in the convent of San Marco in Florence.

double-sided Italian stitches. The tablecloth seen in Ghirlandaio's *Last Supper* was executed in this fashion, using Assisi embroidery in which an unworked design stands out from a solid background of cross-stitches, enriched with a latticework of running stitches.

In the Middle Ages, embroidery from the East was immediately recognizable by its luxuriant colors often highlighted by gold and silver. Both Slavs and Scandinavians, meanwhile, used primarily red, blue, and yellow, reflecting a peasant society that imaginatively transformed garments and household linen by marking them with a stamp of gaiety. This perhaps explains why cross-stitch designs continue to be so appreciated today—they are highly decorative yet within the scope of budding embroiderers, and a wide variety of patterns are available in handicraft shops.

White-on-white needlework first appeared during the Renaissance, along with a growing taste for white undergarments made of linen batiste. Although color had formerly been used on underclothing (the Medicis' inventories include shirts and drawers embroidered with scarlet silk), fashion began favoring white shirts that extended beyond the collar and cuff of the top garments. In order to create a more delicate effect, ethereal embroidery was added to the sheer cloth, through which the skin could be glimpsed. This type of needlework was confided to the agile fingers of women,

including French queens such as Catherine de Medici and Marguerite of Valois, who were known to be magnificent embroiderers. First came cut-thread work and openwork, followed by embroidery on a network of drawn threads (which caught the light better), and finally—the last stage before the invention of lace—lacis embroidery (darning stitches on square meshes placed over plain fabric). This extremely pure decoration adorned the finest church linen, and later household linen such as pillowcases, tablecloths, canopies, and valences. Bedspreads were made of textiles that were heavier or padded, decorated with the famous quilting embroidery so sought after today.

The extravagances of lace soon overtook white-on-white embroidery. Yet at the end of Louis XIV's reign, Madame de Maintenon granted embroidery its title of nobility once more. She was not only an accomplished embroiderer herself, thereby reviving an ancient tradition, but she also founded, in her house at Saint-Cyr, a school of embroidery for poor noble girls.

Throughout the eighteenth century embroidery remained more fashionable than lace. This trend was reinforced sometime around 1760 with the perfection of embroidery frames that made execution significantly easier. Such frames were nevertheless only appropriate for work on a small scale; otherwise, ordinary tapestry frames were used. Embroidery was done in

Empire-style embroidery (right). Laurel wreaths, stars and horns of plenty are motifs typical of the period. The yellow embroidery and green appliqués seen here were executed by the Porthault workshop.

The satin-stitch embroidery and over-embroidered mesh seen on this tablecloth (right) of extra-fine linen batiste demonstrate remarkable skill. The tablecloth dates from the early twentieth century and was donated to the Musée des Arts Décoratifs by Mrs. Seston Thomas.

This fine batiste tablecloth (right) with over-embroidered mesh insertions is a masterpiece of fancy needlework, as evidenced by its subtle composition, extreme refinement, and perfect execution. It adorned an early twentieth-century table, and was also part of the Seston Thomas bequest to the Musée des Arts Décoratifs. The drawing (below) of a richly decorated linen sheet, featuring Colbert embroidery, appeared in the 1921 Galeries Lafayette catalogue.

The most fascinating embroidery is that which reflects the spirit of its own period. This openwork batiste tablecloth (right) by the Melville & Ziffer firm is striking for its turn-of-the-century Art Nouveau embroidery. Executed in silk thread, the embroidery design is the work of architect Hector Guimard (1867–1942), better known for his distinctive entrances to the Paris metro.

white thread and favored designs included not only the timeless themes of leaves and flowers, but also the delights of pastoral life so fashionable under Louis XV. The discovery of the archaeological site of Herculaneum provided more design material by reviving a taste for classical and mythological subjects. Yet embroidery could also reflect historical events, and during the French Revolution Phrygian (or liberty) caps became a popular design, only to metamorphose diplomatically into paisley-type patterns under Napoleon!

In the nineteenth and early twentieth centuries, bridal trousseaux became synonymous with white, as discussed above. Costly sheets and pillowcases were therefore embroidered exclusively with

immaculate linen thread, using the finest points—raised satin-stitch, flat satin-stitch, seed stitch, and Beauvais embroidery. Hems and insertions might be executed in openwork embroidery, Colbert and Richelieu embroidery, and buttonhole-stitched *broderie anglaise*. Certain special items made of airy batiste were embroidered with bluish-gray thread that made the design more legible. These designs of rural and bucolic scenes were often inserted in medallions embroidered on netting.

If a bluish outline can be seen around the embroidery on a bed sheet or tablecloth found in some ancestor's linen chest, chances are that the item was never used. For in order to trace the pattern to be embroidered, a pencil drawing would be retraced in India ink, and this pattern would be loosely hem-stitched to the back of the fabric. Then powdered indigo was mixed in

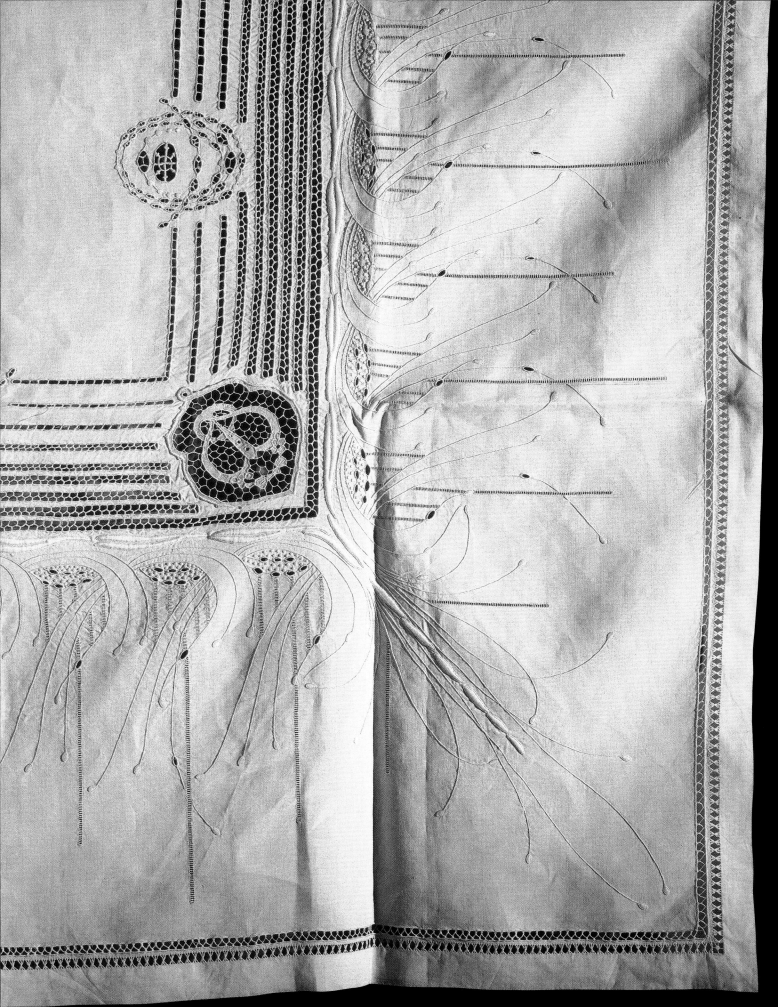

This extravagant centerpiece in batiste (right) dates from the early twentieth century. It is embroidered with raised satin-stitches in gray thread, plus over-embroidered net. The central medallion of over-embroidered mesh shows an antique-style pastoral scene. "Pouncing," a traditional technique for transferring a design to an underlying surface by forcing fine powder through a perforated outline (pictured below), is still used in the workshop of the Zéau firm, founded in Paris in 1902 and now specializing in Beauvais embroidery done on an embroidery frame. The actual embroidery is executed by one of the twenty company employees who do the work in their homes.

a little water along with a pinch of sugar and gum arabic. Dipping a very fine brush into this mixture, the outline of the design seen in transparence would be traced on the front; the embroiderer then had to work fast enough to prevent the indigo from becoming fixed, in which case it would not disappear until washed for the first time.

For thousands of years, all of these stitches, from the simplest to the most elaborate, required hours and hours patiently bent over a needle. In 1834, Thimonnier and Magnin invented an embroidering machine based on the sewing machine. It was not really perfected until 1868, and still could only embroider chain stitches. Embroidery frames that used dozens of needles simultaneously were invented at about the same time. Hand-done embroidery would nevertheless remain the rule for a long time in traditional linen-producing

regions like Normandy and northern France, Ireland, Switzerland, England, and Scotland.

Nowadays, textiles have become a heavy industry in which machines do the work once performed by agile fingers. Alongside automated and even electronic looms, however, there exist what are known as "hand-machines." They distantly resemble the equipment found in many homes, yet in fact are highly sophisticated machines that require four to seven years of training for the embroiderers who operate them. These machines can execute every kind of "point," from raised satin-stitch to bourdon embroidery, and they also do openwork. Only chain stitching must still be done on a separate machine; since this involves embroidering with a continuous thread, "a hand" is required when the thread must cross over itself.

Despite the "talent" of machines and their operators,

How many hours of work did this tablecloth (right) require from the embroiderer seen finishing it in the Porthault workshop? And how many years of preliminary apprenticeship and experience were required?

*A*ll the linen for the yacht Christina, owned by Greek shipping magnate Aristotle Onassis, was embroidered by the Porthault firm. The splendor of marine life serves as a unifying decorative theme (left). The execution is so perfect, especially in terms of shading, that it is hard to distinguish the watercolor sketch from the final embroidered version. A preparatory pattern and finished monogram (right) executed by the Zéau company. The embroidered letters are ringed by a leafy wreath and topped by a knotted ribbon.

166

Embroidery from the Portuguese island of Madeira (right) resembles broderie anglaise in terms of technique, but the designs take a different form. Madeira is known for its concentric, repeated patterns. Recent work has freed itself from these patterns, all the while maintaining high standards of execution. Madeira embroidery was made fashionable by an Englishwoman vacationing on the island in the nineteenth century. She returned home with trunkloads of lingerie, tablecloths and tea cloths. To this day, the Madeira embroidery workshops remain busy (below).

hand-embroidered linen remains an unmatched marvel. This is because, no matter how skilled the hand, stitches are never perfectly identical, thus betraying an emotion that the uniformity of machine stitching can never convey; machine stitching also imparts a slight stiffness to the fabric that manual work does not give.

Hand-embroidered linen has become a rare luxury in Europe, although it can still be ordered for fantastic sums from a few firms who maintain secret embroiderers in countries with ancestral expertise, including France, Italy, Spain, and Portugal. Certain religious orders also keep alive the tradition of fine linen in cloisters where time has come to a standstill. A sign of revival can perhaps be detected in the little workshops and stores that once again offer to hand- or machine-embroider simple designs on linen of the customer's choice, at perfectly

reasonable prices. This embroidery is usually dispatched to Spain, Portugal, or the island of Madeira for execution. Embroidery is also practiced again in rural Portugal, where grandmothers now teach their granddaughters an art that their own daughters had abandoned—the finest examples of this work are currently sold directly at markets and on beaches during the tourist season. Production has recently spread to former Eastern bloc countries and to the Far East, where European manufacturers send their own designs to be embroidered.

Even amateur embroiderers seem to have rediscovered the delights of "plying the needle," as indicated by the popularity of needlepoint in craft stores, some of which offer courses or workshops in embroidery and openwork. There is also increasing demand for brochures with embroidery patterns and

In Portugal, an old bedspread in unbleached linen with over-embroidered mesh insertions appears to wait patiently on a chair in the waning afternoon light (right). Portugal is a country with a rich textile heritage, from Madeira and Nisa embroidery to the Bibros lace still produced in the Douro Valley.

*D*elicate loops *of knotted ribbons and tiny intertwined flowers adorn a hand-embroidered pillowcase done by the Mazzarone workshop in Venice, where the elite of Venice society order their sheets, tablecloths, and place mats of fine linen (right). For several years now, Marisa Osorio-Farinha has brought all her Portuguese embroidering skills and savoir-faire to the Siècle firm. She has managed to produce a harmonious blend of tradition and modernity with this linen tablecloth, hand-embroidered in Portugal using satin-stitches to perfect the lemon-bearing boughs (left).*

advice, which are published by yarn and thread suppliers. Women are once again purchasing short needles, skeins of cordonnet, and corded cotton at department store sewing counters (long ago relegated to the most inaccessible part of the store). With simple equipment, such women are relearning the age-old points such as cross-stitch, chain stitch and herringbone stitch, while the more expert and patient among them progress to magnificent satin-stitching and Beauvais embroidery.

Today, as in the past, nature provides the inspiration for embroidery designs—multicolored bouquets, garlands, or scatterings of harvest flowers and wild flowers, primroses, violets, forget-me-nots, lilies-of-the-valley (characteristic of the Christian Dior linen collection), and even fruits and vegetables such as cherries and strawberries.

Privileged connoisseurs are familiar with the designs of the famous Porthault firm, such as their homage to Catherine Deneuve in the form of tiny bouquets of violets in stem stitching and machine lace. The duchess of Windsor, another Porthault client who was devoted to flowers, ordered a reproduction of the famous flowerbeds of her home near Paris. Tablecloths and wall-hangings in her dining room were executed in satin-stitch and Beauvais embroidery using threads of a hundred different hues. But perhaps Porthault's most amazing commission was a complete linen service for the yacht of shipping magnate Aristo-

tle Onassis. The riot of color and patterns based on the theme of the ocean depths was inspired by images found at the palace of Knossos in Crete. Sheets, tablecloths, napkins, and terrycloth bath linen were hand-embroidered with Mediterranean flora and fauna such as coral, starfish, sea urchins, shellfish, squid, bream, flying fish, dolphins, and mermaids—a masterpiece of Beauvais embroidery.

The satin-stitch, initially designed for colored work, can obviously be adapted to white-on-white patterns, thereby representing the height of refinement. The classic stitches used for white-on-white embroidery are nevertheless seed stitch, bourdon stitch, raised satin-stitch, buttonhole stitch and cordonnet stitch (also used for *broderie anglaise*).

Broderie anglaise is often confused with Madeira embroidery. This is because the embroidery done on

*P*orthault celebrates *summer with a basketful of fruit and flowers on organdy place mats. Lemons, strawberries, and broom are embroidered in satin-stitch (below).*

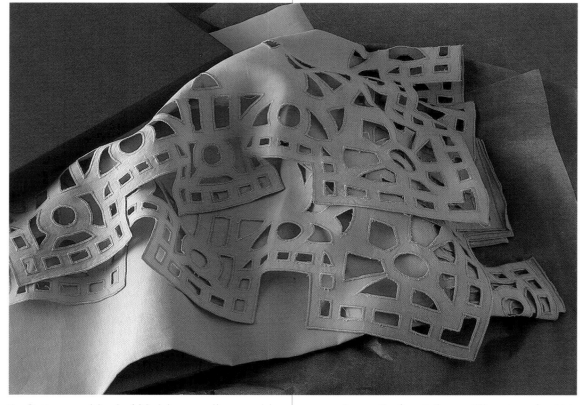

A contemporary design by the Siècle firm testifies to the current vitality of embroidery. This blue linen sheet (right) is edged with an updated version of Richelieu-style cutwork embroidery. Modern society, open to influences from every corner of the world, is able to assimilate varied motifs. The Porthault firm drew on multicolored Aztec patterns when designing these hand-made appliqués for a tablecloth's sides and corners (below).

the Portuguese island of Madeira was discovered in 1850 by an Englishwoman, Miss Phelps, who returned home with trunkfuls of marvels produced by calloused peasant hands. The English upper middle classes all followed suit and had their trousseaux stitched and embroidered in Madeira, where skills were handed down from mother to daughter. Although the concentric patterns became somewhat hackneyed, recent production has managed to reforge its own identity while maintaining high standards of execution.

In 1912, Edouard-Louis Noël—son of the woman who founded the Noël firm famous for its magnificent tablecloths—invented a new stitch, which was named the "Noël knot." Composed of holes and little knots of white stitches, it perpetuated the tradition of hand-embroidery into the 1930s.

Another method of decoration, appliqué work, has been known since the Middle Ages. It was used to provide multicolored ornamentation prior to the invention of satin-stitching and Beauvais embroidery. Appliqué work involves cutting a design out of one or several fabrics (which may be of the

same colors as the foundation or different ones), which are then "applied" to the foundation with backstitches or gimps sewn around the cut-out piece. Insertions, on the other hand, are usually narrow bands of decorative work which are inlaid between two pieces of fabric. Often the inlay is a design cut away from the foundation fabric. Appliqué work was highly fashionable between 1925 and 1950, and was widely applied to bedspreads and lingerie in crêpe de Chine as well as batiste table linen and bed sheets. There are splendid examples from the period showing entwined flowers, ribbons, Art Deco geometric patterns, and initials in the same or contrasting tones. Nighttime lingerie was designed in matching colors and patterns and constituted the first linen creations by couturiers such as Worth and Jeanne Lanvin. In keeping with more recent taste, appliqués are now done in brighter colors; a resolutely modern effect is created by Porthault's bold, multicolored designs based on marine flora, animals, or geometric patterns. Classic white and pastel shades nevertheless continue to set the standard, in matching tones for

Perhaps nothing is so exciting as the marriage of linen and silk. This magnificent set of sheets and pillowcases (right) is made of linen enhanced with satin appliqués and point de Paris (a fine point turc or blanket stitch), creating a delicate vine leaf motif.
Photograph by Frank Kollar for Harper's Bazaar.

Certain items of lace are so richly ornamented and so finely executed that they stagger the mind. Such is the case with this central section of an enormous tablecloth in duchess and insertion lace (left). It was produced in the nineteenth century and has been preserved in the Porthault archives. In making pieces of insertion lace (duchess, Flemish, Brussels, or Milanese), lengths of thread would be left floating behind the design in order to subsequently form the brides linking them to other pieces. Thus, unlike continuous thread-work, the back is not identical to the front.

organdy, lawn, and linen batiste, where varying transparency and layerings enhance appliqués attached with point de Paris (a fine point turc or blanket stitch). Given the delicate effect produced by this technique, it is often used for lace borders and insertions, increasing the visual impression of infinite lightness.

LACE

White lace, weightless and irresistible, was like a drug to which European court society was addicted from its invention in the Renaissance until its fall during the French Revolution. Lace then came back into fashion in 1804 when Napoleon I was proclaimed emperor of France, and held sway throughout the nineteenth century. The development of machine lace in the 1870s and its widespread availability in department stores only spurred the fever, as evoked by the following passage from Zola's *The Ladies' Paradise*:

"The crush at the lace counter grew minute by minute. The great display of white goods triumphed in the most delicate, dearest whiteness. A sharp temptation and mad rush of desire gripped all the women. . . . Tulle and guipure were draped overhead, forming a white sky veiled by

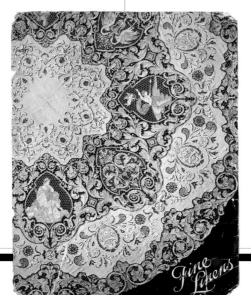

clouds whose fine mesh enfeebled the morning sun. Around the columns dropped panels of Mechlin and Valenciennes lace, as ballerina's skirts fell in a shudder of white to the floor. Then, from every side, on all counters, appeared a blizzard of blond Spanish lace light as a sigh, appliqués of Brussels lace with big flowers on fine mesh, Venice point lace with heavier designs, Alençon lace and royally rich Bruges lace. . . ."

This extraordinary scene involves a customer unable to resist the temptation to steal a piece of authentic Alençon lace; it is set in 1869, that is to say at the end of the Second Empire, when machines had not yet crowded out hand-made lace. Like all Spanish women, Empress Eugénie, wife of Napoleon III, adored lace and brought it back into fashion not only on garments, but also in household linen, so that the trousseaux of aristocratic young women of the day bulged with lace and white-on-white needlework. On Thursday, 1 June 1865, a certain Caroline Brame noted in her private diary that she visited a cousin who had just taken delivery of her trousseau:

". . . Above all there are embroidered lace handkerchiefs that are delightful, finery in Venice point lace, some very pretty dresses, sheets adorned with truly overly lavish lace, a coverlet with her magnificent coat of arms, and an infinite number of small, charming details."

Then, of course, there were the groom's gifts to the bride, which added to the already long list "all sorts of lace" as well as "cashmeres and jewelry."

Cashmeres and jewelry still exist today, but the truth of the matter is that hand-made lace is extinct. That is why lace-decorated linen can command prices comparable to those for antique objects and furniture. Lace, however, can never be more than 450 years old, for this wonderfully fine, snow-like substance only

make a crown for a statue of the Virgin Mary. Soon all of Bruges coveted this heavenly material.

Venice also has its legend. A sailor returning from a long voyage gave his fiancée a piece of finely cut seaweed (some say it was intricate coral). Unfortunately, the sailor was then taken prisoner by a Barbary sailing vessel. While awaiting his release and return, the young woman reproduced the same seaweed design with thread. Her labor lasted until the sailor did in fact come home, so that the first piece of lace ever created was used as a bridal veil.

These two tales illustrate the main feature of lace—namely that its intertwined threads are independent of

Lace on embroidered tulle is light like a caress. Produced at the end of the nineteenth century, this lace is now one of the treasures of the Porthault archives.

appeared in the latter half of the sixteenth century. As Patrice Hugues noted in *Le Langage du Tissu*, "for the first time, an independent invention of needlework appeared in the West, evoking the airy atmosphere and space of the Renaissance."

Needlepoint lace was invented in Venice, of course, while at nearly the same time bobbin lace was developed in Flanders. A Flemish legend holds that a poor young lady took a vow to remain unwed until she could deliver her family from poverty. As she finished making her pledge, gossamer, known as "Virgin thread" in French, floated down from the rafters and formed "subtle patterns of wonderful figures" on her apron. She copied the design with flaxen thread in order to

any fabric foundation. Lace is like "creating from thin air," according to Patrice Hugues. It is produced by a combination of threads worked solely with a needle or bobbins to the exclusion of any other technique, and is not to be confused with mesh and *reticella*.

Mesh and *reticella* were extensively employed for tablecloths and bedspreads until the early seventeenth century. The Musée des Arts Décoratifs in Paris has a 1588 tablecloth in re-embroidered mesh; in the center are a ship and mermaids, bordered by a hunting scene. But one of the most remarkable examples is a bedspread of *reticella* probably produced in Venice between 1595 and 1615. The wonderful imagery represents all the animals of the Creation, surrounded by

Designed by Porthault, the corners and center of this pebble grain tablecloth are decorated with extremely fine arabesques of Venetian gros point lace (right).

figures dressed in clothing from the time of Catherine de Medici. The bedspread is edged with an early lace technique known as *punto in aria*.

This technique emerged from the Renaissance quest for ever greater transparency of materials, which had been obtained by drawing threads from woven fabric. Soon so many threads had been pulled out that the weaver's work was completely undone. Given this dilemma, craftsmen had the idea of attacking the problem from the opposite angle—thus *punto in aria*, "stitch in air," the first needlepoint lace, was simply built on mesh pinned to a temporary ground of parchment that would be removed once the decorative needlework was solidly in place.

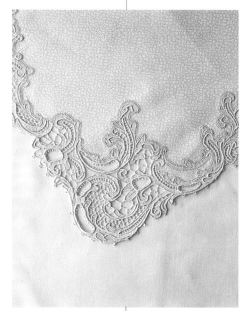

Although this new technique allowed for total independence of design, it long remained dependent on the geometric patterns associated with the *reticella* method. This impersonal geometry perhaps guaranteed Renaissance lace its enormous popularity not only across Europe at that time, but also down through the ages, since it resurfaced in the nineteenth and twentieth centuries via classic designs based on the circle-in-square, lozenge, and herringbone patterns. Although lace was invented to embellish garments by playing on transparency and the contrast between the whiteness of batiste and the ivory color of skin, it also adorned tablecloths, napkins, and towels, and more especially ceremonial pillowcases and sheets. The Musée des Arts Décoratifs has two sixteenth-century sheets from Hungary embroidered in red and edged with herringbone needlepoint lace. Lace was also used for insertions and sometimes served as a highly refined seam to join two breadths of linen. It also adorned the layettes of newborn princes, whose cradles were made up with

lace-trimmed sheets and pillowcases. Soon beds themselves were being covered in lace, as was the canopy of a Venetian courtesan's bed and the entire bed of Charles de Bourbon, with its "tent of linen netting, backrest covered in similar fabric, canopy, post covers, three curtains, sheets of similar cloth with strips of netting, all embroidered with lace."

The Italian infatuation with this novelty was imported into France by Catherine de Medici. She asked Vinciolo, the most famous designer of the day, to join her when she became queen of France. It was to Catherine that Vinciolo dedicated his 1587 anthology of designs, a volume reprinted twenty times. For, like embroidery and figured damask, lacemaking depends on the talent of the designer. While the list of male designers is long, only two female names come to the fore—Mademoiselle Parasole and Lucretia Romana. All the patterns they suggested started with the same basic geometric shapes, to which might be added human figures, animals, and foliage on large pieces. That is why, according to lace specialist Anne Kraatz, it is often very difficult to specify the date and place of production of a piece of antique lace.

Anthologies of embroidery and lace patterns were intended for "noble and virtuous ladies" and "women of good morals" from all walks of life. It had long been understood that needlework would rescue women from idleness and the danger it represented. Even queens such as Mary Stuart and Elizabeth I set the example, and Catherine de Medici enjoyed embroidering mesh with her retinue. Catherine's inventory of belongings included a great number of complete sets of bed linen, plus roughly a thousand unmounted

This Porthault napkin (below) is part of a set in fine linen adorned with Venetian petit point lace, including a tablecloth with a magnificent runner decorated in the same fashion.

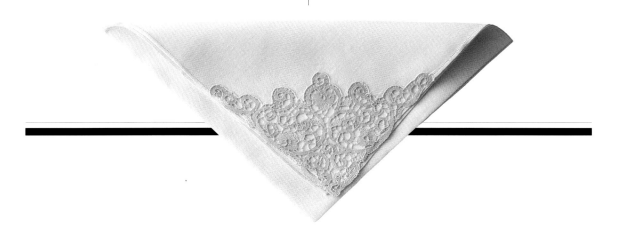

squares of decorative bouquets and rosettes—some perhaps executed by herself—destined for tablecloths and bedspreads.

But it was not only the work of queens, or even of a few craftsmen, that flooded European courts with endless waves of lace. Lacemaking became a thriving industry, organized either by merchants who employed entire families to work at home, or by professional workshops, and sometimes even by convents and charitable institutions.

at all the same as for Venetian lace, however. Flemish lace derived from the craft of ornamental braiding, employing similar tools of pillow, bobbin, and needles.

Although lace was invented in Italy and Flanders, France soon boasted major lacemaking centers in the Auvergne, Normandy, and northern regions. At the same time, Spain specialized in multicolored lace and lace adorned with silver or gold thread, which naturally enough became known by the generic term of "Spanish lace."

The bedspread used by Maria Theresa, queen of France, may be the most outstanding complete piece of lace still in existence. Featuring sprig lace and a great variety of stitches, it was probably made in a Spanish convent between 1660 and 1680. It is currently in the museum at Versailles Château.

During the seventeenth century, the Italian style—and more particularly, Venetian style—evolved toward forms that escaped the strictures of geometry. Stylized flowers would intertwine with garlands of leaves, to which would be added various symbolic decorations such as the fountain of youth, basins, musical instruments, and mythological characters including cupids, satyrs, nymphs, and mermaids.

It was during this period that Flanders was developing what might be called a typically northern style (also apparent in embroidery and damask weaves), comprising stylized tulips, oak leaves, acorns, walnuts, holly, and thistles, or hunting scenes abounding with animals and eagles. The technique employed was not

Although every Western country attempted to promote local production, the market was initially dominated by Italian and Flemish lace, and then by French lace starting in the late seventeenth century. It was Colbert, minister to Louis XIV, who "launched" the French lace industry in the 1660s—it soon surpassed all others. Fashion, as tyrannical as ever, imposed French point lace everywhere, even in Russia.

Since lace adorned every item of clothing, including court shoes, it is frustrating to find so few inventory entries for lace in household linen. In fact, table linen was largely of damask weave during this period, and bathroom linen practically disappeared until the benefits of bathing were rediscovered around 1750.

Only a few sheets, pillowcases, and bedspreads were the object of outstanding lacework. The most important existing bedspread on both an historical and artistic level, according to Anne Kraatz, is one in Venetian flat point lace originally owned by Maria Theresa, queen of Hungary and Bohemia. It is magnificently decorated with the coats of arms of France and Navarre, with additional heraldic figures from the major houses of Europe, plus the symbols of the four cardinal virtues. It was executed in various stitches to create a great diversity of effects, and was perhaps the work of a Flemish or Spanish convent between 1660 and 1680. The bedspread is now in the museum at the Versailles Château.

Generally, however, all that remains are dry lists of inventories or descriptions gathered from volumes of memoirs or collections of letters. Thus the Princess Palatine, sister-in-law of Louis XIV, wrote in a letter that her daughter's trousseau contained "twenty thousand ecus of lace and embroidered linen, all very fine and of grand quality, an abundance of linen adorned with the crests and initials of the couple in lace." The dowager duchesse de la Ferté owned in 1713, according to her niece, "a bedspread of a single piece of Venetian lace," and a set of sheets "in Argentan lace worth at least forty thousand ecus." An inventory for the French crown lists in more laconic style the orders placed with a widow Brion in 1721 for eight pillowcases in very fine semi-Holland adorned with Mechlin lace for Madame de Montpensier, plus another eight pillowcases the following year, in Holland adorned with Mechlin mesh and bride lace.

At that time, the piece of furniture the most heavily decorated with lace was without doubt the dressing table. Vanity tables would no longer be covered merely by a single cloth of *reticella* and *punto in aria*, as had been the case during the Renaissance, but by floods of flounces. The mirror itself was buried behind lace, as were the toiletries. It was above all Valenciennes lace that ruled over this "toiletry" linen in the latter half of the eighteenth century. Resplendently fine and white, it was believed that such lace could be produced only in the fortress of Valenciennes! Somewhat later, when bathing came back into fashion, Alençon lace and point d'Angleterre accompanied the return of bath shirts and robes as well as bathtub sheets, which lined the rough surface of wooden tubs.

Lace became more discreet when the first hints of a Rousseau-like spirit emerged, favoring naturalness and intimacy. But such discreetness could have also been due to cost-cutting dictated by difficult economic times. Whatever the case, starting in 1770, the flounces on pillowcases stacked in the linen cupboard were no longer of lace, but of muslin. A reign of three hundred years was coming to a close, only to end resoundingly with the French Revolution when lace symbolized the obscene extravagance of the *ancien régime*.

Napoleon I tried to restore lace to its throne by having it decorate the trousseau of his wife Josephine and later that of Marie-Louise, not to mention the miles of lace that weighed down the cradle of his son, the king of Rome.

It was during the Second Empire, 1850–1870, that mechanical "hands" began making lace. As early as 1802 an English mechanical loom was already turning out tulle. Such looms were clandestinely brought to France and set up first in Calais and then everywhere in northern France. Once the tulle was available, designs merely had to be embroidered with a needle. Thanks to Jacquard weaving techniques, looms were soon turning out bobbin lace in silk, linen and, of course, cotton. Finally, starting in 1880, the invention of the Schiffli machine made it possible to mechanically produce needlepoint lace of the Alençon and Venetian types. One of the last very fine laces to adorn table and bed linen in the nineteenth century was point d'Angleterre, a bobbin lace made in Belgium from machine-made tulle on which gray-white thread was stitched in point de gaze. There was also a revival of Renaissance lace called Cluny lace, produced in the Puy and Craponne regions of France, as well as the continued presence of Venetian and French point lace.

By the end of the nineteenth century, hand-made lace had become a luxury craft, indeed a genuine art. At the dawn of the twentieth century, the Art Nouveau movement provided new inspiration for lace designs in France and Austria, especially in the workshops at Vienna's well-known school of arts and crafts. The Musée des Arts Décoratifs in Paris has a lace tablecloth designed by Art Nouveau architect Hector Guimard, famous for his Paris metro entrances. The finest pieces of lace were already being displayed as works of art in major exhibitions; in a 1904 exhibition at the Galliéra palace, a magnificent tea table cloth in Venetian point lace depicting blooming poppies was displayed by a lace academy from Puy. At the same time, though, the

increasing rarity of hand-made lace led to the still current vogue for old lace.

During the interwar period, when lace was definitively banished from garments, the lace industry managed to survive thanks to household linen. Tablecloths, bedding and bath towels decorated with lace were manufactured for major linen firms. After the Second World War, the last skilled lacemakers passed away. And by the 1950s fashion designers had turned to machine-made lace which, another twenty years later, was all the rage on tablecloths made of synthetic textiles. Nowadays, mechanical looms can produce a yard and a half of lace per hour, whereas in the past lacemakers progressed at the average rate of a third of an inch per day. And even though machine-made lace has attained a refinement worthy of fine linen, the word "lace" no longer really refers to the same product.

True lace is extinct. It is now part of a historical heritage—or, at most, of a craft learned for pleasure in one's spare time. In short, lace has once again become a pastime of princesses.

DAMASK

Damask refers to a curious weave whose patterns play hide-and-seek with light, for details are best seen when the light catches them at a steep angle. Once a tablecloth is spread, however, whether or not the pattern is evident, the eye inevitably notices the fugitive shimmer of the weave's mat-and-glossy effect that so enhances the sparkle of crystal and the glint of silverware. That is why damask tablecloths became the almost obsessive archetype of distinguished table settings, like the one described in a Thomas Mann novel where, "next to each place setting on the smooth, heavy and sparklingly white damask tablecloth, there were two orchids in a crystal cone."

The secret of damask resides in the weaving technique. It "combines warp-faced and weft-faced twill or satin sections and is always reversible, because a pattern area with warp floats on one side will have equal weft floats on the other," according to a definition by Jennifer Harris in *Five Thousand Years of Textiles*. Traditional damask was always woven white-on-white, and the front—where the weft forms the pattern—appears mat when looked at against the light, but shiny when the light comes from over the shoulder. The effect is reversed on the back.

It should be pointed out that what is meant by damask today is totally different from the "figured" (or storied) damask that was once the only linen considered worthy enough to grace the tables of kings, nobles, and the rich bourgeoisie until the twentieth century. Figured damask entailed magnificent representational images that illustrated various themes and subjects. (See the glossary for a discussion of figured, or storied, damask).

These days, what is commonly called "damask" or even "Jacquard" corresponds to sturdy, traditional table linen, often of cotton, now used in hotels and restaurants. It is closer to what was historically called "diapered linen," documented from the fifteenth century onwards in inventories and invoices. The term was applied to fabrics woven in small all-over patterns, the oldest being lozenge, huckaback, honeycomb, and diamond, or even flowered patterns. Less costly than figured damask, this was the cloth most often cited in estate inventories. Diapered linen is still manufactured today and constitutes the traditional services used in hotels and state residences like the presidential Elysée Palace in Paris.

In the Middle Ages, linen woven in a lozenge pattern was initially imported from Damascus, Syria; starting in the thirteenth century, it was manufactured in Lucca, Italy, and in Amiens, Caen, and probably Paris, France. This lozenge pattern was long known in France as "Venetian weave" (with a distinction made for "big Venetian" and "little Venetian" according to the size of the lozenges) even though there is not a trace of evidence that the aforementioned city ever produced any of it!

In 1477, the death inventory of Charles the Bold, the duke of Burgundy, scrupulously noted a towel

The beauty of damask weave lies in the reversible yet equally attractive nature of the warp face and the weft face: although the tones are reversed, the pattern is the same. This cotton napkin (left) was designed by Primrose Bordier for the Jacquard Français company. Designer and manufacturer have jointly made damask fashionable in France once again, whether of cotton, cotton-and-linen blends, or mercerized cotton.

Damask weave can produce an infinite range of figures with almost the same precision as an engraving. Allegorical themes became a decorative device in figured (or storied) damask during the eighteenth century. This napkin (left) depicts an allegory of the seasons: the charming putti warm themselves before the fire in winter, pick grapes in autumn, and reap wheat in summer.

woven in "Venice-style lozenges." In 1694, the royal warder ordered twenty two-breadth tablecloths in "little Venetian," while under Louis XV (1710-74) the king's personal apartments were equipped with napkins of extra fine Flemish linen from Courtrai in "little Venetian weave" as well as in huckaback and diamond weaves. Huckaback is a textured weave in which yarns are floated on a plain ground to form small all-over patterns that imitate grains or seeds. It is now used chiefly for towels. In fifteenth-century France, there was a sudden rage for "Tournai" weave, which meant linen woven with a small floral pattern.

References to "Damascus weave," or damask, became common in the early sixteenth century, usually accompanied by the name of the specific pattern used in the weave. Despite the geographical allusion, these weaves came mostly from Flanders, where figured damask began its long career.

A special loom called a "drawloom" was required to perfectly integrate large figures into both sides of the weave of a cloth. Drawlooms had long been used in the East and, although damask is usually considered to be a Western invention, it is generally recognized that it was the Chinese who invented the drawloom for weaving silk, perhaps as early as the second century B.C., during the Han dynasty. Damask continued to be woven on drawlooms until the invention of the Jacquard loom toward the end of the nineteenth century.

"Damascus silk," which appeared in Europe sometime around the fifth century, was named after the Syrian town that was a major market for silk yarns and fabrics produced in Persia. By the Middle Ages, "silk damask" was being woven in Venice, Florence, Genoa, and especially Lucca.

Italian silk damask was exchanged in Flemish towns for celebrated Flemish draperies. Apparently no silk was woven in those colder lands, probably due to a lack of raw materials and to the difficulty of obtaining supplies of yarn. Flax, on the hand, was abundant, and the finest linen could rival silk. This supposed, however, a knowledge and mastery of drawloom techniques, probably discovered thanks to sophisticated "readers-in" who were already designing patterns somewhat simpler than true damask (on "readers-in," see "drawloom" in the glossary). Be that as it may, it took centuries to come up with the idea of transposing silk damask techniques to linen, at the same time transforming them to produce highly original examples of figured (or storied) damask table linen (see glossary).

Although figured damask was invented in Tournai, it was another Flemish town, Courtrai, that extensively developed production and became the damask capital during the sixteenth century. Repeated religious persecution, constant warfare and changing borders led to the flight of weavers from Courtrai on several occasions starting in 1567; such disruption, however, did not destroy the damask industry. Weavers simply set up in Sweden, Ireland, Scotland, Germany, and Holland, taking their skills with them.

The most striking feature of the finest Dutch linen production was that it exactly corresponded to the high point of Dutch painting. Thus, apart from universal damask subjects, local designs were directly inspired by themes found in Haarlem paintings, notably still lifes and meal scenes. It is not inconceivable that certain painters drew designs for weavers. The finest damask designs coincided, in fact, with a particularly rich period of artistic creativity, a phenomenon repeated later in Saxony.

Only France and Italy remained strangely aloof from the new industry despite their cultivation of high quality flax suitable for making linen. The many French connoisseurs of truly fine linen had to wait almost until the mid-eighteenth century, following industrial measures by Colbert and Louvois, before the conditions favorable to French production finally existed and manufacturers and merchants could set up in and around Lille and Armentières. Until that point, all napkins and tablecloths were bought in Courtrai, a city that exercised unchallenged domination of linen damask production for two centuries.

The oldest piece of linen from Courtrai still in existence is probably a tablecloth in a private English collection, firmly dated prior to 1556. It is woven with the coat of arms of Courtrai, "argent with gules chevron, border engrailed the same," and the crest of Charles V with his motto, *plus oultre*.

It is no coincidence that Courtrai, which produced linen coveted by the French, became a city coveted by French monarchs. Between 1668 and 1697, the city was conquered and occupied four times. But nothing could put a brake on Courtrai's prosperity, not even the war of the Spanish Succession.

To the contrary, war stimulated trade to the extent that Flemish weavers were indifferent to the jousting between Austria, France, and Spain and employed the

Military feats have always been a favorite subject for figured damask, and Fontenoy was undoubtedly the battle the most widely illustrated. This napkin is like a short history lesson, detailing the different stages of battle, showing the mounted King Louis XV against a ground of fleurs-de-lys, and providing captions for the images. Placing the king in the center and showing the city in perspective are two typical features of damask composition. The napkin is part of the Abegg collection (Switzerland).

same skill in producing napkins to celebrate victories by all sides. They produced no fewer than forty different designs to mark the triumphs of Marlborough, Prince Eugene of Savoy, and the maréchal de Villars. Similarly, the battle of Fontenoy (during the war of the Austrian Succession) inspired so many tablecloths and napkins that the combat is the subject the most often seen today in French and foreign collections of figured damask.

The 1748 treaty of Aix-la-Chapelle (Aachen) led to high tariffs and therefore contraband trade in France. Nevertheless, as the 1760 *Dictionnaire du Commerce* pointed out, "of every one hundred pieces to leave Courtrai, ninety continue to go to France, and ten elsewhere." The French continued to be the largest purchasers since, as the *Dictionnaire* continued, Courtrai was where "table linen is woven in diaper and diamond patterns, damasked in all sorts of designs, as perfectly as in Saxony. The Courtrai manufactory is superior in fineness, whiteness, and solidity of work."

Courtrai nevertheless went into decline around 1792. New designs were no longer being produced, less costly cotton and painted fabrics were providing tough competition, and other countries, notably France, had set up their own linen damask industries. Above all, however, as the *Dictionnaire du Commerce* once again reported, linen was being made in Saxony.

Saxony and Silesia had long been flax growing regions, exporting textile fibers to Holland and England via Dantzig. Weaving centers also sprang up in Upper Lusatia, near Dresden. Starting in 1741, Frederick II gained sovereignty over Silesia and, thanks to his influence, designers and weavers began concentrating in Dresden where their work swiftly gained fame.

Suddenly the wealth of designs, the fine quality of linen, and the idea of adding a silk filling to the warp to make the patterns more visible, made all previous linen, with its occasional filling of colored yarn, seem rustic. After 1824, in addition to rococo and flower patterns, the Romantic art movement provided new inspi-

ration for Dresden damask design, yielding images of castles and abbeys in ruin. Once again it was the French, along with the English, who were the most faithful customers.

France continued to be dependent on imports since, despite its love of fine linen, the industry had hardly evolved since the early sixteenth century. The only exceptions were the production of diapered linen in Amiens and an original weave in the city of Caen. Caen linen was well known thanks to the magnificent gifts offered by the city during official visits of royalty and other high-ranking guests (a tradition practiced by all European textile centers). When Henri IV and Marie de Medici visited Caen in 1603, "the Queen was presented with four sets of table linen, the most exquisite work of high-warp weaving to be seen anywhere."

Given the backward state of the French textile industry, Henri IV followed a protectionist policy and encouraged, unsuccessfully, the establishment of weaving centers at Sully-sur-Loire, Rouen, and Nantes. It was only in the early eighteenth century, thanks to Colbert's industrial policy and the War of the Spanish Succession (in which France won control of the Lys River between Menin and Armentières) that major French damask manufactories were set up. But in spite of the fineness of the cloth produced, only flowered damask patterns were woven.

At the beginning of the nineteenth century, although luxury damask was still hand-woven (and would continue to be so until 1878), standard quality damask was being produced on Jacquard looms. The industry continued to expand in northern France, while linen damask factories were also set up in the Normandy and Béarn regions of France (which, in the mid-eighteenth century, had already begun exporting not only to nearby Spain but also to the Caribbean). A manufacturer of damask cloth in Pau even revived its production of figured damask.

The damask industry in the British Isles was launched by French weavers and merchants in Northern Ireland, and by a number of Flemish weavers and merchants in Scotland.

In Ireland, the industry really only took off after 1765, on the initiative of William Colson, whose factories continue to operate to this day. At the time, the *Dictionnaire du Commerce* described Irish linen as "lacking sturdiness and poorly bleached." Nor was it known for its quality in the nineteenth century. Yet Irish linen, whether plain damask or figured, nevertheless invaded department stores on the old continent due to low prices made possible by low wages. In the early twentieth century, Irish production of fine linen declined as manufacturing emphasis was placed on sewing thread and ordinary household linen. Yet today the most delicate damasks are produced, admittedly on a limited scale, in either Ireland or Italy!

In Britain, Flemish weavers that came from Tournai produced the first linen damask in the region around Norwich in England. But Edinburgh, Scotland, was the true center of high-quality production throughout the eighteenth century.

Then, in 1825, with the invention of flax spinning machines and the use of Jacquard looms for damask weaves, Dunfermline became the Scottish linen capital; in 1859, the Bothwell factory produced a tablecloth illustrating the heroes of the Crimean War, considered to be the finest masterpiece of machine-made damask. It included portraits of Queen Victoria and Napoleon III flanked by generals, and listed the names of the major battles. The corners of the tablecloth were decorated with the entwined symbols of the rose, the fleur-de-lys, the cross and the crescent, while the center contained the British, French, and Turkish crests plus the British royal mottoes *Honi soit qui mal y pense* (Evil be to him who evil thinks) and *Dieu et mon droit* (God and my right). The cloth is extremely fine, and measures three yards by nearly six yards; it is carefully folded in tissue paper and remains in excellent condition in the linen room at the Elysée

Palace in Paris. Strangely, Scottish damask went into a swift decline starting in 1870, and was not even displayed at the 1878 Paris International Exposition.

Southern Sweden is a region that has always produced a very high quality of fine linen; the best local damask factory was founded in 1729 in the town of Flor. A Stockholm weaver had nevertheless produced damask table linen for the royal household thirty years earlier, of which only one napkin remains, bearing the initials of Queen Hedwig Eleonoras topped by a crown. In 1778, a royal manufactory was founded at Vadstena, producing Sweden's best-known damask for over a hundred years. But lack of interest on the part of designers meant that no new patterns were produced, so that the same designs were constantly repeated in the early part of the nineteenth century—crests or initials against a ground of tiny flowers or crowns, or bouquets bordered by foliage. It should be pointed out, however, that all this fine linen was still being woven by hand.

With the development of Jacquard techniques during the nineteenth century, floral compositions became a fully accomplished art. A noteworthy example is a table service produced in 1860 by a factory in Essonne, near Paris. The tablecloth is decorated with the initials "MF" in the center, surrounded by a garland of flowers forming a crest; the ground of the napkins is almost entirely covered with bouquets of naturally rendered poppies, roses, and dahlias, linked by Louis XV-style arabesques, producing a marvellous effect.

All this old linen has now become very rare and very valuable—a napkin depicting the battle of Fontenoy can cost eighty thousand francs (US $14,000). That is why such linen is now found only in museums or major private collections.

Starting in the late nineteenth century, the use of cheaper cotton fabrics meant that even the most modest of tables could be covered with damask. Until 1920, etiquette still required that the cloth be completely white, but then color was timidly introduced on wide

*F*ringed and woven
in a wonderful damask with
grape motif, this tablecloth
and eighteen matching
napkins were made with an
ecru cotton thread so fine it
looks like silk.
Created in Lyon in 1885,
the set is now held by the
Musée des Arts Décoratifs.

borders that might be white-on-red, white-on-blue, or white-on-yellow. The most common patterns were garlands of flowers, birds, or historic revival designs whose names evoked nostalgia for the splendors of a bygone aristocratic era: *petit duc*, Mazarin, Louis XIV, Colbert, Du Barry, Pompadour, Regency, etc. Starting around 1925 and continuing into the 1930s, there appeared lively, multicolored Jacquard designs based on geometric Art Deco patterns. But toward the end of the 1950s, damask found itself relegated to the bottom of the linen pile, having been replaced by printed fabrics.

Today, traditional linen damask, whether old or new, is sought out only by people with either highly conventional or highly refined taste. Italy, which grows no flax, is perhaps the best illustration of this, since it produces some of the most beautiful damask table services, the most refined of which are the work of the Frette firm in Milan.

In order to compete with the recent interior decoration trend that mixes and matches any conceivable print, even transforming wallpaper patterns into tablecloths, Jacquard weaves of up to five different shades are now being produced.

This intricate polychrome effect is most often produced by using two yarns of different colors, varying only the weave. The more the weft floats over the warp, the darker the color will be. If a yarn of a second color is added to the weft, the polychrome effect will be enhanced. To render these Jacquard weaves even more competitive with modern prints, the yarn to be used is chosen for easy maintenance and repeated washings.

This contemporary version of damask has met with considerable success. The revival is notably due to the initiative of the famous French manufacturer Jacquard Français who, with fabric designer Primrose Bordier, has spent the past ten years producing patterns inspired by archive material. These traditional patterns are woven in magnificent colors to make them more contemporary.

At the Porthault firm, models are divided between geometric patterns and large clusters of flowers, while linen or cotton damask continue to be woven in updated versions of classic patterns—dots and ribbons, lattices, wisteria, clover, bouquets and intertwined garlands of flowers.

Even figured damask has reappeared in recent collections. In 1993, Jacquard Français produced fine linen face towels in white and ecru, figured with castle, rider, and crest—a sure sign of renewed taste for traditional household linen. The figured patterns that served as the foundation of table and bath linen for centuries are now once again slowly emerging from the shadows, to the delight of modern-day lovers of fine linen.

THE COLOR OF WHITE GOODS

Never before have taste and color been so personal a matter. Given the range of colors proposed by major linen manufacturers, the eye cannot fail to be seduced by the beauty and choice of colors. From pastels to darks, from cool, muted tones to warm hues, there is something for every taste and mood.

Color can produce a complete change of atmosphere; simply unfolding a tablecloth, sheet or set of towels can make a dinner more cheerful, a bedroom more romantic, or a bathroom more invigorating. As Goethe pointed out in his *Treatise on Color*, given colors are capable of provoking specific moods in people. In the same spirit a witty Frenchman once reportedly commented that "the tone of my conversations with the lady has changed ever since she changed the decor of her boudoir from blue to crimson."

In the United States, lively colors, both solid and prints, became fashionable in the 1960s. The French fabric designer Primrose Bordier still recalls the enthusiasm of her first trip to the United States, when she discovered Fieldcrest top sheets printed with poppies in four colors that were coordinated with solid-color bottom sheets and matching bath towels.

Bordier picked up on this idea in 1965 and timidly presented her own French version of single-color bottom sheets and towels, coordinated with multicolored top sheets in a tiny floral pattern. After the success of the product at the Printemps department store in Paris, Bordier boldly launched the fashion for dark colors in the 1970s—black, brown and navy blue appeared like so many revolutionary flags waved in the face of conventional values.

Now that color itself has become a conventional aspect of household linen, only personal taste and a desire to match the decor of the room ultimately dictate the choice of, say, indigo blue sheets, saffron yellow towels, or a tablecloth of madder root red.

Such color adjectives are a reminder that all dyes were obtained from natural substances until the nineteenth century. Then, thanks to the science of chemistry, active agents in plant dyes were extracted and, later, synthesized from carbon and petroleum derivatives. Today the components of a synthetic color can number in the thousands, and their exact composition is patented and kept secret.

Vegetable dyes are now generally a thing of the past, used only in traditional crafts and small-scale industries in certain countries in Africa and in India, where blue is still traditionally dyed and printed with indigo using stencils and wood blocks.

Although the tools have changed, the art of dyeing textiles still rests on the basic principle of replacing the original color of a fabric with another by getting it to permeate into the core of the fibers. The operation has nevertheless been simplified, and dyestuffs are chosen according to their suitability to a given textile; natural textiles like cotton, for instance, absorb water whereas artificial fabrics tend to shed it.

Another problem which had to be worked out was that of maintaining the uniformity and stability of a dye when dyeing literally miles of cloth or yarn. In order to overcome this problem, fabrics now pass through the dye bath and drying machines at dizzying speeds of up to 400 yards per minute.

An even faster system has been developed in which the fabric is no longer immersed in a bath: dye is applied in the form of a high-pressure spray, excess dye being removed by forcing the cloth between two rollers. Drying is then done either in a vat or in a wind chamber where temperatures can reach 265° F. The whole operation takes only a few minutes.

Manufacturing costs have been even further reduced by employing new techniques based on dyeing procedures originally designed for prints but now used for solid colors. Instead of chemically impregnating the fibers, color is mechanically applied to the surface in thick pigments called gums, mixed with a

The fine art of contemporary damask weave entails skillfully adding color to the unsurpassed refinement of classic damask. These napkins in rich tones with openwork hems were designed by Muriel Grateau (left).

Starting in the 1970s, French linen became synonymous with color. Unrestrained variety and freedom of choice became the rule. Pillowcases and sheets could be mixed and matched according to mood, or according to passing fashion. The linen shown here was designed by Primrose Bordier (left).

Napkins in fan-shaped folds (right). The art of decorative folding, all the rage in the seventeenth century, is now making an elegant comeback thanks to Didier Boursin, the current master.
Primrose Bordier had no hesitation in choosing strong, deep colors for these linen pillowcases with openwork hems (below).

binder, then the fabric is steamed in a vat. Another innovation is the use of special reagents for dyeing or printing toweling fabrics.

The time is long gone when dyers were associated with magicians who possessed the power to change the natural color of things. Certain modern workshops nevertheless cultivate a sense of mystery concerning the alchemy of colors, notably the use of the most sophisticated and reliable colorants, called "indigosols," or "indenthrens". They work wonders on color prints, and are also used to produce solid colors on more expensive linen.

Such colorants are chlorine-resistant and come in the form of powder; when mixed with boiling water, chemicals and gum arabic, the powder produces a pure color, from which a whole range of shades can then be derived. Certain dyes, such as red and orange, are very expensive (just as they were in ancient times) and a kilogram can cost from 750 to 1,500 francs (US $125 to 250). The lab where these colors are "cooked up" is still called the "kitchen" and exudes a magical air, with its boxes and vats of color, which hold an infinite range of shades, all produced by a specialist who "cuts" the colors.

Indigosols reveal their color on contact with air, preferably in muted light, after an interval that varies from a few hours to two days, depending on color and on ambient tem-

perature and humidity. Dark tones "take" quickest, while blue requires a bit more time. The light shades are the slowest to show, with pink the quickest of the group. Just to complicate things, a color like green actually first appears as red, and blue starts out yellow!

According to specialists, the final outcome of this miraculous process is always a source of some anxiety. While waiting, pieces of fabric are hung above print tables some 60 yards long, stacked like long horizontal sails. When all the colors have finally taken, they are fixed by steam saturation at a temperature of 350° F. The fabric is then washed cold, in mildly acidified hydrogen peroxide. The pieces of multicolored fabric are then dried in a high-ceilinged drying workshop, hanging like theater drapes from the flies, billowing in the breeze generated by a theatrical fan.

Colors produced by this method will not "run" or fade. In fact, it was probably ignorance of mordant dyeing (mordants are fixing agents) that discouraged the use of color in household linen for such a very long time, although mordant dyeing was actually first practiced by the Egyptians. Once the technology for successfully rendering color was perfected, the tradition of snow-white linen had been entrenched for centuries. In Europe, this somewhat hindered the acceptance of color by the general public until the end of the 1960s, although it was introduced several decades earlier in the United States.

*A surprising nod to classicism—all it took to invigorate flounces and **broderie anglaise** was a bold splash of color (below).*

A tough choice—but how wonderful to be faced with it! The palette for this jumble of linen napkins designed by Muriel Grateau extends to thirty-two different colors (right).

PRINTS

Printed fabrics are so much a part of today's clothing and interior decoration that it is usually forgotten how recently they appeared. In the West, at least, printing techniques were really only mastered in the eighteenth century.

Cloth with multicolored designs obviously existed in Europe prior to that date, but it was either woven with pre-dyed yarns, embroidered, or hand-painted. It was probably for that reason that the first printed fabrics imported into France by Portuguese sailors in the mid-sixteenth century were dubbed "painted cloth." A 1577 inventory of items belonging to a Marseille resident named Pierre Bouquin carefully noted "a bedspread made of several colors." It is no coincidence that Bouquin lived in Marseille, for that was the very port where such fabrics were unloaded. Women soon seized upon these materials to make delightful skirts for themselves. Calico prints were later produced locally based on original designs that ultimately became the traditional dress and the quilted blankets associated with Provence.

Within a century, the rage for calico prints had spread across all of Europe. The exotic feel and drape of such fabrics, as well as their exuberant, colorfast designs, fascinated Westerners.

The West had figured out how to print colorful initial letters on paper, using successive runs of red, blue, and yellow, as early as the fifteenth century. But it was another three hundred years before printing on paper was successfully translated into printing on fabrics. The problem was the system of mordants, or fixing agents. Furthermore, whereas paper was smooth, fabrics were composed of criss-crossing fibers that did not accept colors as well, especially if those colors were to be superimposed on one another. Only effective mordants could make this possible; but mordants differed according to color used, and could not be mixed when colors were printed simultaneously. Since early French dyers were unaware of all these factors, their initial efforts ran or flaked.

In India, however, dyers knew that when using madder root, for instance, iron salts could be used to produce shades from black to purple, whereas the addition of aluminum oxide salts would produce reds and pinks. Even the Indians lacked a good mordant for yellow derived from turmeric, which would fade in time (as would green, being a combination of blue and yellow). The blue produced by indigo needed no mordant, for it oxidized on contact with the air. Areas of the cloth that were to remain white would be painted with liquid wax, so that the color would not take. The wax would later be removed, exposing the undyed areas. The opposite effect could be produced by using stencils. These techniques, still used today, are generally thought to have been invented in India in the fourth century B.C. In China, printing on silk done with engraved stone or wooden plates probably dates from the sixth century A.D. One extraordinary archaeological find yielded twenty thousand squares of cloth, probably a thousand years old, bearing the portrait of a goddess printed in black and white.

The "painted cloths" that were unloaded at Marseille in the sixteenth century came from Aleppo and Turkey, and were made using a technique originally developed at Masulipatam in India. In order to produce these prints, completely hand-painted methods gave way to block printing, in which the design to be produced was engraved on wooden plates, one plate for each color. The hollow sections of each plate were filled with mordant or pure pigment mixed with gum binders. The plate was subsequently pressed to the fabric and tapped with a mallet. The plate would then be placed right next to the first impression, with the pattern lined up, and the operation would be repeated. After the dye had dried, a decoction of cow manure was used to remove any overlap of color, and then the cloth would be rinsed. This technique was used right into the eighteenth century, and some of the plates are still being used in certain workshops.

In the late fifteenth century, Marseille printers possessed a perfect woodcut technique for producing colored playing cards. They were therefore the first to attempt to print colors onto cotton and imported fabrics. Engravers and printers merely adapted their traditional techniques to cotton goods. But the colors were not always "fast" and the technique was only really perfected after the French Revolution thanks to Christophe Oberkampf (who founded the famous Jouy-en-Josas textile works outside Paris). Although far from perfect, early French calico prints satisfied the average customer, because authentic calico prints imported by the English, Dutch, and French East India companies were sold at exorbitant prices. This partly added to the glamor of the product, and infatuation

The plain white ground of this eighteenth-century calico print bedspread is studded with a multitude of flowers that could be contemplated for hours on end. Although the rage for calico prints no longer provokes protectionist laws, a renewed fashion is making them harder and harder to unearth at antique dealers, even when more recent and less sublime than the one pictured here.

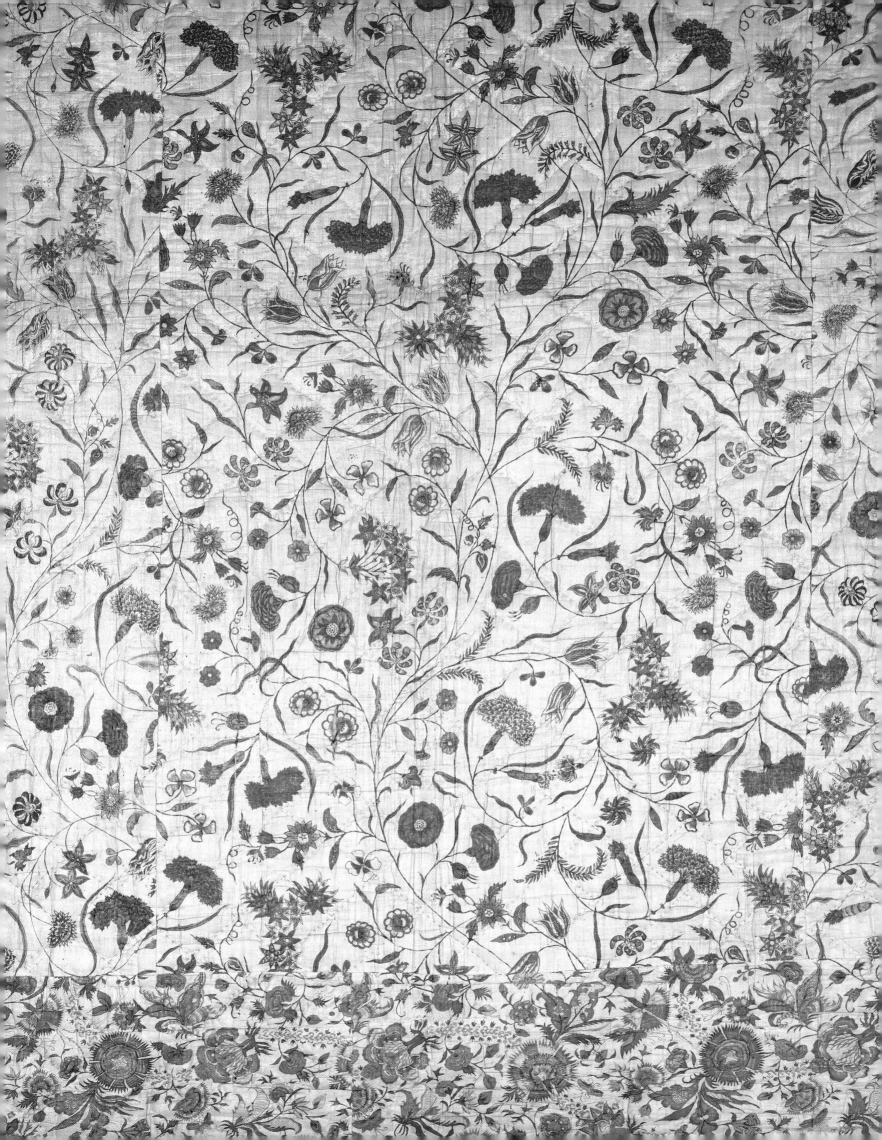

with calico prints became an affair of state in several Western capitals. The success of these prints unleashed the wrath of Europe's entire traditional linen and wool industry. Thus in 1686 Louis XIV's influential adviser, the marquis de Louvais, not only banned calico imports from Holland, Germany, and England, but also local production.

Prohibition hardly dampened the appeal of delightful fabrics that were light, colorful and printed with

allies like that, it was not long before the ban on prints was lifted. Given the impossibility of crushing the fashion, it was decided to transform printed cloth into a national industry. Unfortunately, the year was already 1759, and after seventy-three years of prohibition there were hardly any skilled craftsmen left.

It was in Mulhouse, an independent city, that the printing industry was revived. The first factory had been founded there in 1746 by Samuel Koëchlin,

exotic designs. The French paper *Le Mercure* reported in 1700 that a celebration given by Monsieur le Prince, son of Louis XIV, in honor of the duchess of Burgundy was enlivened by tables that "had rich calico prints for tablecloths," as did the sideboards, whose "borders were bedecked in gold and colors."

While Marseille remained a free port, it was not hard to procure contraband calico prints. And when Marseille was no longer free, people got out their engraved plates and clandestine local production began again.

The Musée des Arts Décoratifs in Paris holds several table napkins from the reign of Louis XV, including one belonging to the de Grassin family, printed in red, blue, and ochre on white. Some people closest to the king, including Madame de Pompadour, adored prints and even owned their own workshops. With

J. J. Schmalzer, and J. J. Dollfuss. That was where Oberkampf learned the trade of engraving, before becoming the head of the famous fabric-printing establishment in Jouy-en-Josas. After the French Revolution, Oberkampf would improve product quality by using copper plates that permitted extremely fine designs, and copper rollers that could turn out 5,000 yards of printed cloth a day!

In the days of Louis XVI, the Jouy textile works shared the market with firms in Rouen, Nantes, and especially Mulhouse, which, in addition to paisley prints, promoted original patterns not only from Alsace but also from Provence, thereby taking up the slack left by bankrupt southern workshops. The Japanese, in the second half of the nineteenth century, went to Mulhouse to learn Alsatian techniques, but after the First World War it was Europe that adopted Japanese frame-printing methods derived from modern silkscreen and ancient stencil technology.

Printed fabric was originally employed only for garments and home furnishings. Yet since the eighteenth century it has also been used for the most decorative items of bedclothing—incomparably charming coverlets which are now so sought after by collectors. Nowadays, printed fabrics have been fully integrated into the realm of household linen. The fashion arrived in Europe from the United States at the end of the 1950s. The earliest printed sheets were nevertheless designed long before in France. As early as 1925 Madeleine Porthault created a collection destined for American high society. The flower pattern she used was heavily inspired by Impressionism and was printed using plates for each of the four colorfast dyes: blue, yellow, green, and red. Porthault began producing printed toweling in 1935, but only wealthy, avant-garde customers in France adopted the fashion. It was not until 1955, when more sophisticated machinery reduced production costs, that prints could reach the general public. And even then, they did not really sweep the "white goods" sector until the 1970s.

Customers are now offered an unlimited choice of prints—period designs or original designs, flowered or geometric, big or small, pretty or ugly, stripes of every shape and description. Manufacturers are bursting with creative ideas. Two main trends have emerged, however—traditional paisley, calico, and flowered prints on the one hand, and prints developed by bold stylists and fashion designers on the other. Yves Saint-Laurent's label is associated with bold colors, Kenzo has highly distinctive and colorful flowered prints, Ungaro uses roses, while Cerruti employs his ever-present stripes. But the most famous original prints in France, in terms of the harmony of colors and quality of the printing, have always been those produced by Porthault. The firm's best-known prints include the clover pattern so dear to Louise de Vilmorin (inspired by the swirls of her signature), and the hearts designed by Madeleine Porthault in 1965. Audrey Hepburn, whose favorite color was blue, always ordered the same blue-on-white printed sheets. Homage should also be paid to Paule Marrot, who, in the sixties, was already designing delicate floral prints which resembled watercolors on fabric.

A cloth-printing factory in Germany, 1837 (above). The craftsman, using a wood block, is inking a new color onto the design already printed on the fabric. In order to align additional colors accurately, the block had a tiny mark at each corner that appeared on the cloth and discreetly indicated the point of alignment.

A modern printing operation— the Porthault works in Alençon (left). Pieces of fabric are hung above the printing table while they dry. They have just been printed with indenthren and indigosol dyes that attain their final color slowly on exposure to light and air.

Thus more than two centuries elapsed before there emerged a renewed taste for patterns echoing the splendid oriental arabesques that so captivated the eighteenth century. The fashion returned via English-speaking countries, notably Great Britain, where they were first imported and appreciated. Britain was not a major flax-growing country, and the long tradition of pure white linen had not been so firmly rooted there. The British have always been more attracted to deep colors and bold designs on dark backgrounds than have continentals, who are more drawn to smaller patterns on light backgrounds. Primrose Bordier intuitively respected this cultural distinction when she cautiously launched her first printed sheets in 1965.

The vogue for prints has led to a certain amount of digging into the archives of museums and manufacturers who have preserved original sketches and engraved plates. These designs are then adapted to various items of household linen and are reproduced. Thus certain original patterns from the famous Jouy-en-Josas works once again enliven pillowcases and sheets. Textile traditions and heritage are nourished thanks to museums like the Musée des Arts Décoratifs in Paris and the Musée de l'Impression sur Etoffes in Mulhouse, not to mention manufacturers like Souleïado in Tarascon and Beauvillé in Alsace (who specialize in wonderful traditional patterns from Alsace and Provence). Some designs are still being printed using old-fashioned plates—at the rate of two yards of fabric per hour!

The fashion for authentic patterns has even led to designs inspired by certain ethnic weaving traditions, such as *kilims* from Anatolia

and textiles from native populations in North America, Peru, and Guatemala, whose geometric designs translate into highly decorative bedclothes. Nor should age-old paisley prints from India be forgotten. All these patterns, in fact, are very similar to those used for home furnishing fabrics. Major manufacturers have grasped this point, including Canovas who produces sheets with a Jouy wallpaper design. Many design firms like Frey, Etamine, Agnès Comar, Daniel Hechter, and Chevignon are now offering household linen that plays on the current taste for highly coordinated interior decoration, with bed linen matching walls, curtains, and other household accessories from lampshades to storage boxes.

Why are prints so popular? Answers to this question generally stress the gay, decorative impact so distinct from the solemnity of white, not to mention the fact that dirt is less visible. Prints conveniently dress up and cover up. Yet in addition to these logical explanations, prints may be an elegant and indirect way of escaping the intimacy of traditional white linen that inevitably bore traces of its direct contact with the body. It is easier to expose printed linen to others. People now live in a world where the gaze of outsiders is more and more present—in the conviviality of vacation residences, in increasingly small urban apartments—yet criteria of being presentable, feelings of modesty, and notions of privacy have never been so strong.

In other words, printed fabrics both adorn and mask intimate physical acts—indeed, they allow them to blend into the environment when wallpaper is coordinated with tablecloth, sheets with night attire. Given the way daily life is now appareled, bodily intimacy has become invisible.

From treasured trousseau to throwaway linen

Just try, for a moment, to imagine life without fine linen. The shelves of "linen" cupboards would be stacked with paper sheets and plastic tablecloths—no textiles in sight. Already, paper towels are elbowing damask napkins off the dinner table. In restaurants as well as in private homes, increasing use is made of Kleenex, paper place mats, tablecloths, napkins, and disposable plates and cups.

In the fast food era, time and hygiene have become paramount. "More convenient" and "more hygienic" are the new criteria surreptitiously reinforcing new habits that are thoroughly unromantic and tradition-free. Already, in certain hospitals and highway motels, sheets are thrown away after use. Linen manufacturers themselves have succumbed to the phenomenon by producing paper napkins and place mats that match their printed fabrics. This substitute "linen" copies the original, but produces a shift in values. A society of quick consumption and quick disposal is devoid of popular memory; this amnesia is the very antithesis of the concept of linen. Authentic linen bears the trace of human contact in its folds. People remain etched in its fibers long after they have departed.

At the end of the day, if we make our beds with paper, we may just have to lie in them. The time might come when our descendants will look back nostalgically on the era when linen was part of human culture, when its reassuring presence accompanied daily rituals, anchoring their existence in time much more firmly than paper could ever do. When that day comes, people may turn once again to the delight afforded by fabrics, to the beauty of decorative touches; they may finally understand that delight and elegance are essential to a fully realized life. As Hector Bianciotti noted, "in this world, nothing is superficial or profound. Nature recognizes no differences except those between beauty and ugliness."

The contemporary art of linen feeds simultaneously on tradition and imagination. This "sculpture" by the Meridiem firm represents a resolutely new line in the age-old material of linen. The sober austerity of pure white linen seems transformed by the frivolity of the raised appliqué designs.

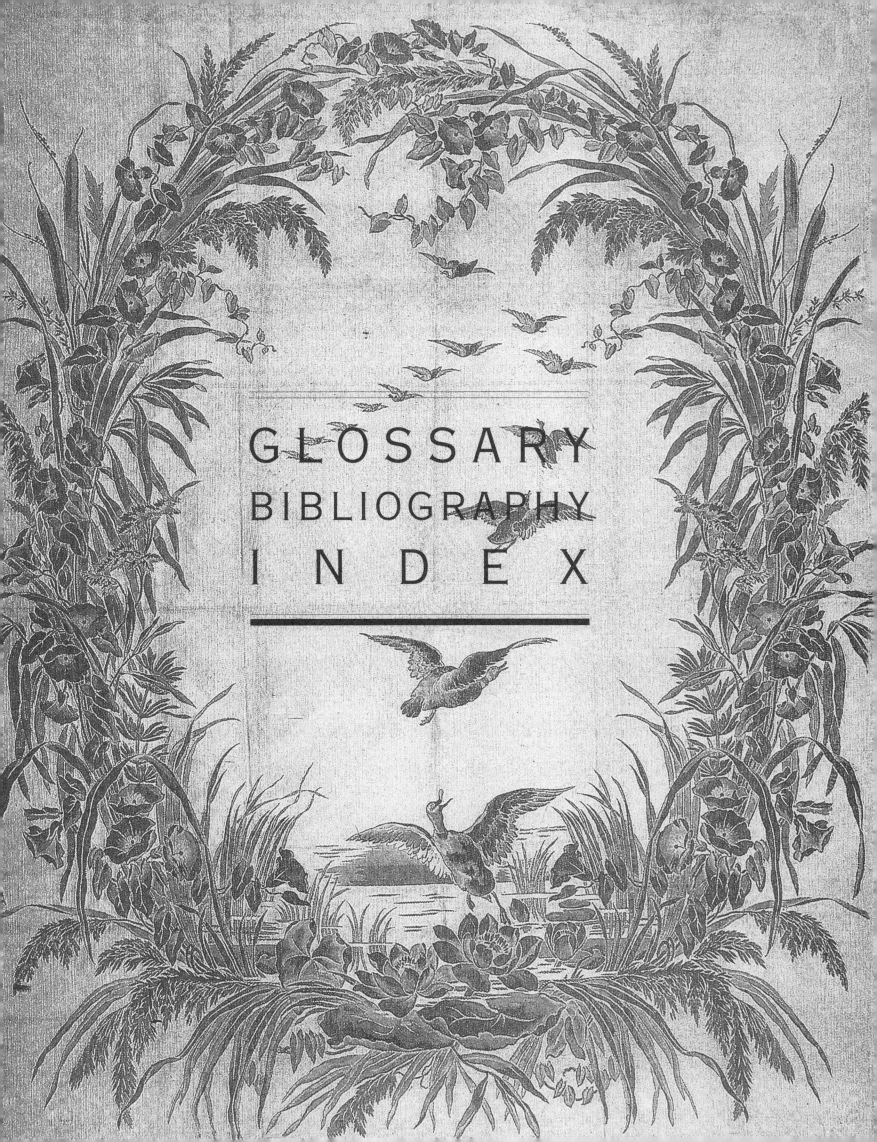

GLOSSARY

BIBLIOGRAPHY

INDEX

G L O S S A R Y

ALENÇON LACE: A needlepoint lace in which fine designs of flowers or leaves are made on a delicate mesh ground, outlined with cordonnet and linked with brides without picots.

APPLIQUÉ LACE: Pieces of lace made separately and sewn onto a ground of fabric, net or lace.

APPLIQUÉ WORK: This consists in placing fabric cutouts onto a unified fabric ground. The edges of the cutouts are stitched on with embroidery stitching or overlaid with gimp or braid.

ARGENTAN LACE: A needlepoint lace similar to Alençon lace, but with bolder designs, a coarser mesh and brides with picots.

ASSISI EMBROIDERY: From Assisi, Italy. Embroidery in which the designs themselves are left unworked, and stand out in white from a solid background worked in cross-stitches.

BACKSTITCH: A hand stitch using a single thread made to imitate a machine seam stitch. In embroidery it is used to outline a design, sometimes to make the stem of a flower, or is made in rows as a filling stitch.

BASIN: A close twill weave with a linen warp and a cotton filling, resembling fustian. The fabric used to be known by its original French name of *bombasin*. However, in France it was misunderstood as *bon basin* (good basin) and became simply *basin*. In England it was developed into a silk and wool mixture, the ubiquitous "black bombazine" of countless Victorian novels.

BEAUVAIS EMBROIDERY (STITCH): Beauvais embroidery consists of extremely delicate chain stitches made with a tiny crochet hook on an embroidery frame. A bouquet of flowers in Beauvais embroidery can have up to 80 different colored threads.

BINCHE LACE: A Flemish bobbin lace made in Binche, Belgium. It has designs of scrolls and flowers made in closely woven strips, on a coarse mesh ground which is more tightly knit to form star- or snowflake-like "whorls" at alternate intersections.

BLANKET STITCH: A blanket stitch is made in the same way as a buttonhole stitch, except that the stitches are wider apart.

BLOND LACE: A bobbin lace whose fine silk mesh ground is made concurrently with patterns in heavier silk. Originally unbleached, it is now often bleached white or dyed black.

BOBBIN LACE: Probably first developed in Flanders, bobbin lace is made by twisting threads wound on an even number of bobbins round pins that mark out the pattern laid on a pillow. The threads can be twisted together in twos or threes beforehand by the manipulation of the bobbins, or used singly, thus achieving a great variety of textures. Bobbin lace is known as "continuous-thread" lace when it uses a constant number of threads and is made in relatively narrow strips (up to four inches wide) which can be placed side by side. If it becomes necessary to add threads when going from one motif to another, these are attached with small running knots and the lace is called "cut-thread work."

The best Flemish lace was produced when the lace-makers began to work portions of the design separately, joining them up with brides to produce larger pieces. This is known as "insertion lace." This type of lace was produced all over Europe with a great many stylistic variations, such as Bruges, Milan, point d'Angleterre or the "Brussels" laces. It can be made in any width or shape, and is characterized by the fineness and variety of the meshes which make up the different flowers and the plain or picoted brides that join them to each other.

The best known "continuous-thread" laces are Mechlin, Lille, Chantilly, and Valenciennes, all characterized by a fine hexagonal mesh and the use of cordonnet or gimp to outline the patterns, and Binche and Cluny laces, which have a coarser mesh and no cordonnet.

BOURDON EMBROIDERY: A close, narrow stitch, generally even in width, often made over cordonnet and used for geometric designs, especially monograms.

BREADTH: The width between the selvages of a fabric determined by the width of the loom used in weaving it. In describing the width of a cloth, two breadths meant a length of cloth comprising two pieces sewn together at the selvage, and so on.

BRIDE: A small bar made of twisted threads, or threads bound with a tight buttonhole stitch, that is used to link the various parts of a needlepoint lace to give it an openwork effect.

BROCADE: Rich, colorful, oriental silk with raised embroidery, frequently in gold and silver thread.

BRODERIE ANGLAISE OR EYELET HOLE EMBROIDERY: Eyelet and small cutwork designs worked in white-on-white, with scalloped edges finished with buttonhole or cordonnet stitching.

BRUSSELS LACE: Needlepoint or bobbin laces, usually with fine floral designs.

BUCKRAM: Initially a fine linen or cotton fabric used for the vestments worn by priests. Today, it is stiffened with size and used for interlining suits and coats, or gummed together for greater stiffness and used in bookbinding.

BUTTONHOLE STITCH: A closely spaced stitch for binding the cut edges of a buttonhole, forming a line of closely spaced loops at the edge. It is used in embroidery for purely decorative purposes.

CALICO: From Calicut in India. When it was first imported, calico was usually printed, but the name now always means a plain, bleached or unbleached cotton unless otherwise stated.

CAMBRIC: A very fine, thin, plain white linen fabric, woven wet, with an 80 to 100 metric count yarn spun from the best and longest fibers.

CANVAS: (for embroidery, tapestry): A stiff, plain material with a highly visible weave, making it easy to count threads or draw them in even lines.

CARD: 1. Any of the perforated boards or plates in a dobby loom (for weaving small figures) or a Jacquard loom for operating the wires that lift the warp threads. 2. Comb used in carding.

CARDING: To remove impurities and disentangle them, fibers are combed with a primitive comb with rows of bent wire teeth set in a thick piece of leather called a "card." Carding is used to prepare fibers of relatively short length such as cotton, and is done in particular to inferior fibers in order to improve their quality.

CHANTILLY LACE: A delicate bobbin lace using silk or linen thread with a hexagonal mesh ground and scrolled, floral motifs outlined in cordonnet. It is generally dyed black.

CHINTZ: A glazed, plain weave cotton fabric printed in five or more bright colors. It is similar to cretonne, except that it is printed with smaller designs. Like cretonne, it is mainly used for interior decoration.

CLUNY LACE: A durable bobbin lace of linen or cotton thread produced in the locality of the Abbey of Cluny in France, where it was used by the monks. It has wheat or wheel designs made up of numerous points d'esprit on a coarse mesh ground. It is commonly used on household linen and curtains.

COMBING: The use of large metal combs to align fibers and remove the shorter from the longer. Only quality fibers are combed.

CORDONNET: A thread or fine cord used to form a raised outline round an embroidery or lace motif.

CORDONNET (EMBROIDERY): A straight or slanted stitch made over a cordonnet that follows the outline of the pattern, often used to finish the edges and openings in cutwork embroidery.

CRÊPE: A lightweight fabric with a surface that is more or less crinkled according to the method used (hard-twisted yarns, weaving in various tensions, etc.). Crêpes are made in every variety of fibers.

CRÊPE DE CHINE: A soft, plain weave crêpe of silk, cotton or wool used for luxury clothing. It is woven with very fine thread (300 denier), often hard-twisted, to give it a flatter, silkier face than other crêpes. Produced from ancient times in the East, it was adopted in the West following the crusades.

CRETONNE: In the eighteenth century, cretonne was a sturdy fabric woven from hemp or flax produced in Creton, a village in Normandy. Nowadays it is mainly woven from cotton in plain or fancy weaves and is mostly used for garden tablecloths and for country-style curtains and bedspreads that keep their shape, hang straight and have a "rustic" feel. It bears printing very well and is made from a carded yarn of a 30 to 50 metric count for a weave of 30 threads per square centimeter. Similar to chintz, it is usually printed with larger floral designs.

CROSS-STITCH EMBROIDERY: General term used to describe all embroideries which involve the counting of threads in the ground material and are embroidered with cross-stitches, plain or double-sided Italian stitches, chevron stitches and backstitches.

CUTWORK: An embroidery in which the design is formed by cutting away fabric from openings which have been outlined in buttonhole stitching.

DARNING STITCH: Running stitches of variable lengths made in parallel lines or long, interlacing stitches giving a latticework effect. Used to fill in a design or background in embroidery.

DENIER: A metric unit used in determining the quality or fineness of silk, rayon or nylon yarn. The less the yarn weighs, the finer it is. This unit is so fractional that commercial deniers are calculated in grams per 9000 meters of yarn: 9000 meters of a 15-denier yarn weigh 15 grams, thus a 15-denier yarn is finer than a 30-denier yarn.

DIAPER SILK: A rich silk fabric usually woven with diaper patterns.

DIAPER: To weave with an allover "diaper" pattern consisting of small, repeated designs that overlap, connect or are otherwise linked into an overall continuous fretwork.

DRAWING OR ROVING: To twist textile fibers together and draw or pull them out into a "roving" preliminary to spinning.

DRAWLOOM: A drawloom is a handloom formerly used for figure weaving that had a more complicated superstructure for guiding, raising and lowering the warp threads than an ordinary handloom. A highly specialized and somewhat archaic vocabulary exists to describe every detail of the weaving process. In weaving with a handloom, the warp yarns are wound on a "warp beam," stretched over a "tenter," and threaded through the "mails" of "heddles" attached to a "harness" by a "drawer-in," "heddler," or a "drawboy," who then pulled the cords activating the harness which lifted the yarns into a "shed" through which the weaver standing on one side of the loom "shot" the shuttle of filling yarn to the weaver standing on the other side. To put it more simply, the warp yarns are rolled on a batten or roller and stretched onto a frame or endless track. They are then threaded separately by a specialized worker through a metal or glass eye attached to one of the parallel cords or wires set in a frame and used to guide the warp threads—in a plain weave this simply entails threading all the odd warp yarns on one set of parallel cords, and all the even yarns on a second set. The worker then activates the frame holding the parallel cords, lifting the warp threads attached to it sufficiently for the weaver to pass the shuttle under them to another weaver standing on the other side, who then repeats the process in the opposite direction under the next set of threads. The shuttle was mechanized in 1733.

With the drawloom the process was complicated by the vagaries of figure weaving. It required a complex set of heddles controlled by separate strings for which the assortment of threads to be lifted were selected by a reader-in. The reader-in broke down the design into thread numbers and then read these numbers "in" from a card to the drawboy. The drawboy had to be very dextrous indeed to be able to follow these instructions with the precision required to produce the design.

DRAWNWORK, OR DRAWN THREAD EMBROIDERY: Embroidery used for insertions and for finishing hems and seams, especially in table linen. It is made by drawing out threads from the weave of a fabric and grouping and stitching the remaining threads together, leaving an opening. The basic styles are ladder drawnwork (in which the drawn threads are sometimes completely bound in stitching to resemble a ladder), Venetian drawnwork (when several threads are gathered together with a hemstitch at the base of a drawn section), and fagotting (in which a greater number of threads are drawn and the exposed ones are grouped into hourglass or zigzag shapes).

DUCHESS OR DUCHESSE LACE: A Flemish bobbin lace with delicate designs of flowers and leaves, characterized by fancy bobbin-made brides.

ELL: Archaic unit of length used for cloth. It varied from country to country: the English ell was 45 inches, the Flemish ell was 27 inches, and the French, or "Paris ell," was 47 inches.

EMBROIDERED TULLE: Tulle is generally embroidered with a darning stitch, both for the filling and the outline of the design.

EMBROIDERY FRAME: Also known as a tambour frame, the simplest frame is made of two circles of wood that fit exactly into one another. The larger of the two has a screw for tightening. Fabric is laid over the smaller, inner circle, and the outer circle is fitted over it and tightened until the fabric is stretched tight.

FANCY NEEDLEWORK: Invariably done in white-on-white, it includes quilting, drawnwork, raised point embroidery (buttonhole, cordonnet, bourdon stitches), cutwork (*broderie anglaise*, Madeira embroidery, reticella), and insertions of raised point or guipure laces.

FIGURED or STORIED DAMASK: From the sixteenth to the nineteenth centuries, the real originality of what is known as figured or "storied" damask lay in the fact that it reproduced a painting or contained a complete narrative tale. In the earliest examples this was generally presented in three or four episodes, woven one above the other and repeated the length of the fabric. For aesthetic reasons, it was then decided to reproduce this series of drawings symmetrically about a median axis on the width of the cloth. This gave a mirrored effect, but if the design included texts, these inevitably appeared upside down. This is the most common layout and is what makes storied damask so unique. Over the years this type of design was replaced with a central tableau drawn in perspective. Because it was expensive to make, damask was initially used for altar cloths, which is why early themes, woven at the cusp of the Middle Ages and the Renaissance, are often religious. The Annunciation, the four evangelists and scenes from Christ's Passion appear most frequently.

Besides religious themes, coats of arms are the earliest designs found in damask. Of the two most famous napkins made, one—known as the Tudor napkin—is in the Victoria & Albert Museum. Henry VIII's coat of arms covers the entire napkin and is surrounded by a highly decorated border with balustrades, putti and Italianate arabesques. The other is in the Conciergerie Museum in Paris and is known as Marie-Antoinette's napkin. It is woven with an exceptionally fine weft and bears the arms of France and Navarre, and the initial "L" interlaced with a laurel leaf below it.

During the nineteenth century, coats of arms were gradually replaced by intertwined initials. Today it could be said that the tradition survives in hotel linen, as many establishments have their crest, logo or initials woven into their damask tablecloths and napkins. Historical scenes are the most prevalent subjects of damasks. The most unusual tablecloth to have survived celebrates a gesture of peace between Spain and France on the death of François I, when the Order of the Golden Fleece passed to Spain. The cloth has full-length portraits of the Holy Roman Emperor, Charles V of Spain, and Phillip the Good, who created the order in 1429. They are surrounded by the emperor's motto, *plus oultre*, on a pair of Hercules columns, and the coat of arms of the Holy Roman Empire and the Order of the Golden Fleece encircled by the escutcheons of the Spanish royal family and those of the seven Dutch provinces. This luxurious tablecloth dates from 1616. At times solemn political events gave way to a "births and marriages column," of which the wedding of Louis XIV and Marie-Thérèse of Austria must have been the most popular, with the royal couple in the foreground and the entire family of each standing behind them. Among military deeds of valor, the most frequently portrayed battle must be the Battle of Fontenoy (Belgium) in 1745, at which Louis XV beat the English and the Dutch. After the French Revolution, historical subjects diminished.

Other subjects include hunting, which appeared in damask from its invention up until the nineteenth century. During the eighteenth century it also became fashionable to represent stories and allegories. Another common subject has been flowers and fruits. They appear in infinite variations and are still used in damasks today.

FILAMENT: A yarn of great length such as silk, or of indefinite length in the case of man-made yarns. The opposite of fiber.

FILLING OR WEFT: The thread or yarn that is carried by a shuttle in weaving and interlaces the warp yarn at right angles from selvage to selvage.

FLOAT: A weft thread that is "floated" or passed over two or more warp threads, or vice versa, during weaving to form raised patterns and different textures.

FRENCH KNOT: A backstitch in which the thread is wound round the needle or otherwise decoratively knotted before the needle is drawn back through the material at the same point.

FRENCH POINT LACE: A needlepoint lace similar to Alençon and Argentan lace, except that it is made on a network of interlocking brides covered in buttonhole stitching.

FUSTIAN: A strong twill weave usually with a linen warp and a cotton filling. When woven in cotton, it has a pile face and twill weave.

GAUZE: An often transparent fabric loosely woven from silk, linen or wool, in which the weft yarns are held apart by the "snaking" of the warp yarns.

GIMP: A coarse thread for embroidery made by twisting a heavy thread around a finer thread, used in the same way as cordonnet.

GUIPURE LACE: The name derives from the medieval French verb *guiper*, meaning to cover with silk or wool. During the seventeenth century the term denoted all raised point lace, especially the Venetian laces. It later came to mean any lace without a mesh background whose patterns are large and bulky and joined by buttonholed brides.

HACKLE: A board with long teeth, also called a flax comb, used to separate the long threads of natural fibers and to remove their impurities.

HARL: A fiber in the stalk of flax or hemp.

HEMP: A plant which produces a very resistant fiber, used for making coarse cloth, matting, and rope.

HEMSTITCH: A stitch that is invisible on the face and crossed on the back of a fabric. It is looped round two or more exposed threads in drawnwork, grouping them to form various designs, generally made on or near stitching lines of hems.

HOLLAND LINEN: A fine cambric shirting that used to be made in Holland.

HONEYCOMB WEAVE: A weave with a pattern of small squares, oblongs, or diamonds with raised edges made by floating several threads during weaving.

HUCKABACK: An absorbent, durable fabric made from cotton, linen, or both, with a textured weave made by floating yarns to form small patterns that imitate grains or seeds. Used chiefly for towels.

INSERTION LACE: See bobbin lace.

INSERTION WORK: For large or irregularly shaped pieces, one uses the same methods as for appliqué work, except that once the pieces of fabric or lace are sewn onto the ground, it is cut away from under them.

INSERTIONS: Narrow, straight bands of decorative openwork, lace, or embroidery with finished edges used to join previously cut pieces of fabric.

ITALIAN STITCH: A running stitch used in cross-stitch embroidery to form straight lines or squares. A double-sided Italian stitch is a running stitch worked twice (often in different colors) on the same line to make a continuous reversible pattern.

JACQUARD LOOM: A drawloom equipped with a Jacquard, which is a mechanism for weaving figured fabrics invented by Joseph Jacquard in Lyon, around 1800. It is controlled by a chain holding cards, known as "Jacquard cards," which are perforated with the design and ensure that the warp threads are lifted in the required order automatically.

JACQUARD WEAVE: Any of the intricate designs made on a Jacquard loom in brocade, tapestry, and especially damask.

JUTE: A glossy fiber used to make sacking, burlap, hessian, and cheap twines.

LACIS EMBROIDERY OR FILET LACE: Derived from the French *filet* (net) or *lacis* (mesh). Square meshes made with a single thread and knotted together at the corners form a network. This is then embroidered entirely in darning stitches. Filet has been made since antiquity, but the idea of embroidering over it did not occur until the fifteenth century.

LAWN: A sheer cotton or linen fabric plainwoven from the finest quality yarns, used for clothing. It is lighter and more transparent than cambric, and is finished with varying degrees of crispness.

LILLE LACE: A bobbin lace made in Lille. It has simple patterns outlined with gimp on a hexagonal mesh ground.

MADAPOLAM: Originally a strong, smooth calico used for making feather pillowcases, it is now made in various weights for different uses.

MADEIRA EMBROIDERY: White-on-white eyelet and cutwork embroidery done in buttonhole stitching, usually on linen. It is distinguished from *broderie anglaise* by its larger, floral designs.

MECHANICAL EMBROIDERY FRAME: Mechanical embroidery frames can be as much as thirty feet long and work up to 700 needles at a time on two levels. The design to be reproduced is transferred to the cards in its memory. To do this, the design is enlarged six times and its outline is traced with a pantograph, whose oscillations are converted into holes on the cards. This perforated card is programmed into the loom which then activates the needles accordingly.

MECHLIN LACE: A delicate bobbin lace with floral designs on a hexagonal mesh ground.

MERCERIZATION: The treatment of cotton yarn or cloth with caustic soda to give it luster and softness.

METRIC COUNT: Yarn counting or numbering is a system for measuring cotton, linen and wool yarns to establish their size, strength and fineness. Because the textile industry was spread across the globe long before the industrial revolution brought uniformity, not only each country but also each manufacturing region developed its own system of counting, just as the number of inches in an ell varied from country to country. The yarn count of wool, for example, appears to have been based on the convenient weight of wool for the spinners to take back to their homes for hand or "jenny" spinning. The metric system of measuring yarns commonly used in Europe today represents the length of yarn per kilogram: the more meters of yarn per kilogram, the finer the yarn. Thus a cloth with a metric count of 100 or 200 (meters per kilogram) is finer than a cloth with a metric count of 80. There is also another method based instead on the weight in grams per kilometer of yarn. The quality of a yarn is also determined by its breaking length, the point at which it will break through its own weight if hung vertically. Lastly, the quality of yarn is determined by the speed at which it deteriorates, which is established by its degree or rate of polymerization. Linen is a cellulose yarn and, with wear, the cellulose deteriorates. A well-preserved cloth has a higher polymer rate than a worn cloth.

MILAN LACE, *PUNTO DI MILANO*: Scrolled or floral patterns formed of fine braid or flat needle-woven tape, the pieces of which are connected by brides.

MIXTURE: A general term used to describe any fabric woven with different yarns in the warp and the weft,

most frequently a cotton warp with a linen, silk or wool weft.

MORDANTS OR MORDANTING SALTS: Iron or aluminum salts that used to be spread on calicos and chintzes before the colors were applied, and which had the property of fixing the colors.

MUSLIN: Muslin weaves range from the coarse mull used in bookbinding to sheer, light fabrics like chiffon (when woven in silk) or delaine (in wool), and loose-woven cheesecloth. Cotton muslins are made with a very fine, hard-twisted yarn, with a metric count of 100 to 200, and the weft yarns are finer than the warp yarns.

NAINSOOK: A lightweight, plain weave cotton fabric that is given various soft finishes and is used both for clothing and curtains.

NEEDLEPOINT EMBROIDERY: A counted-thread embroidery worked in the simpler stitches on canvas. One of the best-known styles originated in Venice, using large or small tent stitches (gros point, petit point), which are slanted stitches worked over the canvas to produce large or small lozenges.

NEEDLEPOINT LACE: Lace worked entirely with a needle and thread over a pattern instead of a permanent foundation such as net. These patterns were initially pricked out on parchment or "vellum." Nowadays one uses a piece of cardboard, still sometimes called a "vellum," with the pattern drawn on it, which is attached to a strip of strong canvas backed with wadding. A thread is then pinned round the contours of the pattern and the decorative loops and whorls made by the lacemaker are stitched to this thread. Needlepoint lace is always worked with a single thread at a time.

Needlepoint laces were first developed in Venice. They are all made on the same principle, with non-geometric designs featuring festoons of leaves and flowers, finished with cordonnet and connected by plain brides or by brides with picots. The principal laces of Venetian origin are Venetian point, raised point (sometimes also called gros point) and rose point.

A number of French laces are derived from Venetian techniques, and have a network of interlocking brides forming hexagonal meshes of different textures. The brides are plain, buttonhole-stitched or ornamented with picots. The principal French laces of this kind are point de France, Alençon lace and Argentan lace.

OPENWORK: Any embroidery in which there are openings in the foundation made by drawing threads, cutting the foundation away after embroidering, or a lace not made on a prepared foundation such as net.

ORGANDY: A very fine, light cotton muslin that is given a finish that makes it very crisp and almost translucent.

ORGANZA: A sheer fabric in plain weave, usually of silk or man-made fibers that is thicker and stiffer than organdy.

PERCALE: A closely woven cotton that is as smooth and firm as cambric, most commonly used for making sheets. It is woven with a 50 to 60 metric count yarn and has 70 threads per square centimeter. To improve its quality, many luxury linen manufacturers weave it with a slightly finer yarn in a slightly closer weave and give it varying descriptions according to the brand. To check the stated number of threads in the weave, one can use a thread counter or a magnifying glass.

PICOT: A small ornamental loop used to finish off brides and edges of lace.

PILE: A mass of raised loops on the face of a fabric produced by weaving a greater number of warp yarns (or vice versa), resulting in a surface that ranges

from velvet to toweling, according to the proportions of the yarns and the tightness of the weave.

PILLOW: A cushion or pad made of tightly stuffed canvas, used as a support for the pattern and pins in making bobbin lace. A pattern for a piece of lace is laid on it, ready pricked out with the holes for the pins that will guide and hold the threads. The bobbins onto which the threads are wound are attached to the top of the pillow and manipulated in pairs. They serve both as reels for the thread and as counterweights.

PIQUÉ: A stiff, durable, ribbed fabric, generally used for parts of clothing such as collars, cuffs and fronts. It is usually white with diagonal ribs, though it also exists with lengthwise ones and figuring.

PLAIN OR TAFFETA WEAVE: The oldest and the simplest of the weaving techniques, in which the weft yarns are passed alternately over and under the warp yarns.

POINT D'ANGLETERRE: A bobbin lace of Flemish origin, made of needlepoint or bobbin motifs applied to a mesh ground, or connected with brides made to resemble meshing.

POINT D'ESPAGNE: A needlepoint lace featuring heavy designs on a contrastingly fine ground, generally using gold or silver thread.

POINT D'ESPRIT: Decorative stitch in needlepoint or bobbin lace that resembles a grain of barley.

POINT DE GAZE: A delicate Brussels needlepoint lace, with flower motifs laid on an extremely fine, "gauzy" net ground.

POINT PLAT OR FLAT POINT LACE: Any needlepoint lace with flat designs instead of raised or padded designs.

POINT PLAT OR FLAT STITCH: A plain, close, unpadded stitch.

POINT TURC: An embroidery stitch. The effect is achieved by threading a thick, coarse needle with a very fine thread, then pulling the thread tight to further stretch the hole left by the needle's passage.

POUNCING: Method of transferring a pattern onto a fabric for embroidery. The design is traced onto paper and pricked out with a pantograph. The tracing is firmly pinned to the fabric and a fine pulverized chalk or charcoal is then forced through the perforations onto the fabric with a pouncing pad, and fixed with methylated spirit.

PUCKERING: A puckered, crinkled or rippled surface produced in a fabric by alternately slack- and tight-woven yarns, or by using a shrinking process that does not affect all of the groups of yarns.

PUNTO IN ARIA: A lace consisting of threads decoratively woven through a meshwork pinned onto a temporary ground, which is removed once the mesh is held together by the stitching. The resulting patterns are predominantly geometric and the technique is the basic method used for all needlepoint laces.

RAISED POINT LACE: A Venetian needlepoint lace in which the floral designs have been padded to make them stand out.

RAISED SATIN-STITCH: Used for embroidering very fine scrolled or plumed motifs and flowers. It is made with very close straight or slanted stitches over a filling usually of flat stitches. RENAISSANCE OR BATTENBURG LACE: A figured guipure lace made of braid or tape whose motifs are linked by buttonholed brides.

RETICELLA: Cutwork and drawnwork embroidery. Geometric shapes made with buttonhole stitching and drawn thread embroidery are combined on a fabric foundation. The foundation of the embroidered sections is then cut away, forming a lacy *reticella*, which is Italian for "little net."

RICHELIEU EMBROIDERY: Embroidery with the appearance of bobbin lace, but much stronger, connected by brides decorated with picots.

ROD OR STAFF: A unit of length equal to 5 1/2 yards.

ROSE POINT LACE: A Venetian needlepoint lace of rose motifs embroidered in low relief and connected by brides.

ROVING: See drawing.

SATIN-STITCH EMBROIDERY: Satin-stitch embroidery is generally done in silks using a variety of stitches. The basic stitch is made without padding, is either straight or slanted and is "passed" over and under the fabric so as to be nearly identical on both sides. The stitches are made so close together as to resemble satin, and the contrasts in direction add a slightly embossed effect. Shading is used when embroidering a petal for instance. The nuances of color are achieved by rows of stitches of different lengths beginning in the lightest shade. Each tier of subtly darker thread fills in the spaces left by the shorter stitches of the previous one, blending the colors.

SATIN: A fabric generally of silk or man-made fibers, in a weave in which warp yarns are floated over weft yarns or vice versa and are interlaced at widely spaced intervals, alternately regular and irregular, thereby forming a smooth compact surface. This method can also be used for weaving cotton or wool.

SEED STITCH: A minute backstitch used for background filling in embroidery. The tiny stitches do not touch, giving a pointillist effect.

SELVAGE: The edge of either side of a woven fabric, finished to prevent unraveling and therefore often less flexible than the fabric between. Selvages are frequently woven of different or heavier threads than the fabric and sometimes in a different weave for towels.

SERGE: A sturdy twill made in various weights from wool, cotton, silk, etc. It has diagonal ribbing on both sides and is smooth and shiny on the right side.

SHUTTLE: An instrument made of wood, bone or metal pointed at both ends, that holds the reel of weft yarn and is "shot" or passed between the warp yarns in weaving.

SILK SURAH: A soft, brilliant, lightweight twill weave silk.

SILK SCREEN PRINTING: The design is first separated into as many colors or color overlays as it contains. Each color separation is then stenciled onto a piece of silk or organdy stretched on a frame or "screen" of the exact width of the fabric between its two selvages. The non-printing areas are then blocked out with a lacquered glaze. The fabric is unrolled and fixed on a very long table, usually measuring about 200 feet. The screen is placed on the fabric and the dye is forced with a squeegee through the meshes of the unglazed areas of the silk onto the material. The screen is then moved down and the process is repeated the length of the fabric. This is done with each color until the design is complete.

Since the 1960s, there have been screen printing machines, in which the design and its colors are photographed and then screened onto a roller. The fabric is fed under a pressure pump on a conveyor belt activated by the movement of the roller and sprayed with one of the colors in the design. This method of continuous printing means that over 10,000 yards of fabric can be printed in a single day.

SILKWORM BREEDING: After the female has laid her eggs on her favorite food, the mulberry leaf, it takes 33 days for the hungry larva to grow from a fraction of an inch to 3 1/2 inches in length. It multiplies its weight eight or ten thousand times before it finally becomes a butterfly, leaving behind it a cocoon of about a thousand yards of twisted silk in a single long thread.

In order to gather the thread, the hatching of the butter-

fly has to be prevented, or else it will tear the silk, rendering it unusable except for the production of cheap floss. Nowadays the process is aborted a few days early.

The cocoons containing the butterflies are first smothered and then soaked in hot soapy water to soften them. In the old days a handful of cocoons were put in a basin and stirred with a small fern broom in order to "hook" the first thread for unwinding. Nowadays this is done by a machine that treats many more cocoons at a time and pulls ten silk threads simultaneously. These stick together and form a single thread.

SISAL: A plant producing a strong white fiber that is used in making ropes and twine.

SLIVER: The loose strands of textile fiber produced by carding or combing, ready for drawing into a roving prior to spinning.

SPINDLE WHORL: Small ring of wood, glass or stone used to counterweight the thread on a spindle.

SPINDLE: Small bobbin of rounded wood for spinning flax, wool, etc.

SPINNING JENNY: An early machine for spinning wool or cotton by means of many spindles.

SPINNING WHEEL: A treadle machine driven by hand or by foot, used in the home for spinning yarn. The wheel is activated by the treadle and drives a single spindle.

SPRIG: A lace flower, leaf or similar small motif, made separately and then sewn onto a piece of fabric, lace or net.

STAPLE FIBER: The short, raw fiber of cotton or waste combings of hemp or flax that were spun and twisted to produce a rough yarn from which rustic linen used to be made.

SWINGLE: A wooden instrument measuring about two feet in length, that resembles a knife, and is used for beating the roughage out of flax, hemp, etc., before combing.

TAFFETA: Taffeta is a plain weave fabric of silk, linen, etc. It has a crisp finish and is smooth and shiny on both sides.

TARLATAN: A plain, loose weave cotton that is transparent and heavily stiffened with size.

TERRY TOWELING OR CLOTH: The name comes from the French tiré, meaning pulled or drawn. Terrycloth is soft and absorbent, with loops (or "terrys") of uncut pile. The pile can be plain or patterned, on one side or both. It is used especially for Turkish or bath towels.

TOW: The short broken fibers removed from flax, hemp or jute. It is used to make twine, for stuffing, or else it is spun into a coarse yarn for low-quality fabrics.

TULLE: A stiff net with a round or hexagonal mesh used for veils and tutus.

TWILL WEAVE: The most widely used textile weave after plain weaving. It has an allover pattern of slanting lines or ribs made by floating a warp thread over two or more weft threads (and vice versa). Their incidence is staggered to make the lines fall diagonally. Herringbone is a reversed or pointed twill, gaberdine has a "steep" twill.

TWISTING: To make a yarn thicker and stronger for weaving, two or more threads are twisted together after spinning. To produce different effects in the fabric, yarns are twisted in different tightnesses (light-twisted, average-twisted, hard-twisted), or one thread can be held tightly and the other run in slackly to produce knop or curl yarns, or different colored yarns can be twisted together.

VALENCIENNES LACE: A fine bobbin lace made in the town in Normandy of the same name from around 1640. It was a continuous-thread lace up to about 1830, when it became a cut-thread lace. Initially it had a round, plaited

mesh ground, but later this became square- or diamond-shaped. The pattern is made together with the ground and of the same kind of thread.

VEGETABLE DYES: These are dyes extracted from plants such as indigo, turmeric, saffron or madder. They were used from time immemorial for the dyeing of cloth, until the development of new chemical dyes during the nineteenth century began to render them obsolete. The earliest traces of dyes on linen were found in Egypt and date from 500 B.C. Blue, the color of the god Amon, and red, the color of the god Seth, have been found on the linen bandages wrapping mummies. Cotton was dyed in India and silk in China. In Europe, the first traces of dye date from the end of the first millenium, in tones of blue and green.

In antiquity, Tyrian purple, reserved for those of royal or imperial rank, was imported from Tyre in Lebanon, where it was extracted from the murex, a mollusc that is almost extinct today. The Gallo-Romans extracted the color from madder, which grew in the south of France, but true scarlet red, from the Mexican cochineal, was not introduced until the seventeenth century.

Dyers used a great variety of dye-yielding plants known as "dyers weeds." Dark yellow was obtained from saffron, bright yellows from the Egyptian lotus, turmeric, and from yellow weed, reds from madder root, the cochineal insect and kermes. Brown was obtained from walnut husks. A fast gray and black were obtained from the nutgall of oaks. Greens, obtained from highly non-fast leaf sap or unripe pomegranate grains, were somewhat unsuccessful until mordants were developed.

For blue, indigo has been used in India and Egypt since ancient times. In Europe during the Middle Ages it had to be imported from India at great expense. A cheaper blue dye plant—the woad, or pastel—was also cultivated in Provence.

VENETIAN POINT LACE: Needlepoint lace (raised point, rose point) originally made in Venice using various decorative stitches. They form a honeycomb pattern over which padded or plain floral designs are embroidered in high or low relief.

VOILE: A light, sheer cotton or wool fabric in a fine, open plain weave. In cotton, the metric count of the yarn can reach 200.

WADDING: A soft, fluffy sheet of short, loose, spun fibers manufactured in different thicknesses and used for padding quilts and clothing.

WAFFLE CLOTH: A honeycomb weave usually of cotton or wool, used mainly for towels, dressing gowns, etc.

WARP: The given number of yarns on a loom that form the lengthwise threads of a fabric. Warp yarns are usually twisted tighter than filling, or weft, yarns to hold the shape of the fabric and they are sized to stop their fibers from tangling with those of the weft yarns.

WEAVE: The method of interlacing the warp yarns and the weft yarns that characterizes the texture of a cloth, as in plain weave, twill weave, etc. The word is also used to describe the back of a fabric, for example: "a pile face and twill weave."

WEFT, WEFT YARN: See filling and filling thread.

WORSTED YARN: A yarn spun from the longest wool fibers, tightly twisted to make it compact and even. It is used especially for weaving fabrics with a smooth napless face used for suiting.

YARN: A continuous thread made of carded or combed fibers twisted together by spinning, or composed of a single filament of silk or man-made fiber, or of several of these filaments laid parallel to each other or twisted together.

BIBLIOGRAPHY

ALBRECHT-MATHEY, Elisabeth. *The Fabrics of Mulhouse and Alsace: 1750-1850*. Leigh-on-Sea, 1968.

ALGOUD, Henri. *La Soie: art et histoire*. Lyon, 1986.

ARIÈS, Philippe and Georges Duby. *Histoire de la vie privée*. Paris, 1985-1988.

BECKER, J., with the collaboration of D. B. Wagner. *Pattern and Loom: A Practical Study of the Development of Weaving Techniques in China, Western Asia and Europe*. Copenhagen, 1987.

BECKETT, J. V. *The Aristocracy in England 1660-1914*. Oxford, 1986.

BEZON. *Dictionnaire des tissus*. Paris, 1863.

BILLAUX, Paul. *Le Lin, "textile vivant" au service des hommes*. Paris, 1969.

BOILEAU, Étienne. *Le Livre des métiers*. Paris, 1837.

BOURSIN, D. *Le Pliage des serviettes*. Paris, 1991.

BRÉDIF, J. *Toiles de Jouy: Classic Printed Textiles from France 1760-1843*. London, 1989.

BRIDGEMAN, H., and E. Drury. *Needlework: An Illustrated History*. London and New York, 1978.

BRIL, Jacques. *Origines et Symbolisme des productions textiles*. Paris, 1984.

BRUNELLO, F. *The Art of Dyeing in the History of Mankind*. Vicenza, 1973.

CANIER, Jacques. *L'école des ragoûts*. Lyon, 1680.

CARLANO, Marianne, and Larry Salmon, eds. *French Textiles From the Middle Ages through the Second Empire*. Hartford, 1985.

CARUFEL, Hélène de. *Le Lin*. Ottawa, 1980.

CHERBLANC, E. *Histoire générale du tissu*. Paris, 1935.

CLABBURN, P. *Masterpieces of Embroidery*. Oxford, 1981.

CLABBURN, P. *The Needleworker's Dictionary*. London, 1976.

CLARK, H. *Textile Printing*. Aylesbury, 1985.

CLOUZOT, Henri, and Francis Morris. *Painted and Printed Fabrics: The History of the Manufactory at Jouy and Other Ateliers in France (1760-1815)*. New York, 1927.

CROOKES, W. J. *Practical Handbook of Dyeing and Calico-printing*. London, 1874.

DAVIDOFF, Leonore. *The Best Circles: 'Society,' Etiquette and the Season*. London, 1986.

DELORT, Robert. *La Vie au Moyen Age*. Paris, 1982.

DIBIE, Pascal. *Ethnologie de la chambre à coucher*. Paris, 1987.

DILMONT, Thérèse de. *Encyclopédie des ouvrages de dames*. Mulhouse, 1912.

DISERENS, L. *The Chemical Technology of Dyeing and Printing*. 2 vols. New York, 1948, 1951.

DUBY, Georges, and Michelle Perrot. *Histoire des femmes*. Paris, 1991-1992.

DU FAIL, Noël, *Treize Propos rustiques*. Paris, 1875.

FENNELL MAZZAOUI, M. *The Italian Cotton Industry in the Later Middle Ages 1100-1600*. Cambridge, 1981.

GEIJER, A. *A History of Textile Art*. London, 1979.

GOUBERT, J.-P. *La Conquête de l'eau*. Paris, 1986.

HALL (Janssen), R. *Egyptian Textiles*. New revised ed. Aylesbury, 1991.

HARRIS, J., ed. *5000 years of Textiles*. London, 1993.

HAVARD, Henry. *Dictionnaire de l'ameublement et de la décoration depuis le XIII siècle jusqu'à nos jours*. 4 vols. Paris, 1887-1890.

HECHT, A. *The Art of the Loom: Weaving, Spinning and Dyeing across the World*. London, 1989.

HERODOTUS. *Histories*. Trans. A. de Selincourt. Harmondsworth, 1954.

HOWARD, C. *Twentieth Century Embroidery in Great Britain*. 4 vols. London, 1982-1986.

KNECHT, E., and J. B. Fothergill. *The Principles and Practice of Textile Printing*. 4th ed. London, 1952.

KRAATZ, A. *Lace: History & Fashion*. London, 1989.

LEBAULT, Armand. *La Table et le Repas à travers les siècles*. Paris, 1910.

LE BOURHIS, Katell, ed. *The Age of Napoleon*. New York, 1990.

LEVEY, S. M. *Lace: A History*. Leeds, 1983.

LONGFIELD, A. *Irish Lace*. Dublin, 1978.

LUMMIS, Trevor, and Jan Marsh. *The Woman's Domain: Women and the English Country House*. Harmondsworth, 1993.

LYLE, D. S. *Modern Textiles*. New York, 1976.

MARCHAL, Lucien. *L'Or blanc: l'épopée du coton*. Brussels, 1959.

MASSIGNON, Geneviève. *Contes autour du lin en Basse-Bretagne*. Paris, 1965.

MERCIER, Louis-Sébastien. *Tableau de Paris*. Amsterdam, 1781-1788.

MIROT, Léon. *Un trousseau d'Isabelle de France*. Paris, 1902.

MONTGOMERY, Florence. *Printed Textiles: English and American Cottons and Linens 1700-1850*. London, 1970.

MONTGOMERY, Florence. *Textiles in America, 1650-1870*. New York, 1984.

NENCKI, Lydie. *La Science des teintures animales et végétales*. Paris, 1981.

O'BRIEN, Charles. *The British Manufacturers Companion and Calico Printers Assistant*. London, 1792.

PARRY, L. *Textiles of the Arts and Crafts Movement*. London, 1988.

PERROT, Michelle, and Georges Ribeill. *Le Journal intime de Caroline B*. Paris, 1985.

PFANNSCHMIDT, E.-E. *Twentieth Century Lace*. London, 1975.

PORTER, R. *English Society in the Eighteenth Century*. Harmondsworth, 1982.

ROBINSON, S. *A History of Printed Textiles*. London, 1969.

ROCHE, Daniel. *La Culture des apparences*. Paris, 1989.

ROTHSTEIN, Natalie. *Silk Designs of the Eighteenth Century*. London, 1990.

SANSONE, Antonio. *The Printing of Cotton Fabrics*. 2nd ed. Manchester, 1901.

SANTANGELO, A. *The Development of Italian Textile Design from the Twelfth to the Eighteenth Century*. London, 1964.

SAUDINOS, Louis. *L'Industrie familiale du lin et du chanvre*. Toulouse, 1942.

SCHOESER, Mary, and Celia Rufey. *English and American Textiles from 1790 to the Present*. London and New York, 1989.

SCHOESER, Mary, and Kathleen Dejardin. *French Textiles from 1760 to the Present*. London, 1991.

SCHWARTZ, Paul R., and R. Micheaux. *A Century of French Fabrics: 1850-1950*. Leigh-on-Sea, 1964.

SERRES, Michel. *Les Cinq Sens*. Paris, 1985.

STOREY, Joyce. *The Thames and Hudson Manual of Dyes and Fabrics*. London, 1992.

STOREY, Joyce. *The Thames and Hudson Manual of Textile Printing*. London, 1992.

Textile Designs of Japan. 3 vols. Revised ed. Tokyo and New York, 1980.

THOMAS, Mary. *Mary Thomas's Dictionary of Embroidery Stitches*. Reprinted 1981, London. Originally printed 1934.

THORNTON, Peter. *Authentic Decor: The Domestic Interior 1620-1920*. London, 1984.

THORNTON, Peter. *Baroque and Rococo Silks*. London, 1965.

THORNTON, Peter. *Seventeenth-century Interior Decoration in England, France and Holland*. London, 1978.

TUCHSCHERER, Jean Michel. *The Fabrics of Mulhouse and Alsace (1801-1850)*. Leigh-on-Sea, 1972.

VIGARELLO, Georges. *Le Propre et le Sale*. Paris, 1985.

WARDLE, P. *A Guide to English Embroidery*. London, 1970.

WASSERMAN, Françoise. *Blanchisseuse, Laveuse, Repasseuse*. Fresnes, 1989.

WHATMAN, Susanna. *The Housekeeping Book of Susanna Whatman 1776-1800*. Introduction by Christina Hardyment. London, 1987.

WILD, J. P. *Textiles in Archaeology*. Aylesbury, 1988.

YANG, S., and R. M. Narasin. *Textile Art of Japan*. Tokyo, 1989.

YOUNG, Arthur. *Travels in France During the Years 1787, 1788, 1789*. Edited by Jeffry Kaplow. Garden City, 1969. First published in London, 1794.

YOUNG, T. M. *The American Cotton Industry*. New York, 1903.

TRANSLATIONS CITED

BACHELARD, Gaston. *The Poetics of Space*. Translated by Maria Jolas. Boston, 1969.

CHATEAUBRIAND, François René de. *Travels in America*. Translated by Richard Switzer. Lexington, Ky., 1969.

ELUARD, Paul. *Last Love Poems*. Translated by Marilyn Kallet. Baton Rouge, LA. and London, 1980.

FLAUBERT, Gustave. *Madame Bovary*. Translated by Francis Steegmuller. New York, 1992.

FRANCE, Marie de. *The Lais of Marie de France*. Translated by Robert Hanning and Joan Ferrante. New York, 1978.

RONSARD, Pierre de. *Lyrics*. Translated by William Stirling. London, 1946.

ZOLA, Émile. *L'Assommoir*. Translated by Leonard Tancock. London, 1970.

PICTURE CREDITS

Cover, pp. 1-6 J. Boulay; p. 8 0. Mesnage; p. 10 Rijksmuseum, Amsterdam; p. 11 Bibliothèque Forney; p. 12 above: Galerie Paul Vallotton; below: Bibliothèque Forney; p. 13 J.-P. Dieterlen; p. 14 Bulloz; p. 15 L'Illustration/Sygma; p. 16 above: J. Boulay; below: Bibliothèque Forney; p. 17 J. Boulay; p. 18 above: Retrograph/Martin Breese; left: Roger-Viollet; right: Bibliothèque Forney; p. 19 above: BAD (Bibliothèque des Arts Décoratifs)/Maciet Coll.; right: Bibliothèque Forney; below: Musée de la Publicité; p. 20 above: The White House/London; left: Bibliothèque Forney; right: BAD/Maciet Coll.; p. 21 Roger-Viollet; p. 22 Bibliothèque Forney; p. 23 above: BAD/Maciet Coll.; below: Alinari/Giraudon; p. 24 RMN/H. Lewandowski; p. 25 J. Boulay; p. 26 Musée de la Publicité; pp. 27, 28 J. Boulay; p. 29 above: FMR/Frette; below: Musée des Arts Décoratifs/Sully-Jaulmes; p. 30 A. Martin; p. 31 Musée des Arts Décoratifs/Sully-Jaulmes; pp. 32, 33 J. Boulay; p. 34 R. Mazin/Top; p. 35 Roger-Viollet; p. 36 C. Sarramon; p. 37 G. de Laubier; pp. 38, 39 J. Boulay; p. 40 above: FMR/Frette; below: G. de Laubier; p. 41 J.-L. Sieff; pp. 42-44 B. Touillon/Stylograph/Côté Sud; p. 45 BAD/J.-L. Charmet; p. 46 BAD/Maciet Coll.; p. 47 The Bridgeman Art Library; p. 48 center: BAD/J.-L. Charmet; above and below: D. Bordet Coll.; p. 49 M. Tulane/Rapho; p. 50 above: Larousse/Giraudon; below: Silvester/Rapho; p. 51 Bordet Coll.; p. 52 RMN/Musée d'Orsay; left: J.-L. Charmet; below: David Messum Gallery; p. 53 J.-L. Charmet; p. 54 Musée de la Publicité; p. 55 above: L'Illustration/Sygma; right: BAD/Maciet Coll.; below: J.-L. Charmet; p. 56 above: Roger-Viollet; below: J.-L. Charmet/B.N.; p. 57 M. Fraudreau/Top; p. 58 above: Cinémathèque Française; below: Bordet Coll.; p. 59 CRCT/Centre de Recherches Techniques; p. 61 RMN/Musée d'Orsay; pp. 62, 63 J. Laiter/A. de Dives/Madame Figaro; p. 64 Phelps/Rapho; p. 65 F. Kollar/Ministère de la Culture-France; p. 66 above:

C. Sarramon; below: Bordet Coll.; p. 67 above: J. Boulay; left: Bordet Coll.; p. 68 Rijksmuseum, Amsterdam; p. 69 Victoria & Albert Museum, London; p. 70 The Bettmann Archive; p. 71 Nelson Atkins Museum of Art/W. R. Nelson Trust; pp. 72, 73 Josy Broutin; p. 74 J. Boulay p. 75 E. Lessing/Magnum; p. 76 Bulloz; p. 77 Musée des Arts Décoratifs/Sully-Jaulmes; p. 78 Victoria & Albert Museum, London; p. 79 Musée des Arts Décoratifs/Sully-Jaulmes; p. 80 D. Turbeville/Courtesy of R. Gallois; p. 81 J. Boulay; p. 82 Musée des Arts Décoratifs/Sully-Jaulmes; p. 83 RMN/Château de Versailles; p. 84 above: Musée des Arts Décoratifs/Sully-Jaulmes; below: L. Ricciarini; p. 85 L. Ricciarini; p. 86 above: E. Lessing/Magnum; below: Retrograph/M. Breese; p. 87 Bibliothèque Forney; p. 88 Scala; p. 89 Artephot/Oronoz; p. 90 Scala; p. 91 J. Boulay; p. 92 E. Lessing/Magnum; p. 93 Bulloz; p. 94 Bibliothèque Forney; p. 95 The Bridgeman Art Library; pp. 96-97 Giraudon/Musée des Beaux-Arts de Tourcoing; p. 98 Bibliothèque Forney; p. 99 Roger-Viollet; p. 100 ACL/Brussels; p. 103 Giraudon/Musée des Beaux-Arts de Caen; p. 104 J. Boulay; p. 105 Bulloz/Musée de Chantilly; p. 106 FMR/Frette; p. 107 Private Coll.; p. 108 Top/Histoires de Table/P. Hinous; p. 109 F. Kollar/Ministère de la Culture-France; p. 110 Boymans-van Beuningen Museum, Rotterdam; p. 111 above: Bulloz/Musée du Petit Palais; below: Scala; p. 112 BAD/Maciet Coll; p. 115 E. Lessing/Magnum/Musée du Louvre; p. 116 J. Boulay and Bibliothèque Forney; p. 117 J. Boulay; p. 118 J. Boulay and Bibliothèque Forney; p. 119 J. Boulay; p. 120 J. Boulay and M. Breese/Retrograph; pp. 121-123 J. Boulay; pp. 124, 125 Bibliothèque Centrale du Museum d'Histoire Naturelle; p. 126 above: Fouque/Explorer; below: Ege/Schuster/Explorer; p. 127 C. Sarramon; p. 128 The Linen Hall Library, Belfast; p. 129 Mauritshuis, The Hague; p. 130 F. Kollar/Ministère de la Culture-France; pp. 131-134 J. Boulay; p. 135 D. Jouanneau; p. 136 P.-L. Martin/Ets Tur-

pault, Cholet; p. 137 P.-L. Martin; pp. 138, 139 above: FMR/Frette; p. 139 below: Archiv für Kunst & Geschichte; p. 140 J. Boulay; p. 141 above: ATP/RMN; below: Retrograph/Martin Breese; p. 142 Musée de l'Impression sur Etoffes, Mulhouse; p. 143 The Bettmann Archive; below: Bibliothèque Centrale du Museum d'Histoire Naturelle; p. 144 The Bridgeman Art Library; p. 145 above: Los Angeles County Museum of Art; below: The Bridgeman Art Library; p. 146 J.-M. Durou; p. 147 H. Cartier-Bresson/Magnum; pp. 148, 149 J. Boulay; pp. 150, 151 Leong Ka Tai/Cosmos; p. 152 J. Boulay and Retrograph/M. Breese; p. 153 F. Kollar/Ministère de la Culture-France; p. 154 J. Boulay; p. 155 Bordet Coll.; p. 156 the Noël firm; p. 157 J. Boulay; p. 159 above: Musée des Arts Décoratifs/Sully-Jaulmes; below: Scala; p. 160 J. Boulay; pp. 161, 162 above: Musée des Arts Décoratifs/Sully-Jaules; p. 162 below: Bibliothèque Forney; p. 163 Musée des Arts Décoratifs/Sully-Jaulmes; p. 164 J. Boulay; pp. 165, 166 G. de Laubier; p. 167 J. Boulay; p. 168 above: B. Touillon/Stylograph; below: C. Sarramon; p. 169 J. Darblay; pp. 170-172 J.Boulay; p. 173 F. Kollar/Ministère de la Culture-France; p. 174 J. Boulay; p. 175 above: Overseas/A & M; below: The White House/London; p. 176 G. de Laubier; p. 177 J. Boulay; p. 178 RMN/ Château de Versailles; p. 180 J. Boulay; pp. 181, 183 Abegg Stiftung; p. 184 Musée des Arts Décoratifs/Sully-Jaulmes; p. 185 FMR/Frette; p. 186 above: Abegg Stiftung; below: Bibliothèque Forney; p. 187 Musée des Arts Décoratifs/Sully-Jaulmes; p. 188 above: J. Boulay; below: FMR/ Frette; p. 189 above: J. Boulay; below: The White House, London; p. 190 J. Boulay; p. 191 Primrose Bordier; p. 192 above: P. Pascal/Elle Déco; below: Primrose Bordier; right: Descamps/Primrose Bordier; p. 193 J. Boulay; p. 195 Musée de l'Impression sur Etoffes, Mulhouse; p. 196 Musée des Arts Décoratifs/ Sully-Jaulmes; p. 197 above: Archiv für Kunst & Geschichte; below: G. de Laubier; pp. 198-200 J. Boulay; p. 201 FMR/Frette.

ACKNOWLEDGEMENTS

The author would like to thank the editor Ghislaine Bavoillot and her assistant Anne Fitamant Peter; Jacques Boulay, who took the photographs especially for this book, assisted by Jean-Michel Tardy; Sabine Arqué-Greenberg, Marc Walter and Sylvie Bednar for their help in the creation of the book; and Lucette Landré for her invaluable work on the Macintosh.

In particular, the author would like to extend her gratitude and recognition to Marc Porthault who, with tremendous kindness and patience, made available his competence, archives and all his linen during the time of the book's preparation. Similarly, she would like to thank Marc Porthault's colleagues, Georges Hanotel, Claude Valentin, Danielle Lefloïc for generously sharing their knowledge, and Dominique Bougault, Séréna Picat and Laurence Lécuyer for their help in the choice of old and modern pieces of linen to be photographed.

She would also like to offer her heartfelt thanks to Josy Broutin, who had the kindness to organize the photographing of her own linen and that of the Jules Zéau firm.

The author is equally grateful to all those who helped her in her research, either indirectly through their books, notably Patrice Hugues and all the authors of the different articles in the Revue de la Société d'Ethnologie Française (vol. 16, no. 3) which was devoted to linen, or in person, notably Miss Marguerite Prinet for her matchless knowledge of

damask and her infinite courtesy; Mrs. Daniel, specialist at Hôtel Drouot, for her unparalleled familiarity with lace; and the sociologists Daniel Roche and Michelle Perrot.

Similarly, the author thanks all those who allowed her access to certain documents or to exceptional collections: Danielle Burguburu, Marie-Noëlle Sudre, Maguelonne Toussaint-Samat, Florence Coblence, Madeleine Roiron, Josette Hoffmann, Adeline Fourmon-Dieudonné, Martine Roy et Joëlle Serres; Véronique Belloir, archivist in the textile department of the Musée des Arts Décoratifs; Paule Andrée Moselle, head-librarian at the Bibliothèque Forney; Jacqueline Jacqué, curator at the Musée du Textile at Mulhouse; Evelyne Gaudry-Poitevin, curator at the Musée Historique des Tissus de Lyon; Danielle Moreu, for Monsieur Ménage, for access to the linen at the Elysée Palace and Thierry Balesdent, for Mr. Casa Soprana, for access to that of the Ministry of Foreign Affairs; Mr. Tardif, owner of the Jules Zéau firm; John de Lierre, owner of The White House shop, London, the Jesurum firm, Venice, and the Frette firm, Paris.

Finally, the author would like to express her appreciation to the antique dealers and designers of linen who agreed to meet her and who also gave her numerous pieces to illustrate the book: Michèle Aragon, Josy Broutin, Muriel Grateau, the Noël firm's shop, Renata for la Maison de Renata, José Houel, Edith Mézard, Catherine Memmi, Micheline

Parrault for Le Temps retrouvé, Francis Leplus for Jean-Vier, Claire Dumail for Meridiem, Marisa Osorio Farinha for Siècle, Sabine Marchal for Nuit Blanche, La Paresse en Douce shops, Liwan, La Maison Douce, The Conran Shop and the 14 Juillet agency for Primrose Bordier's creations for Descamps and le Jacquard Français.

The publishers would like to express their gratitude to all those who shared their love of beautiful linen and to all the shops and collectors who lent their linen to be photographed for the book, in particular Mr. Marc Porthault, Mrs. Toussaint-Samat, and Mrs. Mayer.

We would like to thank Mrs. Suzanne Lowry, FMR publications, Mrs. Sonia Hédard of the Musée des Arts Décoratifs, Mrs. Cathelineau of the Alexandre Turpault firm, Mr. John Dellière and Mrs. Francesca Rena of The White House, Mrs. Elisabeth Loir-Mongazon of the Musée du Textile Choletais, Mr. Mohamed al Fayed, president of Harrod's, Mr. Daniel Bordet for their help with the picture research.

For their precious advice and attentive reading of the manuscript, the publisher would like to thank Christelle Hilger, Hélène Gaudin and Béatrice Vignals.

Finally, warmest thanks must go to Jacques Boulay, Jean-Michel Tardy, Sylvie Bednar, Sabine Arqué-Greenberg, Margherita Mariano and Olivier Canaveso for their collaboration on the book.